Pastor's Opportunities

The Pastor's Opportunities

EDITED BY
CYRIL S. RODD

T&T CLARK
EDINBURGH

T&T CLARK LTD
59 GEORGE STREET
EDINBURGH EH2 2LQ
SCOTLAND

First published 1990

ISBN 0 567 29167 7

British Library Cataloguing in Publication Data
The Pastor's Opportunities.
1. Christian church, Pastoral work
I. Rodd, Cyril S. (Cyril Stanley), *1928–*
253

Typeset by C R Barber & Partners (Highlands) Ltd, Fort William
Printed and bound in Great Britain by Page Bros (Norwich) Ltd

Contents

THE PASTOR'S OPPORTUNITIES

The Contributors

THE Reverend James B. Bates has just retired after being being Chaplain at Southlands College, a Constituent College of the Roehampton Institute of Higher Education, for 27 years.

The Reverend Marcus Braybrooke has served for many years on the Council of Christians and Jews and edits *Common Ground*.

The Reverend Christopher P. Burkett is Team Vicar of St Luke's in the Leek Team Ministry, Staffordshire.

The Reverend M. H. F. Forward is Secretary of the Methodist Church Committee for Relations with People of Other Faiths.

The Reverend Dr Leslie J. Francis is Senior Research Officer at Culham College Institute, Abingdon, Oxfordshire.

The Reverend William D. Horton is a Methodist Minister, and holds the Lord Rank Chair of Practical Theology and Methodism in Wesley College, Bristol, after being a circuit minister for 35 years.

The Revered Antony Hurst is a civil servant and is a non-stipendiary priest in the Church of England

The Reverend Alan le Grys is Vicar of St John's Church, Stoneleigh, Epsom, Surrey.

The Reverend Dr Kenneth Lysons is a supernumerary Methodist Minister in the Methodist Church at St Helens, Merseyside.

Bishop Lesslie Newbigin has retired to Birmingham after serving for many years in the Church of South India and in the World Council of Churches, and is minister of Winson Green United Reformed Church.

The Very Reverend Dr Edward H. Patey has recently retired from being Dean of Liverpool Cathedral.

The Reverend Dr Graham A. Patrick is a Methodist Minister at Alsager, Cheshire.

The Reverend Trevor N. Stubbs is Vicar of St Cross, Middleton, Leeds.

The Reverend Michael G. Townsend is a Methodist Minister at Huddersfield, West Yorkshire.

The Reverend H. W. Webb is Chaplain to Deaf People in the Surrey Office of the Royal Association in Aid of Deaf People.

The Reverend Dick Williams is Rector of Christchurch, Croft, Warrington.

Preface

ONE of the most successful series of articles in *The Expository Times* was 'The Pastor's Problems'. It ran for nearly four years and was subsequently published in book form[1]. When it ended there were still many pastoral issues left that had not been discussed, and several readers wrote to me, making suggestions for possible topics or offering articles. Reviewers of *The Pastor's Problems* were generally kind, but some questioned the title, which they suggested failed to point up the *opportunities* of ministry today.

After a short break, therefore, a new series was started with just that title. The aim was essentially the same as in the earlier series: to offer severely practical advice and suggestions to clergy and ministers. This series ran for 32 months, and now that it has come to an end it also is being published in book form, although only twenty-four of the thirty-one articles can be fitted in.

There are again five sections, rather different from those in the previous book.

Ministers deal with the spoken word, and their relations with literature have always been close. Poetry, novels, and biography are singled out as providing opportunities for enjoyment and for lighting up the gospel in fresh ways.

But in these days of television the visual image has once again come into its own, and the second section offers thoughts on various kinds of visual aids and the place of art in the life and worship of the church. Many clergy are expected to assist in the running of a church magazine, and help is also offered with this.

In *The Pastor's Problems* articles on visiting, hospital visiting, and ministering to the dying found a place, but it was largely a matter

[1] *The Pastor's Problems* ed. Cyril S. Rodd (T&T Clark, 1985, ISBN 0 567 29117 0).

of the pastor ministering on his own. In the present book we find the church organizing itself to care for mothers and tiny children, the mentally handicapped child, those who are hard of hearing, and the confused elderly. These are groups within our society who stand in special need of the church's ministry.

The largest section is devoted to various forms of evangelism. Some of them will hardly be recognized as such by many, yet when the minister attends various 'secular' societies he is bringing the church there in positive ways as well as finding relaxation and interest for himself, when lay Christians go to their work they are living out their faith and need to be understood by their minister, and when working people help their neighbours in spontaneous ways they need to be shown that they are doing God's work. More familiar ways of outreach are also included.

Finally, friendships across the barriers of different faiths are seen to be a way of living out the Christian life and discovering new depths of truth in our own religion as well as learning about the spirituality of others.

I hope that these two books will spark off ideas, provide practical help, and enable ministers to be more effective pastors to their people. I am deeply grateful to all those readers of *The Expository Times* who have contributed in one way or another to the development of this little book, and offer special thanks to those who wrote the articles.

Part I
Literature

The Use of Poetry in Worship, Preaching and Small Groups

MICHAEL J. TOWNSEND, B.A., M.Phil., B.D.
Huddersfield

It is striking how often in reading obituaries of ministers who have died in their eighties or nineties one encounters a sentence such as this: 'He delighted in the poetry of Browning and Tennyson, much of which he knew off by heart and which he quoted copiously in his sermons'. It usually was Browning or Tennyson, of course, for that generation. They were considered Christian poets *par excellence*, and books about their religious teaching continued to be published well after the turn of this century. Many ministers of an older generation entered theological college with a fairly rudimentary general education (this is more true for Nonconformists than it is for Anglicans) and the theological colleges saw it as part of their task to encourage students to explore the world of culture as well as theology. In many cases this left Christian preachers with a lifelong love of poetry, and of the more accessible Victorian 'Christian' poets in particular. Gerard Manley Hopkins, who might have been expected to rival Tennyson and Browning in that respect, was a Roman Catholic and thus suspect, a bit 'difficult' and generally less well-known.

These days sociology and psychology seem to have replaced the arts as extra-theological reading in theological colleges (quite properly, no doubt), and it is assumed that students will find their own way into contemporary culture. The aim of this article is to encourage busy pastors to explore the possibility of enriching worship and preaching as well as small group work, by using some of the rich store of poetry now easily accessible to us. In the process they may expect their own understanding of the faith to be deepened and enriched as well.

Why Poetry?

In the famous preface to his 1780 hymn book, John Wesley did not hesitate to claim that in some of the hymns he included there was 'the true Spirit of Poetry, such as cannot be acquired by art and labour, but must be the gift of nature'. Wesley was, of course, chiefly concerned to stop other people reprinting the hymns of himself and his brother in altered form (something he was nonetheless quite capable of doing himself). He doubtless wished to make them feel ashamed of the practice by claiming a high degree of artistic merit for the original. But then, almost as if aware that merely to commend a collection of hymns on the ground of its artistic excellence is to miss the main point of the matter, Wesley hastily adds that the collection also contains 'the spirit of piety' which is 'of infinitely more moment than the Spirit of Poetry' and concludes: 'When Poetry thus keeps its place, as the handmaid of Piety, it shall attain, not a poor perishable wreath, but a crown that fadeth not away'. And therein lies the rub! What *is* the proper relationship between poetry and a confessional faith? If we want to use poetry in worship or in preaching, can we use any poetry at all, or does it have to be 'Christian' poetry? And what *is* Christian poetry anyway? Is it poetry written by professed Christians? John Donne was a great poet and a professed Christian, yet whilst one might use the 'Hymne to God the Father' in a sermon, one might hesitate about the 'Elegie: To his Mistris Going to Bed', marvellous though it is. So that model won't do. Is it then poetry which has an overtly Christian subject-matter and is written with sincerity? That, I fear, will do even less well. There are one or two writers (who had better not be named) whose religious verse appears not only in books and magazines but on cards and bookmarks and other strange places, whose sincerity and Christian subject matter is not in doubt, but whose writing is of such a quality that it makes the sensitive shudder. As Elizabeth Jennings put it, 'No amount of good will or orthodox belief in the world ever managed to produce a good poem'. Just as you can be sincerely wrong so you can be sincerely bad! If we are to use poetry in the context of Christian ministry we have first to come to terms with its essential untidyness. A poet is not necessarily a systematic thinker, much less a systematic theologian. Poets draw upon, often in a manner of intellectual magpies, all kinds of systems and ideas. We may think of the often tortuous – and ultimately somewhat pointless – debate which has taken place around Dylan Thomas's claim in the preface to his *Collected Poems* that 'My poems are written in praise of God and man, and I'd be a damn fool if they weren't'. Whole books have been written to try and prove that Dylan Thomas is a 'Christian' poet, whilst others who knew him well have denied that he had any substantative Christian belief at all. Such debates and definitions, though often interesting, do not help us very much. We have to attend to the poem *as an artefact*. Poems explore the nature of reality. They also offer moments of illumination and interpretation which may or may not be useful to the pastor in his work. Some of the poems which do this for us will be by professed Christians, but equally some will not be. What matters is the imaginative engagement we, and our hearers, bring to the text before us. C. S. Lewis once recalled the great impact that reading a book by George Macdonald had upon him by saying that it 'baptised his imagination'. For many people in our times the problem with Christian belief is that they cannot imagine it. They cannot imagine (or, if you prefer it, image) the God about whom we speak so readily. Since poems move, on the whole, not on the level of intellectual argument, but in the context of what Walter Ong has beautifully called 'one presence calling to another', they may help us to encounter and wrestle with a God who, in our century, often seems to hide himself.

The Uses of Poetry
1. In *sermons*. Robert Graves once defined poetry as 'the best words in the best order' and where a poem is indeed this it will often be useful in preaching. Preachers struggle constantly with words, trying to make them describe the essentially indescribable, the nature and love of God. The poets have much to teach us here. One example will have to suffice. If a sermon were being preached on 'The Christian Attitude to Death', it could end in this way: 'To die is, as we are taught by our faith, to pass to that realm where we await our share in the resurrection. Because of the death and

resurrection of Jesus Christ we have been promised that the power
of death has been broken and the final victory belongs not with
death, the last enemy, but with God who will give us new and
risen life.' Or, it could end in this way:

One short sleepe past, we wake eternally,
And death shall be no more, Death thou shalt die.

That is how John Donne ends the sixth of his *Holy Sonnets*, and
very effective it is too.

   Two brief comments on using poetry in sermons seem in order
here. The first is that because the congregation will usually only
hear this read once, it needs to be kept simple. Poetry which uses
archaic or obscure words should be avoided, as should poetry which
has to be explained before it is used. As with any good illustration
in a sermon, a poem (or part thereof) should make its own point
succinctly. If it doesn't, don't use it. The second comment is that
we should always, as with any text, respect the context of any
excerpt we use. The present writer has heard Swinburne's line,
'Thou hast conquered, O pale Galilean', used in a sermon to
illustrate the contention that even non-Christians have recognized
the eventual triumph of the crucified. The preacher who so used
that line presumably did not know (or did not trouble to find out)
that the next line of the poem runs, 'The world has grown grey
from Thy breath', and is in fact about Swinburne's concern that
Christian faith and morals had sapped the vitality of the human
race. Such use of poetry is dishonest. It also discredits the preacher
who does it in the eyes of those hearers who know better.

   2. In *worship*. The fashion for the 'fourth lesson' seems to have
come and gone. In some ways that is a pity, though it is always
important not to give the impression that non-biblical material can
be given the same status in worship as the canonical writings. If
poems are to be used in formal acts of worship, ways have been
devised of doing this naturally, and that is not easy. In such contexts
a poem is best read after a short period of silence following the
sermon or following one of the scripture readings. At the eucharist
a poem might be read after all have communicated and before the
final prayers. All-Age Worship or any act of worship which makes

less use of set forms of liturgy will lend itself more readily to the use of poetry. Indeed, there are particular opportunities in All-Age and Family Worship, because in many cases children and young people are much less self-conscious about poetry than are some adults. Poetry is often part of school life, with creative writing groups encouraging young people not only to read, but to write their own poetry. In some schools the results are used in assemblies and on other corporate occasions, or put up in poster form around the school building. Indeed, there are some excellent collections of children's poetry, some of which can be used in Christian worship. One of the great merits of this kind of poetry is that children often observe perfectly ordinary things in new ways, and in their poetry give fresh voice to what we all know and experience. This can be a helpful sharing for all ages within the worship.

The major festivals of the Christian year tend to be the times when poetry can be used in worship with greatest ease and the least sense of strangeness. This is particularly true of Christmas, when Betjeman's 'Advent' or T. S. Eliot's 'Journey of the Magi' have become almost compulsory additions to the biblical readings in the carol services. Both of these are good poems, but it would be good to have a change! Clive Sansom's 'The Shepherd's Carol', R. S. Thomas's 'Lost Christmas', George Mackay Brown's 'The Lodging', even Thomas Hardy's 'The Oxen' (though note the poet's wistful inability to accept the truth of the legend on which the poem is based) would all make acceptable alternatives, and there are many more. Passiontide and Easter are more difficult, partly because the material is less tractable for poets, partly because the dark depths of the passion narrative often call forth (as in the poetry of Donald Davie), dark deep poetry which finely explores the human condition and what the crosss has to say to it, but requires careful reading before it yields its secrets. Frank Kendon's 'The Merchant's Carol', Charles Causley's 'The Song of the Hours', 'Terce' from W. H. Auden's *Horae Canonicae*, many of the poems of R. S. Thomas, perhaps especially 'The Coming', all these are suitable for use in Passiontide. For Easter try Gerard Manley Hopkins's 'Easter' (one of the few pieces by this poet intelligible at a first reading), or Elizabeth Jennings's magnificent 'The

Resurrection'. Older poetry tends to be more satisfactory for this season. Poems suitable for use at Harvest Festivals can be found in any good anthology. Otherwise it is only by browsing through collections that the worship leader will discover the treasures. Worship on the third Sunday after Easter when the controlling lesson for the second year is John 11:17–27 would be greatly lifted by the inclusion of Elizabeth Jennings's 'Lazarus', and the same poet's 'The Annunciation' could make worship on the Sunday before Christmas unforgettable for some:

> It is a human child she loves
> Though a god stirs beneath her breast
> And great salvations grip her side.

3. In *small groups*. All pastors are familiar with the telephone call which begins: 'This is Mrs X of the Bethesda Women's Fellowship/All Saints Mother's Union. Can you please come and speak to us next session?' Women's meetings, men's meetings (in some places), housegroups and external organizations (Darby and Joan Clubs etc.) all clamour for speakers, preferably those not requiring a fee. Pastors quickly learn to distinguish between those which seem to have genuine purpose and those which simply need to fill a speaker-rota no matter with whom or what! In some cases these are meetings of a devotional character where the participants genuinely appreciate something which feeds their discipleship. Other groups represent an opportunity to present the Christian faith, though it usually has to be done in subtle ways. As the Secretary of a Young Wives Group once said to me when issuing an invitation, 'Nothing too religious, please'. Poetry can be used with both kinds of groups. The devotional meetings will often appreciate a selection of poems on a theme, interspersed of course with hymns and prayers. Prose passages could be included too. The popularity of poetry programmes on the radio (such as BBC Radio 4 *With Great Pleasure* where distinguished guests present their personal selection of poetry and prose) can encourage us to use the same technique with small groups of this kind. Other groups have to be approached more carefully, but I have used selections of poetry with non-church organizations and have been invited back!

Subtlety is sometimes called for, even a touch of serpentine cunning! The person who telephones the pastor will often want a title for a printed syllabus, or to be announced the week beforehand. If the pastor offers 'The Poetry of the Passion' there is likely to be hesitation, or worse. At this point of the proceedings it is advisable to offer some such title as 'An Evening with the Bards' or, if you are using the work of only one poet, 'An Hour with R. S. Thomas' (or whoever). My experience is that by and large people respond extremely well when actually confronted by the material. Of course, there will be those to whom poetry does not appeal, and they will no doubt say so. But it is worth putting up with that for the sake of those for whom doors will be opened. With astonishing frequency, after such a meeting, someone – sometimes several people – will come up and shyly admit that they not only read, but write poetry. Indeed, sometimes you will have the joy of being shown some of those poems and asked to comment on them, for they 'just happen' to be in someone's handbag or wallet! When using poetry with small groups the initial resistance is because people fear it will be too difficult for them to understand, or sometimes, because they hated poetry at school. There isn't much you can do about the legacy of bad teaching except ask them to keep open minds on this occasion. But the former fear can be allayed by your choice of material. The same rules apply with small groups (unless it is a study group where you can have the text in front of everyone) as apply in the use of poetry in worship. It helps greatly if some of the material has humour. This breaks the ice and reassures the uncertain. Sir John Betjeman's work is a blessing in this respect, and indeed, 'An Evening with Sir John Betjeman' is often a good introductory session to attempt. Non-church groups will take Betjeman's humour readily enough, which gives the pastor hope that they will take his Christian faith along with it.

Practical Points
One of the most distinctive qualities of poetry is that it is intended to be read aloud. Many people who read poetry privately for pleasure read it this way. Yet many pastors might be shy of engaging in public poetry reading. It goes without saying that

poetry must be read well if it is to have proper impact. But this applies to any public reading, and if pastors apply the same techniques as they have learned for reading scripture and the liturgy to their reading of poems, they will not go far wrong. The cardinal rule is to pay attention to the punctuation. The full modulations of the voice should be used and the tone and pace should reflect the character of the poem being read. If a poem is not graspable when the pastor has read it through twice it is probably not suitable for public reading anyway. Of course, the actual reading may not be the pastor's task. In many churches there will be lay people who love poetry and have good speaking voices. The pastor will get to know who they are within a fairly short time of commencing ministry in that church. Many of these people are delighted to come to a meeting to read the poetry they enjoy and a variety of voices helps audience appreciation. The same rule applies in worship. Whilst only the super-organized would want to appoint a church poetry-reader, there are opportunities for partnership here which should be explored.

The Resources

It is quite impossible to list all available collections and anthologies, or even to mention all the poets whose work can be considered as a pastor's opportunity. I limit myself here to 20th-century work, with a few exceptions. This is not because 20th-century work is inherently better (such a judgment would be manifestly absurd) but because a great deal of earlier poetry requires prior explanation. In some cases this is well worthwhile, and I have found that people much appreciate George Herbert, for example. But those wishing to venture into what is for them a new area of expressing the faith may do better to stick with the contemporary. I indicate therefore a few of the poets whose work merits consideration, and suggest how their poems might be most easily obtained. In some cases volumes of poetry are expensive and those on stipends might consider ordering them through the inter-library loans service at the local public library to have a look first and see if a volume appeals and is therefore worth purchasing.

R. S. Thomas is a Welsh poet-priest with a dark vision of life, whose poetry often wrestles with God. His *Selected Poems 1946–1968* (Hart-Davis, MacGibbon [1973]) supplemented by his *Later Poems 1972–1982* (Macmillan [1983]) would provide all that the pastor needs from this important poetic voice. T. S. Eliot is perhaps the most influential poet in the English language in this century, but he is not always easy either to read or to understand. Some of his shorter poems are well worth using, but it is more difficult to extract satisfactory passages from the longer works such as *Four Quartets*. His *Collected Poems 1909–1962* (Faber & Faber, [1974]) offer all that is required, and the paperback edition is astonishingly cheap! Fortunately that edition does now include 'The Cultivation of Christmas Trees' (1954) which could well be used at Christmas. The vivid and colourful poetry of Charles Causley, the Cornish schoolmaster poet has won many friends, and has an immediacy which is very attractive. Many of his poems deal with religious themes and the ballad form which Causely often favours make him easy to read in public. Pastors should in any case enjoy his description of the hospital visitor who is

> . . . a melancholy splurge
> Of theological colours;
> Taps heavily about like a healthy vulture
> Distributing deep-frozen hope

in 'Ten Types of Hospital Visitor'. His *Collected Poems 1951–1975* (Macmillan [1975]) is splendid value in every way. The Orcadian Roman Catholic poet George Mackay Brown is too-little known in the rest of Britain. His faith is rooted in the correspondence of the cycle of the year with the church's seasons and his writings pungent and thoughtful. Unfortunately most of his poetry seems to be out of print at the time of writing. Pastors who can lay their hands on his *Selected Poems* (Hogarth press [1977]) have a treasure-house which will repay constant reading. The poetry of Elizabeth Jennings is fresh and beautiful and often born out of personal experience. Her work has won several major literary awards. Her *Selected Poems* (Carcanet [1979]) offers a compassable selection of all but her most recent poems. W. H. Auden is an enigma. A convert to Christianity, argument still rages about how deep his Christian faith actually went. His overtly Christian poems are few, but striking, and there are those who find him helpful. His *Collected Shorter Poems 1927†1957* (Faber & Faber, [1966]) will provide all, or more than, is reasonably required. Sir John Betjeman's work has sold (by the standards of most poetry books) incredibly well, and his *Collected Poems* (John Murray) has run through several editions with new poems being added each time. Any good local bookshop will probably carry the latest, though earlier editions are still around and in that case you may need to add the *Uncollected Poems* (John Murray [1982]) which is a bit expensive, but contains the superb 1955 poem on the 'Conversion of St. Paul'.

Like the writer to the Hebrews, there is not time for me to give an account of David Gascoyne, Anne Ridler, Donald Davie ... But a mention must be made of anthologies. The trouble with them is that the poem you want never seems to be included. Nevertheless, they are good starting places. For an anthology of both poetry and prose by children and young people try Donald Hilton (ed.), *Fresh Voices* (NCEC [1979]). R. S. Thomas has edited *The Penguin Book of Religious Verse* (Penguin [1963]) and it offers much of merit. An older anthology, long out of print yet containing much that is extremely worthwhile is G. Lacey May's anthology of *English Religious Verse* for the Everyman's Library series (J. M. Dent [1937]). This should be sought out eagerly in secondhand bookshops. This series tends not to be too expensive secondhand and not many people know the value of this particular volume. For my money though, the best currently available anthology is edited by Charles Causley and called *The Sun, Dancing*. Published by Penguin books under their children's Puffin imprint [1984] it is nevertheless not a collection for children alone. A hundred and fifty poems, wide ranging in style and date, and roughly arranged in subject sections, make a most rewarding book. Causley's introduction is itself an education in the religious value of poetry. If through some of these volumes we can help people to discover in what sense poetry can be the handmaid of piety there will be many who will have cause to be grateful.

The Pastor and the Novel

GRAHAM A. PATRICK, B.A., B.D., Ph.D.
Alsager

In Jane Austen's *Northanger Abbey* a young woman is asked what she is reading. 'Oh! it's only a novel!' she replies. The author comments with asperity: 'Only some work in which the most thorough knowledge of human nature, the happiest delineation of its varieties, the liveliest effusions of wit and humour are conveyed to the world in the best chosen language.'

This high claim for the novelist's art, justified in the case of Miss Austen if not of many lesser novelists, is a good starting-point for us. It is probably fair to say that most clergy today do not need to be convinced of the value of reading novels. It has not always been the case. In 1936, John Oman, in his classic *Concerning the Ministry*, could argue that the chief defect in contemporary theological education was an 'ignorance of literature, and more particularly English literature'.[1] Oman was thinking primarily of the great 19th-century novelists and poets, and made the suggestion that acquaintance with such literature would have a beneficial effect on a preacher's style and inspiration. Whether we accept that argument or not, his laying the finger on this particular area as lacking in theological training is significant.

Since then, the climate has changed. There is a widespread appreciation amongst Christians today of the rôle of the imagination in the apprehension of religious truth. Where once the main emphasis was on reason and logic, it is now recognized that aesthetic awareness is for many people a more significant element in the creation or confirmation of faith than logical argument. It is possible to trace such a shift of awareness back to the Romantic movement of the 19th century, to Coleridge and Newman, who were responding to the rationalism of the Enlightenment. In our own time, such a change was heralded by Howard Root, who in his article in the celebrated *Soundings* of 1963 made a plea for a new natural theology, whose starting-point should be 'not argument but sharpened awareness', and for Christians to take much more seriously modern literature and art as subject-matter for theology.[2]

We appear to have learned that lesson today. Theological students are encouraged to read as widely as possible in literature, and courses such as 'Theology and the Arts' are more widely available than they were thirty years ago. The fact that there are separate articles in this volume on poetry, fiction and biography is itself significant.

Given this change of atmosphere in the theological world, what precisely is the value of reading fiction for the pastor, and what use can he make of it in his work?

There is, first, the simple matter of *enjoyment*. This may seem to many quite the wrong place to begin, for enjoyment is a suspect word for many pastors. We carry an irrational guilt feeling here. We feel at peace with ourselves only if we are 'working'; if we are enjoying ourselves we feel guilty. We forget, in all this, what happens to people who never have any recreation in their lives. There was an interview in the April 1988 edition of 'Gramophone' with the concert pianist, Imogen Cooper, who spoke of the danger for her of allowing music to become her whole life. There were so many demands on her for concerts and recitals that unless she was careful, there was no time left for enjoying herself or studying new repertoire. 'What should feed your playing, namely your life experience, goes out the window because the only life you have is jumping on to planes and going to concert halls. It's very insidious . . .' Her words seemed very relevant to the life of a pastor, who can so easily become stale and jaded because he spends all his time working, and has little or no time for enjoyment or the equivalent in our profession of 'studying new repertoire'.

For some of us, there are few things more enjoyable than becoming absorbed in a good novel, caught up in its action and story. I find this a humanizing experience. To have a novel to look forward to on a day off or at the end of a day is one of the things that helps to keep me sane. How do we know what to read when there is such a vast range of fiction available in bookshops and libraries today? We will all have our own preferences, of course. It helps very much, however, to have stimulus from other people. I am fortunate to have a Chairman of District who reads and recommends fiction to his colleagues. My wife and I recently joined a local WEA group meeting weekly on a Monday evening studying 'Novels of the '80s'. It was difficult to keep up the reading (one novel per week!) and to keep the night free each week, but it was good to have a long list of novels recommended, and we are still working through them.

Secondly, novels *enlarge our experience of life*. It is one of the qualities of art that it enables us to live vicariously a much wider range of experience than is normally open to us, and this is certainly true of fiction. Through fiction we may enter into the lives of people who are quite different from ourselves, and that can only be beneficial for the pastor. The novels of Barbara Pym, for instance, help us to get 'inside the skin' of single people, lonely spinsters whose dreams are unfulfilled, who are aware of something missing in life, resigned to its unsatisfactoriness. Graham Greene helps us to enter the world of failure, the inside of the person who has failed in life's most significant tests, and is struggling to maintain his self respect. There is a moving testimony in Father Harry Williams's autobiography, *Some Day I'll Find You*, to the helpfulness of Greene's novels in the author's darkest hours.[3] David Cecil sums it up in this way: 'No one person can ever know in practice what it is like to be both a man and a woman, a mystic and a materialist, a criminal and a pillar of society, an ancient Roman and a modern Russian. But books can teach us to be all these things in imagination'.[4] That is surely true of novels above all. Such writers enlarge our experience and that makes us more sensitive and aware in our pastoral work.

Third, there is what I want to call the novelist's *vision*. It has been said that all art is a means of restoring dignity to life through detachment and repose. This is part of the novelist's art. He or she isolates a segment of life from the flux of time, fixes it in the framework of the novel's form, and holds it there for our contemplation. We, in reading it, become observers of, and participate in, the action. In his fine short novel, *A Month in the Country*, J. L. Carr isolates a fragment of time in 1920, after the

Great War, when two war survivors meet in a Yorkshire village, one to restore an old wall painting, the other to find a lost grave. Their recovery of sanity and health through communion with the landscape, history, and the village inhabitants is movingly told. Here is that 'arrest of time' which enables us to contemplate, and to reflect upon the universal human themes of suffering, judgment, love and salvation.

The pastor, who spends so much of his time in frenetic activity, needs to stop from time to time, to step aside from life in order to see more deeply. He cannot see its significance if he is always immersed in it. The novelist helps us to step aside in this way. He enables us to see more deeply, to contemplate in the same way as the best devotional writers help us to do. I am reminded of Frank Wright's argument that 'vision', in the sense of looking, seeing, and attention, is at the heart of the pastor's task.[5]

Fourthly, novels *illuminate the theological and moral issues of their time*. Many examples could be given of this. The problem of evil has been explored by novelists in every age, but it is not surprising that it has been a particular preoccupation of those living in the 20th century. It is one theme in the novels of William Golding, whose early novel, *Lord of the Flies*, is often regarded as a parable of the human condition. In *Brighton Rock*, Graham Greene appears to take a similarly radical view of human nature, the lettering in a piece of seaside rock permeating it as deeply as evil and sin permeate human nature. In his novel *The Sanctuary*, William Faulkner reflects on the effect of the absence of God on morality and evil and society. Where people can no longer believe in God, no one is responsible since no one and everyone is guilty of the evil in the world. The consequences of this for society are frightening. The thriller, too, often despised by the literati, is very much concerned with the issue of evil. C. A. Lejeune once said: 'The thriller is the most moral of stories, because it seeks to discover what has thrown a mind out of gear'. The beautifully-written thrillers of P. D. James (e.g. *A Taste For Death*) amply illustrate this.

The problem of suffering, always a dominant theme in Russian literature, has been explored in recent times by Alexander Solzhenitsyn. His two novels set in prison camps[6] examine the various human responses to deprivation and hardship. *Cancer Ward* is a study of suffering in a different context, a cancer hospital in Tashkent. In the face of the threat to life, the patients come to the knowledge of their true selves and discover whether or not they have the inner resources to cope with their suffering. One conclusion drawn is that adversity can be accepted, and even welcomed, by those who have discovered the spiritual dimension to their lives. One of the patients, Kostoglotov, discovers this through reading Tolstoy's book, *What Men Live By*, and passes it on to others in the ward.

The feminist debate is, as we should expect, amply reflected in contemporary fiction. Several women novelists challenge myths of femininity. Angela Carter, for instance, explores in *Nights at the Circus* the pathological effects of passivity in women. Not all women novelists are supporters of the feminist viewpoint, however. Anita Brookner's heroine, Edith, in *Hotel Du Lac*, stands for the personal principle of domestic happiness rejecting both the feminist viewpoint and the complacent consumer of men.

These are just three examples of our general point. This is not to argue, of course, that novelists set out deliberately to discuss such issues. The insights they bring into the contemporary theological and moral scene are usually a by-product. Further, caution is always necessary in determining exactly what the novelist's own viewpoint is. It is indisputable, however, that novels provide the pastor with a great deal of insight into contemporary theological and moral issues, which are his constant and central concern. Barbara Pym was once asked to write an article about her spirituality. She refused, on the grounds that her spirituality was to be found in her novels. A recent study of the novels of Iris Murdoch suggests that fundamental to her art is 'the experience of renewal and grace, the mystery of the Good, the strangeness of the ordinary, the possibilities of self-transcendence. Her imagination encompasses ... a traditional concern of theology, identifying and attributing significance to the essence and the boundaries of the given'.[7] Not every pastor will find Miss Murdoch's novels palatable, but there is no doubt that as with other modern novelists, they are the source for a great deal of theological reflection.

These, then, are some of the reasons why the pastor should read fiction. We conclude with some suggestions as to how this can be used in his work. In one sense we have touched on this already in suggesting that reading fiction enlarges a person's experience and deepens his vision and sensitivity. All this has obvious consequences for a person whose work is centred upon preaching and pastoral work. We shall try, however, to offer a few practical suggestions in this section.

First, in *pastoral work*. Sometimes in a pastoral situation it is possible to recommend that a person reads a novel to help them to come to terms with what has happened to them. One example must suffice, from my personal experience. I have on several occasions given people who have recently been bereaved, and are finding it hard to accept, my copy of Susan Hill's novel, *In the Springtime of the Year*. The latter is a moving and beautifully-written account of a bereavement, which captures superbly the pain of loss, and the variety of emotions and moods which follow it. Clearly, it would not be appropriate to recommend this to every bereaved person, but I have found a number of people have been grateful for having read it, and they were the kind of people who would probably not have read a theological or devotional book about bereavement.

Part of the universal appeal of the story is that it is a means of helping us to come to terms with our situation. Here we touch on the role of myth in literature and religion and on the current emphasis in New Testament studies on 'narrative theology'. The Christian faith itself is based on, and arises out of, a story, so that there is a fundamental affinity between the gospel and the story. One interpretation of St Mark's gospel, for example, is that it is a story told to help Christians deal with persecution. Of course, there is the question of historicity here, which is not an issue in a novel (although it is clear that Susan Hill's account must have some basis in personal experience). But the point we are making is that there are times when a novel, with its story, can help people to whom we are ministering to come to terms with their problem.

Second, in *talks to groups or larger meetings*. It is not so easy to use fiction as poetry in these situations; reading poetry to a group of people is acceptable while reading extracts from novels is not. It is possible, however, to use our reading as material for talks which will introduce an author to the group, and perhaps encourage them to read his books themselves, and will also provide an insight into a current or long-standing theological or ethical issue. If we have read all the novels of one particular author, that can give us an excellent subject for a talk. 'The novels of Graham Greene', for instance, is one that I have given, and I am currently preparing a similar one on those of Barbara Pym, another favourite author. My experience is that groups respond very well to this kind of topic. If you are enthusiastic about a writer, this will communicate itself to others. It is possible to give short synopses of plots and to combine this with comment on wider issues raised by the story or the characterization.

Another approach is to take one novel, and do a kind of 'review' of it. This has a special appeal if it is a recent one which nobody in the group will have read, but it does not have to be of this kind. Again, it will depend on the pastor's personal preference, and on what he has been reading in recent months.

In either case, it is good for people to know that we have serious interests outside a narrow 'religious' world, and important that they are able to see that we can relate our theology to our wider reading.

Third, in *sermons*. In his classic work on homiletics, *The Craft of the Sermon*, W. E. Sangster warns the preacher against using fiction as a source for illustration if he can possibly avoid it.[8] There are dangers in illustrating sermons from any source, but it would be a pity if the pastor took Sangster's advice and avoided bringing material from novels into his sermons. The latter are surely enriched by drawing on as wide an experience of life as possible, and fiction of whatever kind is many people's favourite reading. Those who are familiar with the radio talks of Richard Harries, now Bishop of Oxford, will know how effectively he is able to illuminate a quite heavy theological or ethical issue with an apt illustration from a novel or a play, or by a quotation from a poem. If we read novels, we ought to use them in our preaching if they illustrate a theme, or seem relevant to a particular festival or doctrine. Of course, we need to do it sensitively and concisely; a long reference or quotation can do more harm than good.

For example, I have used George Eliot's novel *Silas Marner*, which tells of the influence of a child upon a soured and bitter man, to illuminate the Christmas story, and *The Brothers Karamazov* at Easter. *Lord of the Flies* can be used if you are preaching about original sin, and there are some fine insights into doubt and its relationship to faith in Graham Greene's *Monsignor Quixote*. The novels of Primo Levi and Elie Wiesel, which are concerned with the Jewish holocaust, can be helpful on Remembrance Sunday, and those of Nadime Gardimer, set in contemporary South Africa, can illuminate the theme of race and prejudice. These are a few personal examples. Every pastor's reading will be different, and while it is good to have recommendations from other people as to what we might read, the best illustrations come from reading and experiences which have become part of us.

Perhaps enough will have been said now to convince the busy pastor that he need not feel guilty about reading novels. It is time well spent. Such reading will enhance his preaching and his pastoral work, and enrich his theology. It will also bring pleasure and enjoyment to a life too often lacking in such diversions.

---

[1] *Concerning The Ministry* (SCM [1936]), 166.
[2] 'Beginning All Over Again', *Soundings* (CUP [1962]), 19.
[3] *Some Day I'll Find You* (Mitchell Beazley, [1982]), 297-8.
[4] *The Fine Art of Reading and Other Literary Studies* (Constable [1957]), 15.
[5] *The Pastoral Nature of the Ministry* (SCM [1980]), 9-11.
[6] *One Day in the Life of Ivan Denisovich* (Penguin [1963]) and *The First Circle* (Collins [1970]).
[7] Norman Vance, 'Iris Murdoch's Serious Fun' (*Theology*, November 1981, pp. 420-7).
[8] *The Craft of the Sermon* (Epworth Press [1954]), 255.

The Pastor and Biography

GRAHAM A. PATRICK, B.A., B.D., PH.D.
Alsager

'THREE passions, simple but overwhelmingly strong, have governed my life: the longing for love, the search for knowledge, and unbearable pity for the suffering of mankind. These passions, like great winds, have blown me hither and thither, in a wayward course, over a deep ocean of anguish, reaching to the very verge of despair.'[1]

'As I come near to the end of my days, the one thing that haunts me more than anything else is that I have been so unsatisfactory a husband and father.'[2]

'It takes a long time before one realizes that the interruptions are as much a part of life as the things they interrupt; and I suppose by the time we've quite realized it, we're ready for the last interruption, which is Death.'[3]

Many pastors would regard biography and autobiography as their favourite reading, and the three extracts with which we begin illustrate very well why this should be so. In the first, a great scientist and philosopher expresses in magnificent prose his personal credo. In the second, a popular and successful scholar and churchman voices with great honesty his sense of failure in his most intimate family relationships. The third is the characteristically wise insight of a gifted writer, also a sensitive Christian, who is reacting to the dictum of Einstein: 'People who write or think should be given jobs in a lighthouse'. All three are eminently quotable in an address or talk; all three challenge our own priorities and our convictions about what is important, and what of less importance, in life; all three offer a fascinating glimpse of people's inner lives, the things which 'make them tick'.

It comes as something of a surprise to learn that biography in the modern sense is a young art compared with poetry and fiction. In a famous essay[4] Virginia Woolf pointed out that interest in our selves and other people's selves is a comparatively late development of the human mind. It was not until the 18th century in England that this curiosity expressed itself in writing lives of private people, and only in the 19th century that the art of biography fully flowered. Our own century has seen a number of new developments in an increasingly sophisticated art, foremost among which have been the influence of Lytton Strachey, who challenged the belief of the Victorians that biography should be hagiography; and the even more pervasive influence of Freud, so that the contemporary biographer feels the obligation to be well-grounded in psychiatric theory. Today it is a flourishing art form. Popular bookshops carry large stocks of biography and autobiography in hardback and paperback, and religious publishers similarly regard biographies of great Christians past and present as a high priority. The *Expository Times* continues its long tradition of commending this type of literature to its readers with a full-page review of a biography or autobiography each month.

Given that many clergy read biography, and that it is more widely available than ever before, how does such reading benefit the pastor, and what practical use can he make of it in his work? We have already touched on these questions in our introduction, but we shall now examine them in more detail.

It is no accident, in my view, that so many pastors value the reading and study of biography. In doing so, they are making certain theological affirmations. Indeed, the very principle of *incarnation* is involved here. The Christian believes that human life is the principal medium of God's revelation. If this is true above all of one particular human life, that of Jesus, it is also true that every human life may reflect some aspect of that revelation. The glory of God is seen in the lives of his saints – and in the lives of those who would strongly deny their claim to the title of 'saint'. So it is not just a question of the biographer and the pastor sharing a common interest in human nature. A theological motive compels the pastor to be a student of biography.

It follows from this that biography is an important reminder to the pastor of the *power of influence of one life over another*. A contemporary biographer has suggested that practitioners of her art 'extend our awareness of the possibilities of living'.[5] That is a fine description of the effect that the life of Jesus has had upon generations of Christians, even though it is an axiom of current New Testament scholarship that the gospels are most certainly not biographies. It is also a good summary of the effect that reading and reflecting on the life of an outstanding personality can have. The very beginnings of modern biography are generally held to lie in the mediaeval lives of the saints, whose purpose was to edify and inspire their readers through largely idealized portraits of their subjects.

We do well to remember that reading biography can permanently influence people's lives. We can all recall biographies which have had a lasting effect upon us. I remember, as a student, reading three notable biographies: Paul Sangster's fine biography of his father, *Doctor Sangster*, Iremonger's massive life of William Temple, and Coretta Scott King's *My Life with Martin Luther King, Junior*. All three affected me in different ways. The first, a portrait of an outstanding Methodist minister, was one of the influences which led to my offering for the Methodist ministry. The second, one of the greatest of all clerical biographies, kindled in me not only a respect for its subject, but a conviction that the Christian ministry demanded the highest intellectual commitment. The third, a more impressionistic portrait, has had a lasting effect on my understanding of the social outworking of the Christian faith.

This is not to suggest that the people we actually meet in life may not also have a permanent influence upon us. Biography, after all, is encounter at second-hand. It does, however, enable us to 'meet' a far wider range of people than is ever possible in one human life, and that is surely part of its value.

Another aspect of biography which is significant for the pastor is its affirmation of the *value of the individual*. A distinguished modern biographer claims that biography presupposes 'an intense interest in, and a conviction of the worth of, individual life'.[6] This is surely a reflection of the Christian estimate of man, the belief in the sovereign importance of the individual before God. Some of the greatest biographers spent many years of their lives researching and writing the life of their subject, not for financial gain but because they believed passionately that their subject was worthy of such commitment. The pastor will be aware of the theological presupposition underlying such an interest, which makes this particular literary form of particular interest to him.

Where he will perhaps have some misgivings is in the fact that most published biographies are of well-known people, who have made some mark in public life. He will want to affirm the importance of 'ordinary' people, who have been known often to only a small circle, but whose influence may nevertheless be considerable. R. S. Thomas's poem is a salutary reminder that most of us clergy fall within that category:

> They left no books,
> Memorial to their lonely thought
> In grey parishes; rather they wrote
> On men's hearts and in the minds
> Of young children sublime words
> Too soon forgotten. God in his time
> Or out of time will correct this.[7]

In recent years, there have been signs that a new type of 'multi-biography' may be emerging, which gives more emphasis to the lives of ordinary people. A good example of this is Ronald Blythe's *Akenfield*, which is a portrait of a Suffolk village consisting of dozens of small-scale biographies, accompanied by edited tape-recorded conversations spoken by their subjects. The result is a fascinating series of portraits, which together provide a more authentic picture of a village than that given by notable people who only glimpse such a community through the windows of great houses, or even vicarages. George Ewart Evans, the pioneer of so-called 'oral history', has also strongly emphasized the historical significance of the testimonies of ordinary people.

It is not necessary to underline the relevance of this for the pastor who spends most of his time with 'ordinary' people, and at funerals is often called upon to summarize the salient features of their lives. For him, a conviction of the sovereign importance of the individual is a very necessary foundation for his work. Perhaps pastors should be more willing to celebrate some of these lives in print, as the late Trevor Hughes did in his portraits of some 'unknown' East Anglian saints, *A Progress of Pilgrims*.

A third reason why biography is significant for the pastor is in its underlining of our *common humanity*. This was an axiom of the great Samuel Johnson, himself the author of sixty-three biographical writings, as well as the subject of the most celebrated biography of all. Johnson once wrote: 'I have often thought that there has rarely passed a life of which a judicious and faithful narrative would not be useful. For, not only every man has, in the mighty mass of the world, great numbers in the same condition with himself, to whom his mistakes and miscarriages, escapes and expedients, would be of immediate and apparent use; but there is such a uniformity in the state of man . . . that there is scarce any possibility of good or ill but is common to human kind'.[8]

This is a classic statement of the 18th-century view of biography as essentially moral instruction. If this attitude is rather out of fashion today amongst biographers, it nevertheless remains true that there is nothing like biography to remind us of the humanity we share with all men and women. Discovering, and re-discovering, this can be a liberating experience. We all imagine at times that we are unique, that nobody else has difficulties like us. It is immensely helpful at such times to encounter these very problems in the lives of other people we respect and admire. Those who suffer from depression, for instance, will gain much solace from reading J. B. Phillips's autobiography, *The Price of Success*, in which the famous biblical translator describes most movingly the acute depression and breakdown he suffered late in his life, just when his reputation was at its height. The title of the final chapter, 'Light at the End of the Tunnel', and his affirmation that the whole experience taught him a deeper trust in God and stripped him of his 'pride and pious imaginings', will be an inspiration to pastors and others who wrestle with the demon of depression.

Biography and autobiography can expand our sympathies by reminding us of our common humanity, and perhaps this is something the pastor is sometimes in danger of forgetting. The moral pedestal we often imagine we stand upon can separate us from our fellows, as Jesus was often to perceive in his judgments on the morally upright Pharisees. Study of other people's lives can keep us humble, and check our pretensions.

The relevance of all this to the pastor's preaching and pastoral work is obvious. The Congregationalist, Leslie Tizard, said that one function of preaching is to assure people that they are not alone in their difficulties. 'Nobody who has seen it will forget the look of relief and gratitude which comes over a man's face when he is assured that things which he thought put him beyond the pale are common human problems . . . Until that moment he has felt himself quite alone; now he is in company.'[9] This is why biographies and autobiographies which reveal a person's inmost soul can be of immense value to the preacher.

A fourth aspect of biography which is important to the pastor is the issue of *determinism*. To what extent is an individual's life largely pre-determined by the economic and social milieu of his birth and upbringing, or by his heredity, or by both? This is a live question in a century dominated by Marx and Freud, and one with which every serious biographer must wrestle today. Nobody who writes a life of another can ignore the issue of heredity and environment. Marxists explain human behaviour in terms of the irresistible processes of history. Freudians believe in the formative and lasting influence of the childhood experience. Today we accept that we cannot fully understand anyone's life without some consideration of these factors.

Biography, however, is an affirmation that these forces are not the total explanation of human behaviour. 'To write biography is to uphold a belief in the individual and therefore to retain a humanist stance. Humanists assert the primacy of will over circumstance: anti-humanists argue that circumstances dominate will.'[10] If this is true, this is another reason why this particular literary form has a special significance for the Christian pastor. It is here that he can study the interplay between will and circumstance, and see time after time how the former has triumphed over the latter. A memorable example of this is Neville Cardus, whose *Autobiography*, one of the most beautifully written of all, tells how a boy from the slums of Manchester, whose mother was a prostitute and whose formal education lasted for four years, became England's foremost music critic and cricketing journalist. I recall the late Philip Toynbee reviewing in the *Observer* newspaper yet another biography of Beethoven, which tried to 'explain' the discrepancy between his wretched life and his sublime creative powers. Toynbee wrote that there was only one explanation of this discrepancy in his view: 'The continuous creative process of God was at work in that sad clay . . . Beethoven's works are messages from God to man'.

Here we touch upon the Christian doctrine of grace, a doctrine well attested in the lives of famous and ordinary men and women, and very much at variance with the widespread determinism of our time. The pastor will find in the study of biography a helpful corrective to this. In his classic work on Pastoral Theology, R. E. O. White says of the pastor's distinctive attitude: 'He will frankly concede that most moral problems are due to the way that family, or society, or life itself has treated an individual without doubting that the individual may yet be changed by other moral forces brought to bear upon him . . . he will work in the conviction that human personality is ever open to invasive forces of good as well as evil . . .'[11]

Another important aspect of biography concerns its *limitations*. Students of biography sometimes quote some lines from T. S. Eliot's 'Confidential Clerk':

> There's always something one's ignorant of
> About anyone, however well one knows them;
> And that may be something of the greatest importance.
> It's when you're sure you understand a person
> That you're liable to make the worst mistake about him.[12]

Those words would make an apt motto for an aspiring biographer. Those who write people's lives are aware of the limitations inherent in their work – the source material, the intellectual climate in which they live, the necessity for selectivity, the tension between interpretation and the evidence, the sheer impossibility of really 'getting inside the skin' of another person.[13] This is why every biography is in a sense provisional, to be succeeded a generation later by a fresh and perhaps quite different view of its subject.

Autobiography is no different. In the preface to his own autobiography, *The Art of the Possible*, Lord Butler quoted the view of Virginia Woolf, who had found no one in literature capable of expressing his whole self except Montesquieu, Pepys and Rousseau. What the autobiographer omits, he confesses, is as important as what he includes!

This is surely relevant to the work of a pastor, who is working with people who often, like the autobiographer, show only part of themselves to him. He does well to remember this, too, when giving addresses at funerals and memorial services. How do we ever discover the whole truth about someone? It is impossible to do so, of course; but like the biographer we need to consult a variety of sources if we are to avoid giving a quite inauthentic picture of a person. Modern biography has eschewed hagiography as its model, but the funeral address is often little more than that.

One final point can be made about the value of biography. It is surely when we study and reflect on the lives of others that we gain in knowledge of ourselves. We often see in others' lives the mirror image of our own, and so grow in self-understanding. This is very necessary for the Christian's growth in maturity and grace.

These, then, are some of the reasons why the pastor should be a student of biography. It is not just that pastor and biographer share a common interest in human nature. There are deeper, even theological, reasons why biography and autobiography should be amongst his priorities.

We consider, finally, some of the ways in which this material may be used in his work. Much of what has been said already relates very closely to the pastor's whole outlook, and to his pastoral work and preaching. We will, however, make some practical suggestions drawn from recent biography and autobiography.

The most obvious use of this kind of material is in *sermon illustrations*. Every pastor knows the difficulty of using the experiences of local people, particularly members of his own congregation, as illustrative material. Great care and sensitivity is required if this is ever to be done. He is on much safer ground using the experiences of people whose lives have been enshrined in biography, for they are at one remove, so to speak, from the local situation.

Many of the notable preachers of the past found in biography a deep and rich mine for sermon illustrations. H. E. Fosdick read omnivorously in the field, and many of us recall the late William Barclay's 'Men and Affairs' page in this journal, and how his writings are lit up frequently by biographical illustrations. W. E. Sangster commended a wide variety of biography: 'Saints and sinners, soldiers and statesmen, writers and philosophers . . . it is all a thick vein. If . . . the preacher is commending a way of life to the people, how can he better illustrate the character of it than by showing what were the practical consequences in specific lives of counsel heeded or counsel ignored?'[14] Of course, care is needed in using such material. R. E. C. Browne points out the dangers of using biographical illustrations at the beginning of a sermon; the mind commonly works by association rather than logical processes, and if an illustration early on in the sermon causes people to go off at a tangent reflecting on their own experience, they will take little further conscious interest in the sermon.[15]

Every pastor will have a notebook or a filing index where illustrations of this kind can be jotted down and referred to at a later date. A few examples from my own notebook over the past two or three years will illustrate the point being made.

'Conversion': *Blessings in Disguise* by Alec Guinness.

'There had been no emotional upheaval, no great insight, certainly no proper grasp of theological issues; just a sense of history and the fittingness of things . . . Something impossible to explain' (on his reception into the Roman Catholic Church in 1956).

'Scriptures': *Herbert von Karajan* by Roger Vaughan.

'One of the signs of a great piece of music is that it will never resist further interpretation. It is like a deep well. You can dip and dip and never come to the end of it' (Karajan's own words).

'Problem of Evil': *If This Is a Man* by Primo Levi.

'Today I think that if for no other reason than that an Auschwitz existed, no one in our age should speak of Providence' (Primo Levi was an Italian Jew, who survived Auschwitz, and tells the story in his autobiography).

'Failure': *Six Men* by Alistair Cooke.

On Adlai Stevenson, whom he calls 'The Failed Saint': 'What he

left behind was something more splendid, in a public man, than a record of power. It was simply – an impression of goodness. He had mastered the art, far more difficult and rarer than that of a successful politician, writer, actor . . . success as a human being'.
'Humility': *The Life of Bishop John Robinson* by Eric James.

'Isn't it strange what misconceptions we Christians have of each other, and how personal encounters often dissipate some of our prejudices and fears? . . . I would like to get to know you and Ruth better . . . I am sure there is much I can learn from you' (Billy Graham's comment after spending an evening with the Robinson's shortly after *Honest to God* was published).
Thanksgiving': *Chanctonbury Ring* by Mervyn Stockwood.

'Each day before I get out of bed I think of three things for which I return thanks: a good sleep, bodily faculties, food, a home and security, my garden and animals – and much more.'

Another use of biographical material is in *talks and addresses*. Sometimes, after reading a biography, I have felt that the subject-matter was of interest and relevance to a particular group, and I have used the material to make an address. I recall doing this, for instance, on Studdert Kennedy, after reading William Purcell's biography, and on Leslie Weatherhead after reading his son's biography of him. There is a good deal of material for use in this way in Shirley du Boulay's life of Desmond Tutu, *Tutu: Voice of the Voiceless*, the advantage being that the latter is a household name, and a controversial one.

It is sometimes possible to feature a well-known contemporary figure in a school assembly. I have used the story of Maximilian Kolbé, the Polish priest who sacrificed his life to save a fellow prisoner in Auschwitz, in such a context. There are two very useful collections containing brief biographies of 20th-century Christians by John Searle, the most recent of which, *On the Right Track*,[16] consists of twelve portraits of well-known Christians in sport. There is much useful source material here for talks to young people.

On occasion, I find that a sermon develops from something I have come across in a biography, and jotted down for future reference. In the biography of John Robinson referred to above, Eric James mentions something Robinson wrote in 1969: 'I am seldom happy except on a frontier: and I have a sense of constantly pushing out, or rather being pushed – drawn from ahead, yet held from behind, by a power that will not let me go. The centre remains the same, but the edges are opening and expanding'. Reflecting on this, I developed a sermon about 'living on the frontiers', expressing my own understanding of Robinson's 'frontier' theology. It is a pity that our current emphasis on the lectionary often inhibits us from using and developing themes from non-biblical material.

All this may give the impression that biography should be read purely as a quarry for our preaching and teaching. It would be a pity if this were so. My thesis in this article has been that the pastor should be a student of biography and autobiography largely for their own sake, and because he will find in such literature affirmation of certain fundamental Christian convictions about human life. Such study will inevitably enrich his pastoral work and his preaching.

---

1 *The Autobiography of Bertrand Russell*, Vol. I. (George Allen & Unwin [1968]), 13.
2 William Barclay, *A Testament of Faith* (Mowbray, [1975]), 16.
3 *Helen Waddell* by D. Felicitas Corrigan (Gollancz [1986]), 254.
4 'The Art of Biography' in *Collected Essays* Vol. IV, ed. by Leonard Woolf (Chatto & Windus [1969 edition]).
5 Frances Spalding in a review article in the 'Times Educational Supplement', 13 May 1988.
6 Robert Gittings, *The Nature of Biography* (Heinemann [1978]), 19.
7 'The Country Clergy' in *Poetry for Supper* (Granada [1958]).
8 *Rambler* essay, no. 60.
9 *Preaching* (George Allen & Unwin [1958]), 103.
10 Frances Spalding, *op. cit.*
11 *A Guide to Pastoral Care* (Pickering & Inglis [1976]), 2-3.
12 *The Complete Poems and Plays of T. S. Eliot* (Faber [1978]), 449-50.
13 See, for instance, A. J. Cockshut, *Truth to Life: The Art of Biography in the Nineteenth Century* (Collins [1974]).
14 *The Craft of the Sermon* (Epworth [1956]), 251.
15 *The Ministry of the Word* (SCM [1976]), 85.
16 Marshall Pickering [1987].

Part II
Presentation

The Use of Visual Aids

JAMES B. BATES, B.A.
Ilfracombe

'WHAT I hear, I forget; what I see, I remember; what I do, I understand.' So generations of educators have stressed, urging their students to use visual and creative methods of teaching, and the typical infant classroom is ablaze with work of the children, while they themselves are the proverbial hive of activity. In contrast, with few exceptions, our churches and chapels are bleak and bare with the children compelled to spend most of the time they are there sitting still and listening. Where churches have a rich visual tradition, seldom is it exploited for teaching purposes, and seldom are the children asked to make their contribution. No wonder, then, that so little of what is done in church impresses itself upon children, and so much seems boring and meaningless. In the same way adults, though more accustomed to listening, find that concentration flags and the message is forgotten if they have to depend on their hearing alone.

The brief of this article is to concentrate on the use of visual aids in teaching, rather than to explore their possibilities in worship. Since pastors have opportunities to teach within the context of worship, as well as in groups and classes, it would seem wise to learn from the teacher in the classroom. Few teachers, however, would welcome the situation which faces most preachers in worship, a congregation of diverse interests and of wide age-range in a room seemingly designed to isolate people from one another by awkward furnishings and too much space.

Yet, teaching can take place in church and different ages can be interested and stimulated where material is presented imaginatively. This means, in most cases, presenting it visually, either by getting people to think in images, or by providing them with a visual aid. Pictures, like stories, have a wide appeal, and can fix a thought in

35

the mind more effectively than the most striking or subtle statement. This was acknowledged and exploited both in the middle ages and the Renaissance, partly because people were illiterate, but also because the artist could express thoughts and feelings which reached experiences beyond words and make them memorable. So churches of the 'catholic' tradition are rich in wall-paintings, stained and painted glass, carvings in wood and stone, in exquisite needlework and metalwork. Protestantism in its iconoclastic reaction limited itself almost exclusively to words and music to express and communicate its faith. Listening was all and the sight was starved.

It is, however, a Puritan, who died just over three hundred years ago, who can remind us of the first essential for the preacher who wishes to communicate effectively. John Bunyan thought and wrote visually. We can picture Christian as he journeys on and follow his progress in a series of scenes which can be visualized. In this method, of course, Bunyan followed Jesus, whose teaching is remembered by millions who never open a Bible. The use of visual aids begins by thinking visually. Here words have an advantage over pictures because they allow room for the imagination. One can be surfeited with visual images so that they cease to have an impact. This is true of television which in some cases can be far less effective than the radio in teaching because it leaves nothing to the imagination. It can, of course, stimulate, but too much television saturates and ceases to be effective.

This needs to be remembered when we think of using videos or films in worship or teaching. They can so easily take over and overwhelm so that there is little room for the viewer to make a response. In 'Small is Beautiful' Schumacher draws the distinction between a tool and a machine. A craftsman uses a tool to help him in his work. A machine replaces him. There is a place for the 'film service' but even here the film must be strictly under control, kept short or left unfinished, so that there is some room for a response. Otherwise the congregation is turned into an audience and the preacher into a master of ceremonies. A video or film can be used as a most effective tool, but it has to serve a purpose beyond itself. The preacher must think out why it is useful and what purpose it can serve, how it can help a congregation and to what it can lead. It needs to be built into a service or session with careful introduction, presentation and development. There is no reason why it should not be the dominating feature of the service, but this is why it is so important that it should not exclude the other elements of worship.

It is less likely that the purpose of a service will be lost when slides or pictures are used. A picture, projected or displayed, provides a common focus for preacher and congregation which they can consider together, either in silence or as a conversation piece. It can stimulate questions, details can be pointed out, opinions can be sought. In worship it can lead on to acts of devotion as an aid to prayer. Helping people to explore the visual is just as important as teaching them how to listen. Jesus opened people's eyes in more than one way. The world is constantly speaking to us, appealing to us through sights as well as sounds, and 'vision' includes simple observation as well as mystic insight. We need to be taught to see, and to be taught how to learn through seeing. Here the artist can help us, but not only the painter and sculptor. The photographer and the poster artist, whether employed by the church or the world, offer insights which we could miss. Relief agencies, for instance, know this. You are more likely to evoke a response with a picture of a starving child than by an impassioned verbal appeal. The impact of a picture presented at the appropriate moment, or a picture on display which is referred to at the right moment can both reveal and implant an idea in a way more effective than words. Some pictures, perhaps more especially paintings, call for quiet consideration or contemplation; others will provoke discussion, even controversy. In both the preacher and people are brought together as they look together and seek to express their feelings or thoughts. The good teacher is one who is learning alongside those whom he is trying to teach, and a common object provides an opportunity for this.

As with films, presentation is all-important. Pictures must be large enough and clearly displayed so that all can see. Here slides have the advantage because they can be projected to the size needed, but they also demand a darkened room and few churches are easily blacked out. Nor is it very helpful to interrupt a service by drawing blinds, even during a hymn! So a simple rule could be, slides on winter evenings and pictures in daylight. This may mean that few works by great artists can be used in the daytime because there are few reproductions large enough (though Athena publishes a limited selection). In group work, however, there should be no problem. Posters, on the other hand, are designed to make an impact from a distance and many agencies provide very challenging material, especially the USPG, Christian Aid, and Oxfam.

Pictures must have a decent setting which does not conflict with the layout of the church. Money is well spent on good display boards and proper means of projection. Both should be moveable, but not makeshift. Pictures will not and should not be a feature of every service and a blank screen or an empty display board can unintentionally cause disappointment, especially among the young. They need not be central, but they should be visible. Their position needs to be thought out liturgically (possibly near to the pulpit, since they will most likely be used in association with the ministry of the word) and in relation to the permanent features of worship. Display boards can usefully serve both in the front of the congregation and in the foyer of the church, the one complementing the other. Pictures too small to be used in church can be displayed in the foyer for people to study after the service and a display on the theme of the service can reinforce what the preacher aimed to say. A well-kept foyer with attractive and relevant displays impresses the visitor and can be used to widen the experience of the congregation, especially if it is related to the worship of the church. Displays within the church itself can add brightness and interest to worship and be used directly with the preacher moving around them, or for study after. As with all posters and notices, displays must be removed as soon as they have served their purpose. Few sights are more damaging to the image of a church than the fading remnants of what was done last year.

For many teachers, the blackboard (or its equivalent, the marker board), is still the most useful of tools. Blackboards are seldom attractive to look at and chalk dust does not go well with black gowns or cassocks, so churches may do well to invest in a marker board, or even better, in a flip chart where sheets of paper replace the wipable surface. In all these devices the preacher is able to build up the theme visually, using headings or diagrams. He can refer back to what has already been said and reinforce it by underlining. He can invite the congregation to make contributions, writing up, or getting them to write up what they have said. Even more than a picture it becomes a common focus of interest and at the end there is a visible record of what has been achieved. This, then, can be used most effectively as a source of topics for prayers and devotions.

Care needs to be taken over lettering and layout. The former needs to be bold, simple and clear. Practice makes perfect and preachers, like teachers, need to develop a style which is clearly visible and orderly. It is as well to plan the layout as one plans the sermon, allowing, if needs be for the contributions made by others. This need not stifle originality or unexpected inspiration, but it does prevent a theme getting lost and the display becoming messy. Diagrams are always helpful and can fix an idea in the memory. The preacher who can build up a diagram as the sermon progresses will hold the attention of young and old. Not everyone finds it easy to draw, but 'matchstick' men serve the purpose as well as more elaborate drawings in most cases. If one is unsure of one's ability to draw in public (no easy task, even for the experienced), one can prepare a sheet by outlining the drawing in pencil which is all but invisible until drawn over with a marker during the service. With a flip chart drawings, diagrams, or even headings can be prepared before the service and uncovered at the appropriate moment.

In recent years the overhead projector has become an essential feature in the worship in many churches. Especially in evangelical circles where one worships with gesture as well as voice, the OHP has freed the hands from hymn books so that they can be clapped or waved as inspiration or tradition demands. It also means that when the words are projected on a screen or wall, the worshipper can lift eyes as well as heart and this (so choirmasters will tell us) is good also for the voice. For the preacher, as for the teacher, the OHP has all the advantages of the marker-board or flip chart, with the added benefit of allowing the preacher to face the congregation while he is using it. Its pens are easier to manipulate than markers or chalk. Sheets can be prepared beforehand and points can be revealed as they are needed by using cover sheets. With the help of a photo-copier, prints can be taken from drawings or from books (though copyright needs to be watched here). It can be used in daylight and needs only a blank wall for projection if a screen is not available. This means that it is unobtrusive when it is not being used. Placed by the pulpit it is fully under the control of the preacher, to be switched on or off as the occasion demands.

The range of source material for visual aids is limited only by the imagination of the preacher and can begin with what is about him. In even the plainest of settings there is a liturgical (and therefore theological) significance to what is in the church and how it is arranged. George Herbert found meaning in every part of the church, even the floor. A series of services on the font (or baptistery), the pulpit, the communion table and even the organ could provide a miniature compendium of Christian teaching and practice, and familiar, unnoticed furnishings would take on a new significance. Most churches in their decorations include some Christian symbolism, and from the earliest times, as the IHS and CHI-RHO indicate, the church has taught through symbols. Parish churches are incredibly rich in visual material, but too seldom are their carvings, stained glass or needlework used in worship. Visiting schools are more likely to learn from them than the congregations who attend week by week.

More and more churches are recognizing the significance of the Christian year and both feast day and fast offer opportunities for visual display. Since parson Hawker of Morwenstow first celebrated harvest the preacher has been surrounded by a wealth of visual aids at harvest festivals. Many of these have not only been brought, but grown by members of the congregation. How important then that these gifts should not be ignored, but recognized and used in worship. Christmas is almost universally observed by special decorations, and so is Easter. Both these allow for the use of the visual in teaching and preaching, just as they provide a way in which the congregation can express devotion in creative activity.

Some traditions have reacted against over-elaborate display and ceremonial, but the simplest gathering of people is a form of ceremony and has something to teach. Ceremony fails where meaning has been lost, or where true meaning is lacking, and in most cases this is due to the failure of the preacher to teach from what people display and do.

Artefacts have become a popular means of teaching children about world religions and many children will have become familiar with tephillin and mezuzahs, kirpans and kangas, but remain ignorant of Christian artefacts. The Communion offers obvious examples, not just the chalice or Communion glasses, but the bread and wine. The water used at Baptism as well as the font, the collection bags or alms-dishes, the books used in worship, their titles and contents pages, are all things which are familiar and taken for granted, but which can be used in teaching.

Bible teaching can be helped, but also very much hindered, by the use of visual aids. Bible 'illustrations' are, as a rule, to be avoided, not just because so many are bad (the Victorian Sunday school wall pictures and the Woolworths' children's Bibles), but because their aim is wrong. You cannot re-create the scene as it happened, nor present people (especially Jesus) as they were. Any attempt is an interpretation and valuable only in so far as the artist has had depth of insight into the significance of the event portrayed. So the fact that Giotto dresses New Testament characters rather like friars and nuns, that Brueghel portrays a Jerusalem crowd as a rabble of Netherlandish peasants or Rembrandt sees the Bible story in the setting of Amsterdam Jewry adds to the meaning of the events because they are interpretations not representations. As with the Gospels themselves, we look at Jesus as they saw him, and it leaves room for us to discover Jesus and the Bible characters for ourselves. A modern series of Bible pictures from France leaves the faces of people blank. We form our own impression through understanding and imagination. On the other hand maps and photographs can provide useful background information. Israel today, through archaeology, through the landscape and in many cases through surviving customs can give us a picture of the world Jesus knew (though we must remember that the old city of

Jerusalem, so beloved of Bible illustrators, is Arab and mediaeval and not the Roman city of Herod).

Jesus drew examples for his teaching from everyday life, in the same way as Amos from a plumb line, and Jeremiah from a budding almond tree. For the preacher with eyes to see, there is catechetical material everywhere, both in what things are in themselves and in what they symbolize. Most religious symbols have their roots in the natural world (water, fire, bread, for example), but unless the distinction between the natural and the symbolic is made clear there will be confusion, and unless the natural is made real, the symbol will remain meaningless. So, a candle lit on a dark winter's day, a loaf of bread broken and shared around will help people to experience and understand what Jesus meant in his claims about himself. We can use examples from our homes, from the tools of various trades, badges and signs of all kinds, the world of nature and the world of mankind, almost anything which speaks of the ways of God and man.

'What I do, I understand.' Perhaps the most effective visual aids are those made by the congregation. Classrooms are bright with children's work, and children are delighted and proud to have their work displayed. In worship their work becomes an offering which they are glad to make, and this can become a most useful tool for teaching. They have learned through producing it and can help others to learn from it by talking about it or just by showing it to the congregation. In family services where the church takes up the theme on which the children have been working, their work, brought for display can become a vital part of the worship, both to illustrate the theme and as an aid to devotions. All the more reason, therefore that the church invest in good display stands so that the children's work is properly acknowledged.

In recent years creative visual work has not been limited to children. Many churches have taken to producing banners with which to celebrate festivals and other significant occasions in the church's year, and the dreariest chapels have become bright with colour. This is a most useful medium. It is public and works on a scale large enough for everyone to see. It uses simple and bold patches of colour and so depends more on a sense of design than skill in draughtsmanship. It makes full use of symbolism, and so is an excellent means of teaching as well as being a visual reminder of the message it conveys. It can be folded up and put away for future use, or disposed of when it has served its purpose. Preacher and people can get together to prepare banners so that together they can explore the meaning of the message symbolized and the most effective ways of communicating it. The people can share with the preacher in the presentation in worship so that the sermon, so often a solitary exercise, becomes a communal enterprise in which the visual and oral become one in communicating the faith. This is only one way in which preacher and congregation can share in the offering of worship. Whatever has been made, whatever has been grown, whatever has been received can be a focus and inspiration for worship, so that we maintain the tradition which goes back to the Temple:

> And the glorious majesty of the Lord be upon us:
> Prosper thou the work of our hands upon us,
> O prosper thou our handywork.
> (Ps 90:17 BCP)

Resources
Equipment
  For projectors, OHP's, screens, flip charts
  SELECTASIZE VISUAL AIDS*
  The Corner House
  Brighton Road
  Couldsdon, Surrey CR3 3ES
  07375 54611/2/3

For slides of religious art
  The Slide Centre*
  17 Broderick Road
  London SW17
  01-223 3457

  The National Gallery
  Trafalgar Square
  Westminster
  London SW1

BBC Educational
Michael Benn Associates
P.O. Box 234
BBC Schools Publications
Weatherby
West Yorkshire LS23 7EU
0937 541 001

For posters and prints
SPCK
Holy Trinity Church
Marylebone Road
London NW1
01-387 5282

St Paul Book Centre★
199 Kensington High Street
London W8
01-937 9591

Church House Bookshop
Great Smith Street
London SW1
01-222 9011

★ These issue catalogues

Things that are Seen

WILLIAM D. HORTON, M.A.
Wesley College, Bristol

When St Paul, in his second letter to the Corinthians, contrasted the 'seen' and the 'unseen' (4:18) his purpose was more to affirm the eternal nature of spiritual realities than to deny the importance of material things in God's provenance. He wrote as one who, through suffering, had learned to sit loosely on the ever-changing, dying world around him and to trust in the unchanging, ever-living world of God's spirit. He was encouraging his converts to trust, similarly, their unseen God rather than to pin their hopes on the fleeting, ephemeral world so visibly and immediately at hand.

Of course, if the apostle *were* entertaining any intention of denying the visible world's reality or of denigrating its significance in God's purposes, he could justly be accused of mishandling the 'given' ingredients of the faith he claimed to espouse. A faith which holds the world to be God's creation and proclaims, as the heart of its message, God's incarnation in Jesus Christ cannot dismiss the human, material and visual as irrelevant to its spiritual content. Christian history teaches us that the vast majority of people experience the unseen realities of the spirit through, not in spite of, the ordinary things of daily life. It would be presumptuous to deny that God can and does reveal himself to us in any way he chooses, even directly and 'out of the blue', but the main vehicle of his self-revelation would appear to be the people and things of daily life. The 'things that are seen' may be transient; human life is certainly subject to mortality, but God uses the visible and temporal to bring us into touch (the language of the physical and visual world is necessary even to describe spiritual experiences!) with the unseen and the eternal. Of the many scriptural illustrations of this the supreme example is the use Jesus made of bread and wine at the Last Supper. In his hands, the food on the table became his own shattered body and shed blood, the means whereby the first disciples appropriated to themselves, as countless Christians have done since, the spiritual and eternal blessings of his death and passion. So God's love is 'enfleshed' in human love, his spirit is seen at work in human life and the heavenly vision is mediated to men and women through earthly channels. The invisible is experienced through the visible.

How does this relationship between the seen and the unseen find expression in the church, today? Inevitably, different traditions differ in the importance they attach to the visual content of the church's life. The Catholic and Orthodox traditions, for example, place much greater stress on the visual element in worship than does the Protestant which, broadly speaking, is more verbal and cerebral in its approach. There are, no doubt, good historical reasons for this, not the least being the Protestant concern to take seriously the prohibition of the second commandment. The violent iconoclasm with which the Cromwellian puritans reacted against what they considered to be idolatrous was but one expression of this concern. Happily, the majority of today's Protestants do not have image breaking high on their agenda. None the less, there lingers a suspicion in some circles that visual and sensuous images only serve to adulterate the purity of worship 'in spirit and in truth' (Jn 4:23) and, on that account, are best avoided.

But we live in a visual age! Visual images are thrust at us from every quarter, particularly on the television screen which is now the chief medium of mass communication. Our children are educated in schools possessing sophisticated equipment which enables them to explore every aspect of life from a visual point of view. Where, outside of the university lecture and the church sermon, do people rely on words only to proclaim their message? Any manufacturer selling a product, any promoter publicizing a cause is well aware of the need of a visual presentation; films, videos, flip-charts, acetates, models, colour brochures – these are today's impact makers, not the sales' patter, however silver-tongued the salesperson may be. Increasingly, churches (even those which, traditionally, have been hostile or indifferent to visual things) are coming to recognize the vital importance to their life of colour and form, touch and movement, music and drama, arts and crafts, and the whole range of sensory experiences. These things are not inimical to the spiritual life, they are its allies; God comes to us and we approach him by means of them. There may be, indeed, a danger of over-stressing the visual element in Christian experience for its own sake, but the penalty for taking fright and doing nothing is to exclude from the Christian arena a major area of human life and to increase further the marginalization of the church in society. It is also to restrict the proper celebration of the gospel; the multi-coloured message of life, light, love, hope and joy in Christ cannot be proclaimed adequately in a context which denies these things. What people experience through seeing and feeling has a much greater influence on them than what they hear, even in the kingdom of God!

Chapter 4, 'The Use of Visual Aids' focused on the importance of the visual content of the church's educational programme. Starting from a similar theological and practical standpoint this chapter seeks to take the matter further. It draws attention to three other areas of church life where the 'things that are seen' have a particularly important part to play and, in each case, it offers suggestions for developing the visual side of the church's work.

1. *Worship*

Reference has already been made to the ways different traditions approach the visual element in worship. But whatever their approach, inevitably, *all* traditions are involved with visual things, because worship takes place in buildings and uses ritualistic forms. The lofty, colourful mediaeval cathedrals and parish churches were built to reflect God's majesty and 'otherness' and to draw the thoughts and prayers of worshippers upwards to God, in adoration. Services in them were designed to create a sense of the numinous rather than to appeal to people's intellectual understanding. Within the magnificent setting of the cathedral and its worship present-day Christians still see God's glory revealed. But, equally, the large nonconformist preaching place with its central pulpit, the more homely country chapel and the simple Friends' meeting house reflect the biblical and theological understanding of those who built them. They, too, have a powerful, if different visual quality which influences worship in a distinctive way.

Today, any Christian community which has the opportunity of starting from the drawing board and building a church to meet the liturgical needs of the late 20th century is both fortunate and entrusted with a heavy responsibility. The opportunity ought not to be wasted out of a misguided loyalty to the past; building in the style of a previous generation or providing for a way of worship which no longer attracts is to fossilize both gospel and worship and rob them of their living power. Today's architects, builders and those who furnish churches must be true to today's insights, using the very best materials, techniques and visual forms which speak to today's worshippers.

The majority of Christian congregations, however, already have their buildings and furnishings. How do they best use what they have received from the past, in the present? How can they express the gospel visually, more effectively? Often, much can be done with little effort or expense. A simple spring-cleaning operation to remove grime from windows, dust from lampshades and dirt from walls and paintwork can make a building lighter and more worshipful; it is as basic as that! A blitzkrieg on accumulated rubbish, musty piles of long unused hymnbooks, out-of-date posters and other eyesores removes visual distractions to worship. Taking away one or two of the rarely needed front pews, enlarging the sanctuary area and re-positioning furniture can create space for movement, dance and drama in worship. Increasing the wattage of the light bulbs can banish sepulchral gloom and make the service a more joyful experience for the congregation on a dull winter's evening. Introducing strategically placed spotlights can highlight the building's focal points and benefit worship. Concealed lighting can, in some places, soften a harsh glare and provide a more sympathetic atmosphere for worship.

Of course, some improvements involve greater expenditure than can be met from the church's current account and the members need to count the cost before embarking on them. But, if they are carefully planned and well carried out, the benefit they bring is nearly always far out of proportion to their cost. Good quality, hard-wearing carpet or modern floor covering, for instance, is expensive to lay over a large area but it adds to the visual impact of the building as well as making it both warmer and quieter. Plain or mottled colours are preferable to heavily patterned designs because they are less distracting and easier on the eye, but royal blue and red are not the only colours available! Similarly, curtains can contribute as much to our church buildings as to our homes and, if chosen with a skilful eye to the overall colour scheme, can enrich the decorative appearance of the building and make it more worshipful. Before buying carpets or curtains, however, take advice as to how they will affect the building's acoustics. People still need to hear as well as see! Adults in charge of very young children can do both, and the rest of the congregation worship undistracted by the noise, if part of the building (say, the back of a gallery) is partitioned off with a glass screen and the separate room wired for sound. However! What this says about mutual acceptance and the whole congregation worshipping *together* may not be to everybody's liking.

Another major item of expenditure is the replacement of fixed pews by chairs (though the outlay is not so great if, as sometimes can be arranged, the sale of the pews off-sets the cost of the chairs). Sitting in pews, the eye (if it can see beyond the neck of the person in front!) is focused on a pre-determined spot – the altar or the pulpit. Chairs have a greater flexibility and can be arranged to meet the different visual needs of each act of worship. They can even be set out to encourage eye-contact between the worshippers! Though not cheap to buy, good chairs are visually more pleasing than most pews, more comfortable, more adaptable in use and, therefore, more conducive to present-day worship.

There is much that can be done to enhance the visual quality of worship on a temporary basis. Churches accustomed to vestments, altar frontals, pulpit falls and the like which change with the changing seasons of the Christian year need no reminding of the impact these things make on worship. Churches whose tradition does not include the regular use of such 'aids' can introduce seasonal banners and hangings as the focus for worship on any given Sunday.

Let the banners be colourful, simple in design (and, therefore, eye-catching) and well-produced, employing symbolism that 'speaks for itself': if the symbols require interpretation, their visual impact is lost. The occasional use of paintings, collages, models, statues, tableaux and 'stations of the cross' may be even more effective than having them permanently in place and taken for granted. Crib scenes and Easter gardens provide a visual stimulus for worship as the different festivals come round.

Flowers, too, make a valuable contribution to worship by adding natural beauty to God's house and speaking of his creative power. Floral arrangements need not always be put in the same place week after week (is it right to put them on the holy table?) and different containers and forms can be used to introduce variety. If flowers are left in the church for mid-week services or for the delight of visitors, appoint someone to care for them and remove faded displays; half-dead blooms withering in the vase raise nobody's spirits! At a time when floral art is so widely practised there is usually little difficulty in encouraging a group of devotees to contribute their skills on a rota basis. But always ensure that the art is subordinate to the worship and not vice versa!

With the wide range of visual material available today audio-visual equipment can be used to make the worship-service itself more visual. Why not use transparencies (e.g. 'stills' from the Zefirelli film 'Jesus of Nazareth' produced by the Bible Society) and appropriate music to accompany a meditation based on scripture, instead of a sermon, one week? Done well, this can be a very effective worship experience. Does the congregation always need to pray with eyes shut? Encourage the congregation to look at a picture or some other 'visual' and let that stimulate and inform the spoken prayer. No one would want this approach to worship every Sunday. But an opportunity is missed if it is never tried at all. The popularity of the harvest festival and the Christmas nativity service clearly shows that the more visual the worship is the greater significance it has for many people.

2. Fellowship

The Holy Spirit gives gifts to the church and those gifts are infinitely varied. They are all given to 'build up the body of Christ' (Eph 4:13). But it is a sad fact that while some gifts have been highly prized by the church others have been conspicuously overlooked. Those who have been enabled to preach, to act as pastors, house fellowship and prayer group leaders and to fill the (so called) 'spiritual' offices of the church have been rightly valued for the contributions they make. But those who haven't these gifts to exercise but are gifted with their hands, their artistry, their willingness to serve in other ways are not always given due recognition for the essential part they play.

Every church, however small, is a treasure-house of talents, as the pastor who goes home visiting soon discovers! The pastor's responsibility, therefore, is to encourage every member to contribute something to the common good and to create opportunities for people to exercise their particular gifts in the church's life. Some may be encouraged to give their skills in broadening the scope of Sunday worship; others to use their craft in making furniture or furnishings for the church. Things made especially for a church by its members have far greater significance than any bought-in items can ever have; they become offerings of worship and fellowship in a unique way. But the possibilities of congregational involvement are as many as the number of church members! Why not arrange a 'talents' service with the accent on a display of craftwork and hobbies? The theme could be thanksgiving to God for his gifts. Such a service would encourage a better mutual understanding among the members, a greater sharing of interests and a feeling among the participants that their skills and talents were being recognized and made part of the church's offering of service to God.

The corporate exercise of skills and artistic gifts can also contribute to the church's fellowship. Groups of people can come together in 'working parties' to make hassocks or banners or a variety of soft furnishings for the church. Of course, there is always the danger of an unholy rivalry and competitive spirit creeping into any corporate venture. But given the readiness of people to accept each other's offering, the 'things that are seen' become the means of strengthening the church's unity and fellowship. Then any joint undertaking, whether it be a flower festival, a DIY re-decoration of the premises, or the maintenance of the church gardens brings church members together and produces a sense of corporate identity. No bad thing for any church!

3. Mission

The visual content of the church's life not only contributes to its worship and fellowship, it also has an important role in its mission to the neighbourhood. At the simplest level, what passers-by *see* from the outside matters considerably; the majority never step inside to enquire further. A badly maintained building, overgrown gardens, a notice board advertising last Christmas's bazaar, uneven paths and dangerous steps all speak a visual message, but it is not the message of the gospel! On the other hand, a church which looks cared for and welcoming, which declares its faith by prominently displaying a cross (perhaps illuminated at night) and gives evidence of life within, helps its mission by the way it presents itself to the neighbourhood. Not every church has a prime high street site; but every church can use the site it has to the best advantage.

Regular churchgoers often fail to appreciate how much courage is needed by non-churchgoers if they are to cross the threshold into the church building. A wide gulf exists (if only in people's minds!) between the world of daily life and the strange, religious world of the church; only at weddings and funerals is that gulf bridged to any significant extent. Visual things help to narrow the gap! Installing, where possible, glass doors or a picture window which allow passers-by to see into the church (perhaps right into the worship area itself) helps to break down the barrier between the sacred and secular, to their mutual advantage. Doors which are fully open at service times, a well-lit porch, a comfortably furnished and carpeted welcome area with its flowers and pictures, all help the visitor to feel at home in an otherwise strange environment.

There are special occasions on which, through the 'things that are seen', the community can be encouraged to participate in church life. On Education Sunday a local school can be invited to exhibit some of its work and the staff and scholars asked to share in leading the services. A local factory may be persuaded to display some of its products at an industrial festival service. Students at the art college, technical college or drama school can be enlisted to give their skills towards a church project, to the benefit of both students and church. In these and other ways church members are encouraged to think about their relationship to the community and people who do not normally attend worship or support the church's work are challenged to think about their relationship to the Christian faith.

The importance, for the church's mission, of high quality publicity material cannot be over-estimated. However 'alive' a church may be, if it advertises its life through badly produced, scarcely legible duplicated leaflets, or hand-outs printed in ecclesiastical gothic type, it will not attract the attention of any but its most loyal supporters. Let the church learn from the secular advertiser and use the best publicity it can afford. Shoddy, visually unattractive material is not worthy of the gospel it seeks to commend.

Outside the building, evangelism is no longer centred solely on open-air preaching; visual means of proclaiming the gospel are recognized as being just as, if not more, effective. Christian drama groups explore the opportunities of street theatre; music groups attract people to listen to their gospel songs; processions of witness, at Christian festivals, confront bystanders with the cross and their banners; empty shop windows are used for a temporary display promoting a good cause or illustrating some aspect of the church's work in the community; news items are provided for the local TV and radio stations and the Christian message is spread far beyond the church building. It is for each church to uncover the possibilities in its own locality and then to proclaim the gospel, visually, in every way it can. Through visual things the church engages in effective mission.

St Paul said that the 'things that are seen' are only temporal. No doubt he was right! But visual things are not, thereby, insignificant as this article has attempted to show. They are of crucial importance to the Christian faith and to the life of the church. They provide a God-given opportunity for every pastor to grasp for the sake of the gospel.

The Parish Magazine

DICK WILLIAMS, B.A., B.D.
Croft, Warrington

IMAGINE, if you will, the first Christian congregation in Jerusalem. Among its members would be the Mother and brothers of Jesus. There too would be the Apostles and the rest of the disciples – people who had known Jesus before his crucifixion, many who had seen him after his resurrection. Here was a Christian community – a fellowship and congregation of people whose lives were being re-ordered around that central experience.

Now let us imagine a newsletter reflecting their corporate life and activities, produced for the benefit of all the members and available to anyone else who was interested.

That work of imagination accomplished, we have conceived the basic idea of a parish magazine.

It is, of course, fashionable to deride such publications. But fashion is frequently a substitute for thought. True, some parish magazines are dismal in form and dreary in content. So are many sermons and many weighty tomes. So, indeed, are many examples of any art form. Print does not always reflect the life that it chronicles. The skills which make print transparent to life are not universally nor evenly distributed. More fundamentally, the quality of corporate Christian experience in parish life is likewise variable.

Parish magazines are almost universally unpretentious. That is one of their charms. Nevertheless their purpose and their content demand to be taken seriously. A steady current of new interest in them is a welcome sign of life in local congregations. In the welter of today's religious publications where can people look for a reflection of local and accessible church life? People who want to get a glimpse of Christian faith as it is currently lived in their neighbourhood have a right to find it in their local parish magazines. Local churches have a duty to provide it.

But for the purpose of this chapter the importance of the genre is not at issue. The request is for a consideration of the ways in which parish magazines may be created. But of all practical matters vision, conviction and motivation come first. So for a practical approach I choose to begin with a high doctrine of parish magazines. It really is worth starting 'in Jerusalem'.

Let us begin with aims.

The aim of a parish magazine is to hold up a mirror to local church life so that each member may see his or her own part in it, and see the place of their local church in the world. It must aim to do this in a way that will help them, and any others who may read it, to become aware that here is something about ultimate truth embodied in the loving relationships of people grappling with the basic experiences of human life.

The aim will determine and guide the methodology. A parish magazine is a community paper. The community it reflects must be involved in its production. The weight of that principle does not remove the need for an editor, indeed it reinforces it. However the editor does not need to do everything himself nor should he.

For practical purposes I suggest three fundamental skills. The first skill is that of attracting help. The second skill is that of editing. The third is that of design and production.

I

Let us start by thinking about getting help. On occasion I am invited by a parish to meet a group appointed to think afresh about their parish magazine. I know that I am on to a winner before I go because the vital first step in the process has been taken. The parish council has corporately expressed concern and taken action. The project – whatever the puzzlement may be – is off and running. One such occasion took me to a vicarage where the assembled group felt themselves to be running on the spot. They had energy, but – they said – no talent, no necessary skills, no flare, none of the requisite resources.

The first step, therefore, was the very unliterary one of inviting them to list the occupations of everyone in the congregation. It was an urban priority area parish in which not many had jobs but former jobs were very much to the point as well. As I recall it took about three minutes to discover that in the congregation there was an art teacher and a printer. The coming together of that information with that evening's task had the force of revelation. They were lucky, of course. But the principle of self discovery is at the heart of such things.

In the matter of attracting help the local church must first turn out its own shelves. And it will be looking for help in editorial skills, news gathering, design, production, finance and distribution. It may well be that a decision about the editor may be the last to be taken. It is not one to be taken hastily. If it is not – and it need not be – the parish clergyman, then it must be one who enjoys his entire confidence, and one with whom he will meet frequently and relevantly. As the editor of a Diocesan tabloid newspaper I do not edit my own duplicated parish magazine. That is done by a stonemason, who has the artistic skills of his craft and is also our Sunday School Superintendent.

Care should be given from the very first to all things financial. Many magazines have foundered upon a divided mind in money matters. A budget should be worked out, and this should be based upon at least three considerations. The first is whether or not the magazine should be distributed free as an investment in mission, or whether it should break even, or whether it should aim to show a profit. The second consideration concerns the scale and nature of the magazine proposed. The third is to do with advertising: whether to raise revenue from it, and if so at what rates, from whom, and with what exclusions. Agreement in advance about an acceptable level of financial loss or investment is important. As a minimum requirement a fiscal policy capable of being sustained for at least a year should be agreed from the start.

A parish magazine treasurer needs to be appointed. A recruiter of advertising may also be appointed.

The supply of news is a genuine community commitment. A congregation comprises diverse age and activity groups. It should be the responsibility of each to make sure that its life is represented to the editor. It is his job to create the composite picture. How each group perceives and carries out its communications task is a fair agenda item for its own committee and for that of the church council.

No business is more important than that of distribution. Producing a magazine which fails to reach its readers is self-condemned folly. A list of subscribers should be compiled, divided into manageable 'rounds', and shared among voluntary visitors who will deliver it. This is a matter of much importance in parish life. It deserves a full evening's planning by a founding group. The whole enterprise stands or falls by them. A reliable person should be appointed to coordinate and service this particular activity.

The judgment about the kind of format in which to produce the magazine may well depend upon the availability of local talent. Where there are strong artistic and graphic endowments in the congregation these will be best expressed in off-set litho. Essentially this is a process in which the editor and his helpers arrange a page just as they would like to see it and it is photocopied onto the printer's plate and reproduced exactly – drawings, photographs and all.

Increasingly however there are computer 'buffs', some with their own equipment, anxious to demonstrate the powers of their Apricot machine – or kindred piece of equipment. Different type faces and sizes and other visual effects can be keyed into the programme and multiple copies of the desired pages run off and then collated.

The old fashioned duplicator still throbs away in many a church hall and parsonage. These – or typewriting and duplicating agencies – still turn out smart, unpretentious magazines which win confidence by their unassuming but informative style. Specially printed coloured covers are available for them from various sources, if desired, or the church's own design can be used with advantage. A well designed cover can have a long term influence for good in those who see it many times. Local competitions for a design can foster fruitful habits of thought among those who try their hand.

To create a magazine much help is needed. It should be actively sought.

II

The second requisite skill is that of an editor.

It frequently falls to the lot of the clergyman to act as editor. For many it is a wearisome chore which bounces back each month with unforgiving regularity. Again, however, there are basic skills which are well within the grasp of the busy minister.

Producing a parish magazine is very much a matter of fostering good relationships. The editor must meet those who supply his news. In a small parish it may happen informally in the course of normal routine. It may have to be engineered in the form of a regular special meeting. He must also meet his distributors on a similarly relevant basis. These encounters will not only help stimulate the flow of news, they will also provide feed-back and give him a sense and awareness of how the magazine is being received.

His first duty is to acquire an overall vision of local church life. In the context of this he will need to draw up a diary of events for as far ahead as he can, and on a monthly basis in some detail. This programme will impose its own requirements, first for relevant information, secondly for whatever explanation it may necessitate, and thirdly for inspirational or illustrative comment in the form of feature articles. Knowing in advance what the calendar of events contains he will be able to commission in advance whatever other material will serve to shed light on it.

Within the overall vision he will see certain priorities. The deliberate or instinctive identification of these will set his style as editor. The rest of the magazine contents will arrange itself around those things he deems most important.

In the context of this overall vision and setting of priorities he will need always to pay special attention to the detail of individual lives represented in the births, marriages and deaths columns. I still recall the shock of learning that my carefully polished leader was read well after the baptisms, weddings and funerals columns. This is a fact to learn from and accept. The appearance in print of one's name is a rare event for most people. It can give one a sense of dignity and of belonging. For some it can be a healing experience to see their name in print.

The editor must insist, with all the diplomacy he can muster, that articles are true in purpose and clear in expression. He will need to be aware that most people in England have literary ability estimated to be Grade 4 CSE. He will be properly sensitive to the fact that popular tabloid dailies are written for a reading age of around 8 while addressing a mental age and intelligence quotient as high as may be.

He will do well to build up his resources. One simple device is to have a set of twelve folders, one for each month of the year. Each can have a note of the month's special events. Into each can be dropped anything which may prove in that month to be useful resource material. Casual reading can then be harvested for items not immediately relevant but whose time will come.

He may also wish to subscribe to one of the various agencies which supply regular packages of news and feature items from which to select his 'fillers' or even his major features. In the case of off-set litho productions some of these are supplied 'camera ready', available as they are for paste-up directly onto the pages being constructed in the church hall or vicarage study.

III

The third skill is that of lay-out and design. If the editor feels the lack of his own skill in this area it will be specially worth his while to look out for suitably endowed parishioners. They are more plentiful than one might suppose. A parish with a church school is almost certain to have among its teachers someone skilled in the arts of visual display. It is but a step from that skill to the matters of laying out the contents of a magazine in such a way that the arrangement and display of articles is an attractive invitation to read.

The use of space between headlines and paragraphs and columns helps the page to 'breathe'. The page should have a friendly and open countenance. It should resemble the welcoming face of a friend.

Thought should be given about which regular features go where. Basic information about times of service and availability of clergy, and location of organizational meetings, should be clear and attractive and easy to find. The minister's letter or the editorial comment or main article should be allotted a commanding space –

page three or centre-spread are usually best. Other items may gain in impact from their juxtaposition on the page. For example a note about 'Bible Sunday' services will gain from a neighbouring note about a Bible study secretary. An article about a summer-school or holiday club for children will be helped by a cartoon, or a recollection of Sunday School proceedings from one of its younger members. There is an overlap between editorial and design decisions, and if two people are involved they need to talk such things through. It is usually an enjoyable exercise.

In a former parish we produced an off-set litho magazine and perhaps a brief account of the laying out procedure will be a useful way of summarizing some of the principles involved.

If it were to be a twelve page production that month a twelve page booklet would be created in five seconds by picking up three sheets of paper and folding them down the middle. We would then number the pages 1 to 12, note on each its intended contents, then guided by this master plan we would lay out lengthways six sheets of paper, divided by a fine line in the middle into two pages each — one on the left of the line, the other on the right. Sheet one would then be treated as the cover, its left half marked 12, its right half marked 1. Sheet two–intended to be the reverse side of the cover would then be marked page 2 (on the left) and page 11 (on the right). To left and right the remaining pages would be marked 3 and 10, 4 and 9, 5 and 8, 6 and 7 (6 and 7 forming the centre-spread).

Already assembled would be the type-written columns, the cut out pre-printed items from various sources, letra-set headlines, 'cannibalized' words and letters from various newspapers and magazines, drawings and photographs.

Armed with light spray-on glue the team would assemble each page using the editor as reference and guide and arbiter.

The six pages, duly completed, were taken to the printer for plate making and printing. The involvement of many people fed ideas and information into the whole process.

I have not so far mentioned one important resource, and as the editor of one such in my own diocese, I must not fail to do so. I refer to the various centrally produced inserts available. These often supply an effective supplement of news and features which provides the local news with its wider context, so sharpening its relevance. When these are included in magazines their own physical dimension usually determines that of the home product so that the two match. The question must be asked at the outset whether this is the preferred design option. Some insert magazines print in different sizes to accommodate local magazine sizes.

Diocesan news sheets and tabloids like the one I edit myself express a diocesan design commitment which makes its own demand upon local products. In my own parish we retain the A4 magazine format with our A3 sized tabloid, folded in three, nestling snugly inside.

Parish magazines, then, are community papers best served by some form of community production. Parish Council discussion of parish magazines, properly conducted, involves the discussion of the whole of church life. The work of producing an effective magazine can stimulate the life and worship of a whole congregation. And it can do a very great deal to penetrate society with the salt and light of Christian truth.

They are the Christian gospel's uniquely variable infiltrators into (almost) all the world. Where they lodge month by month they are seen by many eyes. And very often their pages are the hidden springboard by which a good news story comes before the huge audiences immediately contactable today by the world's vast media industry. And all the time, and for the most part, they are the quiet signalling points by which troubled people flying blind in life can find a real and contactable community of faith.

Part III
Caring

Mothers and Very Young Children

CHRISTOPHER P. BURKETT, B.A.
Leek and Meerbrook, Staffordshire

'If I didn't come here I think I would go mad.' 'I need somewhere to talk; it helps talking.' 'We get on each others nerves, we have to get out of the house' (mother speaking of her relationship with her $2\frac{1}{2}$ year old daughter). These are a few of the comments made by mothers of very young children attending our 'Mums and Toddlers Group'. This article will explore why the intensity of the feeling expressed needs to be taken with utter seriousness, and how simple pastoral provisions in the local church can meet a vital social need. What follows is based on the experience of one group over a number of years, resourced by one Anglican congregation. It is written, however, in the conviction that many of the conclusions apply in all sorts of social areas and that most congregations have the resources readily to hand for this work.

Our work with mothers and their pre-school children began as a church initiated follow-up to baptism enquiries. Without entering the complex and often vexed debate about infant baptism, we decided to offer what we thought might be a way into serious Christian commitment for the parent and the child. The group began after a circularized invitation had been sent to all mothers who had requested baptism for their child at least six months previously. At this stage the implication of the planning was that children would be brought who were of an age that could be taught in some more or less formal way. Hence the title we chose, 'The Mums and Toddlers Group'. Experience suggests that this initial premise was wrong. What has developed is not a church alternative to pre-school playgroup, nor is it weekday Sunday School.

The invitation brought a response from more than thirty mothers. Since that starting circular we have never again sought

65

members for the group as it has become self-perpetuating. As one membership of children grows beyond the group, so there are always more wanting to take part. The usefulness of the group to its membership has spread by word of mouth in the local community. We soon discovered that unwittingly we had stumbled upon a major social need in our locality – support for mothers with very young children. The age limit we had envisaged for the membership was soon dispensed with. Some of our so-called 'toddlers' are actually infants still at the breast. We have not jettisoned the Christian content originally planned, but we have had to adapt it significantly to the needs that have become evident. What began with the motive of proselytism, has now become a thought-out offering of Christ's caring ministry, a truly pastoral opportunity. We began by trying to answer a need felt within the congregation, the group has become a way of answering a need felt in the wider community.

Several different motives have shown themselves to be crucial in the mothers' commitment to the group. Above all new, or fairly new mothers need to be able to tell the story of their parenting experience over and over again. Often this centres, of course, on the experience of birth itself. Being privileged to listen-in to these conversations the similarities of feelings expressed to those of bereaved people is all too apparent. As well as the joy of becoming a mother there is also a sense of loss. Some mothers feel that the demands of the child push out their own personal needs and make them feel as if their bodies are no longer their own. Often a crushing sense that things can never again be as they were before the birth is expressed. Others have only recently ceased paid employment, and feel a loss of worth as well as support that formerly the work environment provided. All these heartfelt losses, and more, have been given voice within the group.

These feelings of loss have to be worked through, but too often it seems women feel unheard in the expression of them. Unspoken or unheard these feelings can become a blight on the mother's whole well-being, and in turn affect her child and the rest of her family. Family, friends and the wider society seem to assume that once a woman is safely delivered of a child she should simply get on with the business of rearing and nurturing the infant. Just what a major re-adjustment in life is asked for by the existence of a demanding child is too easily played down. The sharing of these feelings within ordinary conversation in a safe environment with other people who are experiencing similar things can be of immense significance to a mother's well-being. Telling her own story she finds that others identify with her and that she is able to identify with them. A road out of a terrible isolation is one of the great gifts of such conversation. An effective group must provide space for this.

Post-natal depression affects something like one in ten women. This can vary from mild depression to major and very disturbing illness. The onset of such illness can be very soon after birth, or maybe some months later. It cannot be too strongly emphasized that such illness needs medical care and attention. It is beyond the scope of such a group as that under discussion, although the group might be a valuable source of support and encouragement to those being treated elsewhere for this illness. Health workers may refer sufferers to a group if they are confident that it is well run and able to offer the right support. Group organizers in their turn need to be aware of the health service support and care that is available so as to be able to suggest to sufferers where help can be found, although other mothers will often do this themselves when the need becomes evident. Group leaders must aim to distinguish between the widely experienced feelings of loss and the like which the group can handle very effectively, and depressive illness which in every instance needs the attention of a doctor and skilled health workers.

The group also offers a way back into society. Just as motherhood can bring with it emotional isolation, the ever pressing physical needs of the child can make the mother work-bound. There is simply so much to do that there is no space to be out and about. Father's work commitments and distance from family support that many couples now experience add to this burden. The Mothers and Toddlers Group provides a legitimate reason for breaking the circle of effort and getting out of the house. Often this is expressed as a feeling that the child must be given the opportunity to socialize, but that opportunity for mum is just as crucial. It is important, therefore, that the value of the group to the child is plain for all to see. This is one aspect of our group that mothers often comment upon in comparison with others. This is something that has to be worth the effort of going to for both mother and child.

Another motive for attendance is the value of sharing advice, problems and solutions. The group must aim to provide an unhurried and free atmosphere in which mothers can question and inform each other. Once again, this is an area all too easily missed elsewhere. Here is the permission to gossip childcare that can be missed in a busy clinic or doctor's waiting room.

One other motivating factor we have discovered is the provision of a space of time in which the mother is cared for, thus offering a momentary respite from her constant need to care. This is a very simple provision to provide but an essential one for the group to be really effective. For us it has focused on two things: one, mothers attending have a hot drink made for them; and two, there is a definite and distinct period of work with the children and then free play for the children. We have not found separating the children from their mothers either practical or necessary. With very young children the stress of even few minutes separation can cause chaos and disruption for the whole group. Rather, we have attempted to provide space for mum whilst the children are still in view and very close at hand. This usually means the mothers sitting in a circle around the open space in which the children's activity takes place. The enjoyment and fun the children demonstrate is itself a fillip to the group. The increased social skills which we see developing in even the youngest toddlers also provides a powerful reinforcement to the value of the group.

We have discovered that mothers give a high priority to attendance at the group. This in turn has encouraged the local church to place a high value on the work. It is evidently a way of sharing care that is needed and that we can readily fulfil. We believe it fills a vital gap in our local community. It is therefore an outworking of Christ's caring ministry and a proper use of our resources as the local church. But in attempting to address a social need we have also gone some way towards tackling the congregation's original motive in starting the work, namely sharing the gospel. The bearing of children provokes in many profound religious questions. Issues of meaning, the possibility of hope in an all too fearful world, questions of life and death, and the need to be certain of an exterior source of love, all begin to surface. Group leaders must wait for these questions to be raised. This marks a significant change in the tenor of the work from the church's point of view; we now wait for religious questions to be asked whereas initially we had viewed the group as a proper place for the active and formal propagation of the gospel. The change shows a much more deeply felt appreciation of what is actually happening in the lives of those who join the group, and as such is successful in helping some along the road of faith. Leaders need to be ready and prepared for this, and the local congregation must have some positive opportunities to offer those seeking faith. Out of the group's care has come new commitment to Christ.

Consideration must now turn from motivations to the severely practical matters of organization. How well these are dealt with is a further enhancement of the value given to the group by its organizers and sponsoring congregation which in turn becomes another encouragement to the mothers to value the group. Providing a kettle and a cold room at the back of the church and expecting people to get on with it will not produce the positive results wanted. Indeed, unless resources of time, effort and a little cash are available it is best not to attempt the work. Expectations and hopes that are unfulfilled will destroy the credibility of the group.

The group must be timed to fit well with the needs of its members. It is no use starting very early because the physical effort of mum getting herself and a small child ready takes a lot of time. Increasing stress here will be a positive discouragement to people to attend. But also the group must not be so late as to interfere with meals or the needs of other children in the family at school. We have found mid-morning in the middle of the week to be ideal, but other groups successfully operate in the early afternoon. Also we have deliberately chosen a day which is the local market day, so mothers can combine the trip out with shopping needs.

Another aspect of timing is that this is one of the church's activities that most definitely does not start promptly. We have a set starting time and everyone is encouraged to be there for it, but we don't begin until everyone is comfortable and ready. This usually means waiting a little for latecomers. Once again we attempt to make sure that there is as little stress as possible involved in the physical effort of being there.

The room itself needs to be warm. Indeed, if very young infants are to be encouraged to come a higher than usual public building temperature must be maintained. The bearing of costs here are again evidence of the local congregation's commitment to the work. We have found it essential to provide another room where pushchairs and prams can be safely left so that they do not clutter the activity room with potential hazards. The group activity room must be carpeted. Some mothers will feel most at home on the floor with their child, and the children are much easier to work with if they do not have to rely on the availability of small chairs. Those old enough to sit can sit on a chair alongside their mothers if they need to, but most of the activity will be on the floor. Needless to say the leader must be able to sit on the floor with the children!

We have discovered that an unvarying programme timetable from week to week works best. This provides the children with a structure that they soon learn, and from which they draw confidence. So our programme has several distinct phases that are repeated each time. First, a period to settle down and meet each other, during which the older children will often run about. Second, an ordered time of worship and exploration that centres on the children. Third, a time of free play using toys provided by the church. Fourth, a hot drink for the mothers, and a drink and a biscuit for the children. The third and fourth phases provide the most time for conversation for the mothers. The beginning of each phase is marked by a definite action which the children readily respond to as indicating a change of behaviour and activity. For example, the distribution of percussion instruments marks the start of the worship slot, the taking of a collection to pay for the tea and coffee marks the beginning of free play, and the distribution of biscuits marks the quieter time needed to have a drink. At each stage the children themselves are involved as much as possible, and take great delight in telling the leader what should come next.

The worship period itself also has an unvarying structure within which different elements are introduced week by week. It begins with a song from our stock repertoire of eight well known and simple Christian choruses. We have found it important not to introduce new music. Often children make their own requests for what should be sung. The song is unaccompanied, except for the children playing simple percussion instruments like rattles, tambourines, and maracas. Some of the instruments have been made at home by mothers.

After the children have collected together the instruments to be put away we have a short period of exploration and talk. This is introduced by a simple device that keeps the children eager to share this part of the programme. We have a large surprise box, which is very colourful and has a lid. Inside the box is some item that will form the topic of discussion. Guessing what it will be is always great fun for the children. Items focus most often on the world children experience; parts of the body, clothes, home activities, people they encounter, seasons of the year, and the world of nature have all figured. Key symbols like water and light are frequently used. All these things are linked to the thought that this is God's world and these are all parts of his love for us. Sometimes a very short prayer may form part of the topic, on other occasions activities or making something (with the help of mum) may supplement the discussion.

The seasons of the Christian year are a frequent part of the topic, and the stories of Jesus are introduced here. Easter and Christmas are important events in the group's life. Indeed, the Christmas celebration is the only meeting of the year where our programme is varied. Usually we gather in church under the large christmas tree to share the story of Jesus's birth, and then share presents, before a simple party. This has been prepared for by several weeks' topics in the usual group. This linking with what is going on in the regular worship of the church has encouraged some mums to bring their children to all ages worship in church.

Children of such a young age have a short span of attention so the discussion slot never occupies more than ten minutes. During this time some will wander off, or go back to mum, only to return a few moments later. As long as a few children have maintained their interest that is sufficient. No attempt is made to discipline them into paying attention. That is not the function of such an informal group, and anyway we have found it actually to be unnecessary. The secure environment in which children feel very involved means disruptive behaviour is rare and usually easily dealt with by mother. Above all it is never made an issue of in the group, and invidious comparisons between the behaviour of one child and another by the group leader must be avoided at all costs.

The worship slot ends by celebrating any birthdays that the group members or their families have that week. A birthday song and the blowing out of candles are used as we thank God for this particular person. The free play which follows is always eagerly anticipated by the children.

Some might criticize our highly structured programme as too constraining or as boring. Our experience is, however, that it works very well for the children who appreciate the rhythm and security of it. Mothers also find in such a pattern reassurance that what they have made the effort to come to is worthwhile for them personally and their children. Such a programme requires preparation by the leader. If such preparation is missing the children will all too soon spot the fact and lose interest. Personally, I would make a strong plea for such leadership to be in the hands of the minister himself or herself. This sort of commitment by the ordained minister adds further credence to the group, as well as providing the minister with valuable pastoral contacts and opportunities. For smooth running of the group there needs to be another leader as well. This person's particular role is to make sure that the mothers present are pampered a little; things are got ready for them, drinks are made, toys are tidied up, whatever registers that are needed are kept. We have found that this is a role that church members will readily fulfil and gain much from. Certainly, such effort freely given is much appreciated by the group members and new caring relationships can be stimulated by the right character.

One other feature of the group is an annual outing by coach.

This is usually in the summer at a time when the membership of the group is about to change most radically as children move on. It is therefore a way of celebrating what has gone before, as well as providing another space away from home. It is essential that the day out be not too long, and clearly geared to what the children will enjoy and cope with. We have found parks with picnic facilities and play equipment to be ideal venues.

This article has attempted to make plain the necessity of making a church based group for mothers and their young children a warm and secure place where in as unstressed a way as possible experiences can be shared and new skills gained, by both parent and child. Great sensitivity is an essential requirement for group leaders if this is to be achieved. Nothing should be done that reinforces any mother's worries about her own abilities as a good mother. Nothing should be done that draws attention to any one child's disabilities or shortcomings. Comparisons of children present, that may be taken as stinging criticisms although they were not meant in that way, should be avoided. Bad behaviour from a child should draw discipline from no one but the child's own mother. Group leaders need to develop the art of quick distraction so as to draw children's attention towards something else if anyone's behaviour begins to get out of hand.

Such groups, run with care and compassion, can provide an oasis of hope within a period of life that many mothers experience as fraught, tiring and extremely stressful. In the group Christ's love and concern can be shared in a down to earth way through mutual support and conversation. Such groups are a small but nonetheless significant way of demonstrating Christ's promise to share our burdens. We have found ourselves blessed in sharing that task.

Pastoral Care and the Mentally Handicapped Child

KENNETH LYSONS, M.A., M.Ed., Ph.D.
St Helens

PROBABLY about 120,000 people in England and Wales are severely mentally handicapped, of whom some 50,000 are children. Mental handicap may be due to hereditary and cultural factors, injury, disease, inadequate nutrition and complications at birth. The manifestations of mental handicap are many, but those most frequently encountered are Down's Syndrome (mongolism) and conditions arising from defects of the central nervous system.

What can the church offer as a caring community to support and sustain the families of handicapped persons and mentally handicapped persons themselves?

Caring, from a Christian viewpoint, is a manifestation of God's love in action. It is based on a belief in the value of all persons, even though, as with the mentally handicapped, this view may be repudiated by those who base value exclusively on the economic and other contributions that an individual may make to society. Yet, when confronted by mental handicap, ministers and congregations are often confounded for two reasons.

Firstly, lacking first hand experience, they often do not understand either the needs of mentally handicapped persons or the problems encountered by their families.

Secondly, a mentally handicapped person usually lacks the degree of rationality that normal encounters in pastoral work assume. Miles[1] has pointed out that theologians have not concerned themselves with mental handicap, because they presuppose rationality both on the part of their readers and those with whom God can enter into a relationship.

Recently, however, there has been an increased interest on the part of the Anglican, Roman Catholic and Free Churches for the pastoral care of mentally handicapped persons and their families. In 1984, for example, the General Synod Board for Social Responsibility of the Anglican Church published *The Local Church and Mentally Handicapped People*.[2] In 1985 a Baptist Union Working Group on Mental Handicap and the Church issued a most useful book entitled *Let Love be Genuine*.[3] There are also many useful insights from an autobiographical viewpoint in *Face to Face*[4] written by the mother of a severely mentally handicapped child who is also a distinguished theologian.

In the context of this article 'supporting' is regarded as a temporary activity and mainly relates to the initial care by the minister of a family into which a mentally handicapped child has been born. In the words of a well-known prayer by Reinhold Niebuhr this involves working with and through the parents to enable them 'to accept the things they cannot change, to have courage to change the things they can and develop the wisdom to know the difference'.

One of the dangers of supporting, however, is that support can easily merge into dependency, a condition to be discouraged. Sustaining differs from support in that it is long term. It can again be given by the minister. Ministers, however, come and go. The departure of the minister might mean withdrawal of the source of sustenance. This consideration alone justifies the contention that 'sustaining' should be a long term responsibility of the corporate church family.

I. *Supporting*

The three main problems likely to be encountered by the minister at the initial stage when the existence of mental handicap is confirmed, relate to decision making, the removal of guilt and doubt and the provision of help and comfort.

1. *Decision Making*

Decision making is of primary importance, since such techniques for detecting foetal abnormalities as Amniocentesis and Chorion Villus sampling now enable the presence of mental handicap to be detected in the first three to four months of pregnancy. Where this is the case, the minister may be be asked for an opinion as to whether or not the foetus should be aborted. The same request for help in reaching a decision may be made when mental handicap is discovered at or after birth. Parents may be under strong pressure from doctors or social workers to have a child 'put away'. In the latter case, the dilemma confronting parents has been well summarized by Joehnig.[5] He points out that parents with a handicapped child can do no right. The child's appearance reflects on their competence as parents. If they keep the child at home they are accused of emotional maladjustment in failing to 'accept' the child's handicap. If they place the child in residential care they have 'rejected' him or her. Paradoxically the parents also come under pressure from friends and relatives, even from social workers, who conjure up spectres of marital break-up, nervous breakdowns, and damage to other children in the family if they persist in keeping the child in the home. In their bewilderment at such conflicting advice and attitudes, the parents may turn to their minister. What does he say? The present writer believes that three considerations apply to such harrowing decisions.

Firstly, that mentally handicapped persons have the fundamental rights to life, to be loved, to live in their family when this is possible, and to develop to the limits of their individual capacities.

Secondly, that decisions should, in Fletcher's terminology, always be made situationally and not prescriptively. That is, decision making requires the careful evaluation of such factors as the degree of handicap, parental health both physical and mental, economic and social circumstances, housing conditions, parental attitudes to the disability and the apparent stability of the marriage.

Thirdly, the minister should never take the role of decision maker himself. What he can do by consultation with specialized agencies and personnel and, where possible, those have have encountered similar problems at first hand, is to provide parents with the information that will help them to reach their own decision for which they accept responsibility. He may, of course, also present the parents with his own theological and pastoral insights, but never prescriptively.

2. *The Removal of Guilt and Doubt.*

The need for the removal of guilt and doubt may arise. The parents of a handicapped child cannot avoid seeking for some meaning in the tragedy that has befallen them. Miles[1] believes that it is not rare for parents of the mentally handicapped to see their child as resulting from God's visitation of 'the sins of the parents upon the children'. He points out that the possible effects of practically everything during pregnancy provide a miserable field for introspection. Guilt may find expression in anger against God, against the minister as God's representative, against the spouse, or against any event or person who can possibly be involved.

Stubberfield[6] points out that 'attributing mental retardation to God's judgment is not always the result of faulty religious instruction', but can operate at a more profound and unconscious level. In the face of an irrevocable tragedy some parents may find belief in the punitive nature of God's judgment to be a means for the preservation of self-esteem. 'Feeling punished for sins may be more tolerable than to believe that this event has no meaning and is unrelated to one's personal identity.'

Stubberfield also makes useful distinctions between a sense of guilt, genuine guilt, and shame and guilt. A sense of guilt may be related to concrete deeds resulting in a desire to experience forgiveness. Guilt feelings give rise to the consciousness of having transgressed and the need to make atonement. Shame arises when persons feel that they have fallen below their ideals and aspirations. Turner[7] points out that the mother may feel shame because she has not produced a 'proper' child. She may also feel that in some way she has failed her husband. The father may be resentful that the child will not grow up to make a name or even a living for himself. Both parents may experience a certain element of risk and uncertainty about having other children.

Feelings of guilt and doubt need to be countered in several ways.

The minister should endeavour to explain that handicap is part of the risk of being in a world of development and genetic hazards and not to any vindictiveness on God's part. It is also necessary to stress that every mentally handicapped person is a child of God. Such persons may have imperfect minds, but that does not detract from their right to human dignity. Above all, as Turner stresses, the key word of the Christian faith is 'love'. It is love that prompts the qualities and action which we recognize as 'good' and full intellectual, emotional and spiritual development cannot be achieved by the person who has been deprived of love. Some parents may feel guilty because they feel the demands made on them by a mentally handicapped child are too great. Until it is ascertained what, in reality, those demands are, we cannot determine whether the demands that such a child may make upon his parents and family are too onerous. Without being sentimental, the minister can point out that love always looks for a way of being constructive.

The present writer, himself the father of a mentally handicapped child, has found great help in the words of Thomas-à-Kempis, 'love takes a burden and makes it no burden'. It is also through the love they receive, particularly from parents, that mentally handicapped persons obtain a concept of what love is. As it has been well said, 'the mentally retarded never know they are a tragedy until they see it in our faces and our actions'.[8]

3. *The Provision of Help and Comfort.*
In the first throes of grief, however, the parents of a mentally handicapped child are unlikely to be in the mood for intellectual arguments. It is trite, but true, that the best service a minister can give at such a time of sorrow, loneliness and resentment, is that of standing by. In a perceptive paper a paediatrician, Blue[9], has rightly observed that the very first days are crucial. The minister who is ready to listen and support the parents then will produce more positive results than many sessions of counselling later on will achieve. The minister by his concern and sensitivity can provide comfort and the assurance that God is present even in our sorrow and bewilderment.

II. *Sustaining.*
Initially, support in the areas of decision making, the removal of doubt and guilt and the provision of comfort will be the responsibility of the minister. Help is also needed in coping with

the problems of living and in allaying fears of what the future may hold. Such help can best be given by others who can give informed and balanced advice based on their own practical experience of mental handicap.

Sustaining in the sense of long term help is mainly the responsibility of the social services and specialist voluntary agencies, such as the Royal National Society for Mentally Handicapped Children and Adults, with whom parents should be urged to make early contact. There are two areas, however, in which an attempt should be made to harness the concern and resources of the local church to provide sustenance both to parents and the handicapped child, namely, acceptance and imaginative caring.

1. *Acceptance.*

Acceptance is important as a counter to the rejection that mentally handicapped persons and their parents sometimes experience. The church should be the place where both are welcomed and 'belong'. Sadly, this does not always occur. A mother, newly arrived in the area took her mentally handicapped daughter to church. The child attempted, discordantly, to join in the singing, and was restless in the sermon. The mother was conscious of an 'atmosphere' of disapproval from the predominantly elderly congregation. She never returned to that church, but started to attend the Salvation Army where she and her child were welcomed.

Acceptance formally begins when the mentally handicapped child is admitted into the church family at baptism. Baptism provides the minister with an opportunity to stress that the congregational promise 'to maintain the common life of worship and service . . . that all the children among you may grow in the grace and the knowledge and love of God and of his Son, Jesus Christ our Lord',[10] implies a sustaining obligation to the mentally handicapped child no less than to one who is 'normal'.

Baptism further implies that, in due course, the child will receive instruction in the Christian faith and be admitted into the full membership of the church.

Instruction of the mentally handicapped, whether by parents, minister or in the Sunday School, is, of course, a special aspect of all instruction. The difficulties to be overcome may include dual handicaps, i.e. mental handicap accompanied by defects of sight or hearing, difficulties in verbal expression, limited concentration, emotional immaturity, extreme suggestibility, insecurity, lack of acceptance, and possibly anti-social tendencies such as aggression arising from frustration or withdrawal due to lack of confidence. Instruction is too wide a subject for discussion here, but certain guidelines can be given. Bible stories are better told with the aid of pictures rather than read from the Bible. Abstract ideas such as love, forgiveness and mercy need to be explained by concrete examples of which the Gospels contain many and, where possible, acted out or shown in practice. Prayers should be short and simple. Hymns, again, should be simple and those with a chorus or 'actions' are especially suitable. Talks should be brief and related to events that children have experienced, e.g. birthdays, games and holidays. Where possible, participation in worship, such as taking the offertory should be encouraged.

In the writer's experience, with mentally handicapped children, preparation for membership should be by regular participation in the life of the church, rather than by specific classes. This would include the Roman Catholic practice of allowing the child to take communion from an early age since, as Newman[11] stated in another context 'the heart is commonly reached not through the reason, but through the imagination' and symbols can put even the retarded in touch with God in a very special way. In any case, it needs to be remembered that with a mentally handicapped person 'the principal objective of membership preparation is to establish a relationship between the person and Christ and not to pass on knowledge or a moral code'.[12]

A church that by its acceptance sustains both the parents and the mentally handicapped child will receive much in return. The very presence of such a child in a congregation witnesses to the facts that God's love gives worth to all persons and that Christianity knows no untouchables. The childlike innocence, trust and love manifested by many mentally handicapped persons, is perhaps as Frankl says, 'God's reminder that the world must rediscover the attributes that the retarded have never lost'.[13]

2. *Imaginative Caring.*

The impact of a mentally handicapped child on a particular family is difficult to forecast, since many variables are involved. The mental strain on both parents, but especially the mother, may be intense. Siblings may resent the extra attention given to the handicapped child. Social life, especially visiting, may be constrained. It is not strange that a higher incidence of breakdown has been reported in families with a mentally handicapped child. The adage that 'a handicapped child means a handicapped family' is true, even under the best conditions. It is against this background that the sustaining role of the Church Family must be seen. Imaginative initiatives in this regard have been taken by L'Arche and the St Joseph's Centre and both are rich sources of 'good practice' in the area of imaginative caring.[14] The St Joseph's Centre defines its aims as follows:[15]

(1) *To make the parish aware and welcoming*
     To make the parish more aware and understand better:
     (a)   Mentally handicapped children, adults and elderly people, wherever they are living with their differing needs and feelings and especially their spiritual needs.
     (b)   Families with a mentally handicapped son or daughter and their differing needs and feelings.
     (c)   The contribution which mentally handicapped people can make to enrich the life of the church and the local community, thereby enabling parishioners to be more welcoming and involved.

[2] *To become a friend*
     To become an informed friend to mentally handicapped people of every age, especially to those in hostels, group homes and hospitals and their families.

(3) *To offer help*
     To offer families and all mentally handicapped people of every age, especially those in hostels, group homes and hospitals, in accordance with their differing needs and wishes as much moral support, practical help and information as possible.

These aims can be implemented in many ways. Suggestions for giving practical help to parents include: finding ways of providing a break of an hour or half a day; listening to their story; accompanying parents on visits to facilities or at meetings with professionals; assisting with other children in the family; seeking out useful information; staying with the family when parents go out; providing opportunities for parents to share their experiences.

Similarly, help can be given to mentally handicapped persons themselves in such ways as: sharing activities, buildings and resources with mentally handicapped children and adults; finding ways of meeting spiritual needs; going to church together; giving a lift and accompanying; remembering and celebrating birthdays and Christmas; telephoning, writing letters and postcards; inviting mentally handicapped persons to one's home. This list of ways of imaginative caring is by no means exhaustive. The writer recalls reading of a church which organized its own special, single story scripture examination with coaching and a certificate for a Down's Syndrome girl with the object of 'making her feel like the rest'.

Sustaining is, of course, a life-long activity. In due course both parents and the mentally handicapped person will need help with such matters as marriage, and coping with death and grief, and the problem that haunts all parents with such children of 'what will happen to him or her when we've gone'. The opportunities open to the churches for 'sustaining' are immense and have been enhanced by the policy of the present government of caring for mentally handicapped persons in the community, rather than in residential institutions.

Sometimes we pray for 'those who are mentally handicapped'. Less frequently do we remember their families on whom a heavy burden falls. It is useful to reflect, however, that the original sense of the term intercession was that of 'standing between', of taking a step into an area of need and staying there. Richards[15] has observed truly that 'no one can be said truly to inter-cede if he is not prepared to share the burdens of which he speaks . . . Intercession cannot be done at a safe distance. Its very definition implies involvement'.

[1] Miles, Michael, *Christianity and the Mentally Handicapped* (Christian Brethren Research Fellowship, n.d.).

[2] Bayley, Michael, *The Local Church and Mentally Handicapped People* (C.I.O. Publishing, Church House, Dean's Yard, London SW1P 3NZ).

[3] Bowers, Faith (ed), *Let Love be Genuine* (The Baptist Union, London [1985]).

[4] Young, Frances, *Face to Face* (Epworth Press [1985]).

[5] Joehnig, Walter Bruno, *Mentally Handicapped Children and their Families – Problems for Social Policy* (Unpublished PhD thesis, Essex [1974]).

[6] Stubberfield, Harold W., 'Religion, parents and mental retardation' in *Mental Retardation, Social and Educational Perspectives* ed. Drew, Hardman and Bluhm (C. V. Mosby Co., Saint Louis [1977]).

[7] Turner, Leslie, 'The Christian Ministry to the Mentally Handicapped' (*Journal of Religion and Medicine*, 3 [1976], 1–20).

[8] The writer has a note of this sentence, but has unfortunately, mislaid the source.

[9] Blue, C. Milton, *The Minister and the birth of a defective child*, 1971.

[10] These are the words used in the *Methodist Service Book* but similar promises are made by members of other denominations.

[11] Newman, J. H., *An Essay in Aid of a Grammar of Assent.*

[12] *The Church's Response in Norfolk to the Sacramental and Spiritual Needs of the Intellectually Handicapped* (Norwich Diocesan Board of Social Responsibility [1984]), p. 10.

[13] Frankl, V., *The Will to Meaning*, 140.

[14] L'Arche, 14 London Road, Beccles, Suffolk NR34 9NH. St Joseph's Centre, The Burroughs, London NW4 4TY.

[15] *The Parish Ministry to Mentally Handicapped People and Their Families* (Typewritten [1985]). Quotation by permission.

[16] Richards H., *What Happens When You Pray* (SCM. Press [1980]).

Ministry to the Hearing Impaired

HAROLD W. WEBB

The Royal Association in Aid of Deaf People, Dorking

ONE in ten of the population in the UK suffers from hearing loss to some degree: amongst the over 70s the ratio is six in ten. Hearing impairment is the most common and disregarded of disabilities. Probably our congregations and parishes have more hearing impaired people than they have drug addicts, alcoholics, unemployed, abused children, one parent families or any others in the sad catalogue of vexing social disorders.

Hearing impairment is not an exciting subject! However, we are not in our ministry to satisfy our sense of excitement. We attempt to minister to all in need: the drug clinic in the church hall and a good public address system in the church are both ministries.

Degrees of Loss

'Hearing impairment' can mean all or almost nothing: the 'stone deaf' through to those whose loss is slight. The effect of impairment differs greatly according to the degree of loss. Those born with a hearing loss lead a very different life from the vast majority whose hearing loss occurs as part of the ageing process.

Chaplains to the Deaf minister to 'Profoundly and Prelingually Deaf People' who use sign language as their first and most natural communication. If a local pastor is called upon to minister to such profoundly deaf people (at a baptism, wedding or funeral for example) he or she should call upon the help of the Chaplain to Deaf People. It is a matter of negotiation if the chaplain takes full responsibility for the service, or acts as an interpreter to the local minister after discussion beforehand.

Hearing Aids

This specialist ministry to the profoundly prelingually deaf does not include ministry to the hard of hearing – those who become hearing impaired later in life and whose previous life has been in the hearing world. Although the hearing impairment may be severe, ministry to such people normally remains in the care of the local pastor.

Those who became hearing impaired later in life often use hearing aids. These are a great boon, but not a total solution. Two problems often arise. Firstly, 'hearing impairment' does not just mean that sounds cannot be heard as loudly as before. Often the sound quality is distorted so that, for example, vowels are heard but not consonants. Thus the saying, 'Don't shout, I'm not deaf!' The person can hear you quite well, but cannot make out the actual words you use. Amplification through the hearing aid is like turning up the volume on a badly tuned radio. Of course, like the radio, hearing aids have tone controls to help cope with this problem.

Secondly, the hearing aid lacks discrimination, the ability to ignore unwanted sounds. If I were at the moment using a hearing aid here in my study, I would be much disturbed by my daughter's record player, the washing machine down the passage, the traffic outside. As I do not need to use an aid, my natural hearing enables me to ignore all these sounds. For the hearing aid user the problem of background noise is most acute and makes concentration difficult, especially in conversation in a noisy place. Therefore the NHS Guidelines to hearing aid users advises them to take time to become accustomed to their aids, and to begin using them in a quiet room.

The Nature of the Problem

Two experiences will illustrate the twofold problem of hearing impairment. I was talking to a Mother's Union Group. In the front sat three ladies, hearing aids switched on. Behind me (I ought to have known better!) was a window, the sun was shining, my face was in the shadow. Later I moved to one side and my face could be seen more clearly. At once the ladies said, 'We can lip read you better now'. Firstly, practical thought must be given on how to meet the problem. We cannot minister to deaf people in the dark!

Another time I was in contact with two quite young people, both going deaf, who must finally expect to be profoundly deaf.

Both are musical and members of their church choirs. Both were advised that they should resign from the choir as they could no longer hold their place. For one of these two in particular this led to a great sense of rejection and loss of self esteem. So our second thought concerns the great trauma of becoming hearing impaired. The traumatic effect is not just to lose contact with the life known before. Often it is to feel rejected by the world around. The mental isolation of many hearing impaired people is far worse than the physical isolation.

If hearing impairment starts quite early in life, and especially if the loss is sudden and profound, the trauma is all the worse. But mostly the trauma comes to the elderly, who with the dignity, patience and wisdom of age accept it as just part of becoming old. They and all around assume too easily that nothing can be or need be done to help. But in fact the churches can give a lead in offering practical help and understanding to all the hearing impaired of what ever age.

Unhappily I have to say that my hard of hearing friends are of the opinion that churches and clergy are amongst the least understanding when faced with hearing impaired people and their problems.

The Church Formal

By this I mean firstly the church gathered together for worship in the church building.

First we must consider the lighting. Can the people see our faces clearly, and those of all who help lead the worship? The hearing impaired need good lighting if they are to lip read. We all lip read to some extent, however unaware of this we may be. Good lighting helps to make facial expressions clear also. As the elderly may also suffer from poor eye sight, good lighting is a double blessing. The lights on the pulpit and lectern need to be placed so they light up not only the Bible or sermon notes, but the face of the reader or preacher as well. The raised pulpit makes it easier to see the preacher, as well as for him or her to project the voice.

'Dim religious gloom' and beautiful East windows which leave the face in shadow will not help the hearing impaired. They may find it hard to follow intercessions led from the back of the church.

The obvious help for hearing impaired people is the Public Address (PA) system. I, like many clergy, dislike microphones and consider it is possible, with good voice projection, to be heard by those with normal hearing in most churches without a PA system. But obviously the hearing impaired will rely on such a system to help them.

Beware! The microphone does not take away our vocal faults. The voice dropping at the end of sentences – the rapid mutter – the parsonical voice – all become more apparent at the other end of the system. It is a good thing occasionally to record a service so we can hear ourselves as others hear us.

The best PA address system for those with hearing aids incorporates the Induction Loop. This I must try to explain in non-technical terms. A loop of bell-wire encircles all or part of the church and is incorporated with the microphones (and speakers if required) of the PA. The hearing aid users sits within the area enclosed and switches on the 'T' switch – a control on all modern NHS aids but not on all bought privately. The effect is two-fold. First, the sound comes directly from the microphone into the ear – not from some far-off loudspeaker. The sound is clear and free from distortion caused by a resonant building. The second effect is even more beneficial: all background noises from sources outside the loop, or not picked up by a microphone, are eliminated. The creche in the vestry is no distraction!

Guildford Cathedral installed such a loop system and I preached at the inauguration. Afterwards a hearing aid user came up and said 'that was the first sermon I have heard for years'. Any church planning to install a PA system should ensure that it includes the loop. Remember that all speaking points must be through (switched on!) microphones which are inclusive in the system. Call in experienced hearing aid users to check before paying the final account. Some experiment can be needed to find the best place for the mike which picks up organ and choir. Make sure that the firm installing the loop gives an after-care service. Maybe the hearing aid users in the congregation will need to be shown how to use their 'T' switch – including turning it off after the service! Nurses or doctors in the congregation can give this help.

Those with a very profound hearing loss can be guided by a friend at their side helping them through the service. In these days of multiple choice such a friend needs to be well prepared beforehand. Service sheets clearly showing hymn and page numbers also assist. It is perhaps a counsel of perfection to suggest sermon notes be given to the hearing impaired. Visual aids and overhead projectors may help in some churches. In others the first may feel too much like the class room, the second like the lecture hall.

'The Church Formal' includes structured events: committees, study and even 'informal' prayer groups. If hearing impaired people are to join such groups to advantage, they must be arranged with them in mind. The seating is set out so that the hearing impaired can see everybody present. Naturally in the meeting only one person will speak at a time! – and indicate when they wish to speak so that the hearing impaired can look at them. A person by their side can guide them through an agenda. Ideally, and not very expensively, a portable loop could be set up. A church room used regularly for meetings could have one installed permanently.

At all times in group meetings we try to remember what it means to be hearing impaired: for example, that it is hard at the same time to read a paper passed around for discussion and listen to an explanation of it. The objective is not only to let the hearing impaired understand what is being said, however much attention we give to this. The hope is that they will make their own contribution to the meeting. It can be well worth while the chairman repeating questions raised from the 'floor'.

In church we have our special services. Some use the dramatic contrasts between light and dark: Advent Services, Carols by Candlelight, Easter Vigils. The hearing impaired may find these hard to follow, as are services or plays in church which use the whole building. Words from the back can be hard to hear. It may not be practicable to give each speaker a microphone. Understand if the hearing impaired ask with regret to be excused.

The Church Informal

The hum of voices and the clatter of tea cups at almost any church social gathering are no doubt true outward signs of fellowship within the Body of Christ. They are also sources of confusion and even pain to hearing aid users. If the aid is switched off the hearing impaired cannot follow what is being said, especially if the light is not right. If the aid is on, the ear is assaulted by noise from all sides, making one-to-one conversation difficult. Again understand if the hearing impaired make their excuses early.

The Church Pastoral

The Pastor will often visit those who are hearing impaired. The advice I will try to give now will not only, I hope, aid you in this ministry, but also show how you may be able to pass on practical advice to these people.

When we visit them, the first thought must be about light. Can our face be seen comfortably and easily? Do not stand if the hard of hearing person is sitting and can only see you by risking a cricked neck. Make sure no bright light is behind you – not easy if the one you visit has a favourite chair facing the window!

The hearing aid is most useful in the privacy of the home. Even so, the person will lip read you to some extent. The greater the impairment, the greater the reliance upon lip reading. This skill is an art as much as a science. Many consonants have the same lip pattern – 'p' and 'b' for example. Much intelligent guess work – based upon the context is needed to follow – if you are talking about peas or bees!

Avoid bushy beards hiding the mouth, smoking, any movement of hands in front of the face. Look at the person the whole time – much concentration is needed for this! Speak slightly slower than usual but with normal rhythm. *Do not shout* – do not exaggerate your lip movements as this distorts their patterns. Avoid the constant nervous grin.

It helps to speak in short sentences. If you are not understood, then repeat yourself in different words. Make it clear when you change the subject: be sure this is understood before you plunge ahead. At a pinch, there is pen and paper. Use facial expressions. The smile makes it probable that you are talking about the nice weather rather than offering condolences after bereavement. Simple gestures are helpful – to point to yourself or the other person shows who you are talking about.

If other people are included in the conversation, try to ensure that the hearing impaired person can see everybody clearly and comfortably. Talk *to* them, rather than *at* them, over their heads to the family or friend present. This request I address to doctors and nurses also.

It can be difficult for hearing impaired people in hospital to grasp what is going on. Perhaps in your visit you will have time to ask on their behalf and tell them.

There are many environmental aids to make life easier for the hearing impaired at home. The 'T' switch with the proper adaptations helps them use the phone, TV and radio. It is useful to encourage the hard of hearing to explore these possibilities: this is a ministry to their families and neighbours as well. A recent development is the 'directional microphone system'. The microphone is worn on a loop round the neck of the speaker, and the hearing aid user switches on the 'T' switch. The system is proving itself in one-to-one conversations and also in small group meetings.

Encourage a person who complains that their hearing is going to see a doctor. Referral to an audiological department must come through the GP and is the first step in obtaining a hearing aid if this is necessary. It is best to have such a test rather than go at once to a supplier of private aids. The GP and audiologist may find a physical condition which needs treatment, and such treatment may ease the hearing problem. A person may finally decide to buy an aid privately. It is best to buy one with the 'T' switch, with all the advantages it can bring.

Through the Age Groups

Encourage mothers-to-be to have the anti-rubella (or the new MMR) vaccine. German measles and meningitis have been common causes of deafness, either at birth or later in life.

If you meet parents whose child is born or becomes hearing impaired, urge them to contact the NDCS, whose full name and address is listed at the end of this chapter. The NDCS will offer support and advice to the parents, not only at the traumatic time when the deafness is diagnosed but throughout parenthood.

If it is said of some child that he is inattentive and dreamy –
especially at school – encourage the parents to have his hearing
tested. Very likely there is no cause for alarm (not about the hearing
anyway) and if there is a hearing problem the cause can probably
be treated. But the teens are not an age in which to miss out on
pre-exam schooling. It is as well to know that long exposure to the
louder forms of pop music can permanently damage young people's
hearing. One audiologist says that school discos should have
government health warnings!

Working people with hearing problems sometimes believe that
their disability impedes their advancement. The Disablement
Rehabilitation Officer or the Disability Advisory Service (DAS) at
the Job Centre may be able to give advice – about equipment
which can be supplied at no cost to employer or employee to use
the phone for example – and as not all employers seem to know
this, you can perhaps pass this advice on.

If you are a lecturer or teacher, you may find that some of the
students are hearing impaired. Remember always to speak looking
front – your voice disappears as you turn to the blackboard. Try to
stand still: you are hard to lip read if you wander up and down.
Hearing impaired students cannot both look at you and write notes:
the best help you can give them is outline notes of your lectures.
All this will help, even if a loop system is fitted in the lecture
room.

The vast majority of hearing impaired people, become so in old
age. Life, including social life, has not come to an end! The local
Hard of Hearing League will offer them support and social
activities. These include free lip reading classes. Such classes run by
Adult Education courses have to be paid for.

An Opportunity?

Our pastoral opportunities in ministering to the hearing impaired
is two-fold.

First, we can by our practical help and advice encourage them to
live full and satisfactory lives as church members and members of
society.

The 'secondly' concerns them as active church people. What a shame if their wisdom and experience is lost just because their hearing is not as good as before! What a condemnation of us if we give the impression that they have no worthwhile contribution to make to our churches.

But if we offer to them all the practical help I have attempted to describe, we are in fact offering more than 'mere' practicalities. We will be offering a caring heart which 'sees' this invisible disability, and appreciates the positive place within our Christian Fellowship of those who are and remain children of God first and disabled people a long way second. The mere fact of our thought and effort given to the practicalities of helping hearing impaired people will help overcome that isolation and feeling of rejection, which all too often is the lot of those who suffer from this most common disability.

For help and advice

The nearest Chaplain for Deaf People, and his or her Association. The local Social Services Department will supply details of local help for the hearing impaired, including the provision of some environmental aids.

The Royal National Institute for the Deaf (RNID), 105 Gower Street, London WC1E 6AH. 01-387-8033.
The RNID can give much information about environmental aids, such as the leaflet 'Installation Guidelines for Induction Loops in Public Places' and a sign to advertise the fact once your loop is operational, and perhaps a list of firms who have installed loops in your area. They can also supply details about directional microphone systems.

The Breakthrough Trust, Charles W. Gillett Centre, Selly Oak Colleges, Birmingham B29 6LE. 021-572-64471.
Local branches will have a display of environmental aids, and will advise which are best suited for a particular hearing impaired person.

The British Association of the Hard of Hearing (BAHOH), 7/11 Armstrong Road, London W3 7JL. 01-743-1110.
Two leaflets help to relate to the hearing impaired, and to help them lip read you: 'The Severely Deafened' and 'Sound Advice'. BAHOH will also put you in contact with your local Hard of Hearing League if you cannot otherwise find it.

The National Deaf Children's Society (NDCS), 45 Hereford Road, London W2 5AH. 01-229-9272, supplies information about local NDCS groups.

'Link', The British Centre for Deafened People, 19 Hartfield Road, Eastbourne, Sussex. 0323 638230. Helps the rehabilitation of those who suffer from sudden or increasing hearing loss. Their leaflet 'Golden Link' advises churches in helping the hearing impaired.

Deafness – the Journal of the National Council of Social Workers with Deaf People, Vol 4, no 1 contains further information about hearing impairment. Available from Ken Jones, Lincolnshire C.C. Social Services, Wigford House, Brayford Wharf East, Lincoln LN5 7BH. (Tel. 0522 552222)

The Confused Elderly

CHRISTOPHER P. BURKETT, B.A.
Leek and Meerbrook, Staffordshire

EDITH can be seen walking the streets in her night clothes all too often. If you approach her and ask her why, her reply will be that she has locked herself out. What is she doing in her nightdress in the middle of the day, and why did she leave her flat anyway? Such further questions will get no more adequate response. She is too concerned about her lost keys. On returning her to her flat you discover one door wide open and the other one locked and bolted. In the kitchen the cooker is red hot although nothing is cooking on it. In the front room the radio blares away, whilst the remnants of numerous uneaten meals are scattered about. Settling Edith down in her front room might work, or you might find her walking the streets again only minutes later. Edith is a sufferer from senile dementia.

This is a disease shrouded in ignorance, fear and taboo. The very name itself is enough to cause panic and misery. Who wants to admit that someone they love is demented? But the name conjures up the suggestion of completely deranged behaviour which is far from an appropriate description of many sufferers' troubled lives. Sometimes it is little more than forgetfulness and a not too disturbing vagueness, although sometimes total disorientation and a radical change of personality is evident. In its most severe forms the behaviour it leads to can be very offputting and frightening to those who encounter it. It produces not only a marked change in the life of the sufferer, but also a disturbing challenge to those in the wider community. One of the products of this is a reluctance to admit what has happened. Isolation causes further deterioration in the quality of life of the person ill and those who care for him or her.

The disease is the consequence of irreversible changes in the brain, it usually lasts for between two and ten years. It may be properly thought of as a terminal illness, but of much longer duration than most illnesses so labelled. This is perhaps one of the most disturbing qualities of the illness. The disease is increasing in the western world. As more people live longer so its incidence increases. Sometimes people only in their forties are affected by dementia, but it is much more common in the elderly.

Its incidence means that every community will have its share of sufferers and families struggling to cope. Unfortunately, but understandably, the disease is often hidden. Families are reluctant to admit that mother is a sufferer, or that grandad is no longer the amiable and capable person he used to be. The fantasy world sufferers often live in makes them very hard to cope with. Turning day into night, and night into day, as so many sufferers do, makes living with them very burdensome. Simple tasks and appliances that have been used for years suddenly become danger points. Carers feel that they need to be on guard and watchful for twenty-four hours a day. The toll of care means that those with the disease not infrequently out-live the person who has the primary responsibility of caring for them. Alongside the physical stress of such caring must be ranked the emotional stress of the change in the loved one and the knowledge that there is no cure. Maybe as many as two-thirds of those with symptoms go untreated and unrecognized. Sufferers themselves often remain convinced that there is nothing wrong, and resentment at the suggestion that they need assistance can lead to further isolation and more severe confusion.

Just as carers for those with dementia must come to terms with the hard fact that the problem is never going to go away, so too the wider society must be made more aware of the disease's occurrence and the concurrent need for support and assistance. This is a disease that cannot possibly be coped with solely by statutory services simply because of the pressure of large numbers and limited resources. Most families are eager and ready to care for their elderly confused members but the nature of the illness makes outside support and assistance vital. Such outside help is frequently provided by the Health Services and Social Services, often by very able and dedicated staff, but once again the pressure of numbers often limits the degree of aid available. Even the best support, with periods of hospitalization and regular home visits from health and social service professionals, can still leave a carer exhausted and hemmed-in. The project described in this chapter is one local attempt to provide voluntary assistance to sufferers, and thereby to carers, in such a way that the statutory services can use it as a reliable adjunct to their provisions. It is viewed as standing in the best tradition of church supported pastoral work that aims to offer services that are not available otherwise, in close cooperation with professionals involved in the problem, and offering the possibility of structured loving service for volunteers. Any church congregation is able to offer help with shopping and the possibility of sitting-in with Granny whilst the first line carer has a couple of hours off. And every Christian community must concern itself with ways of making sure such assistance can be sought from it easily and without embarrassment or fuss. But the project described here is of a much more structured nature for reasons which I hope will become apparent. It provides an opportunity for worthwhile and appreciated service to the community by a church congregation that sees itself as having a commitment to a pastoring role in its locality.

Our group began as an initiative by a local charitable foundation and our community psychiatric nurses in drawing together likely volunteers. It has quickly developed as a self running and autonomous community group with a large measure of church support. It is offered in this series of articles in the hope that other congregations, once alerted to the need and the possibility of going a little way towards meeting it, might be prompted to attempt similar work. This is a pastoral caring scheme that demands first and foremost a building and a body of people, these are just the resources that the church often has available.

The project aims to provide care for just one day per week to those suffering from dementia so that their usual carers can rely upon having those hours off. Sufferers who live alone can be given the added chance to socialize and the certainty of a good cooked meal. The clients are brought to the church centre by car, and spend the day there in a structured but convivial atmosphere until they are returned home, again by car. Activities during the day aim to preserve what skills the group members have.

One of the great difficulties the group has had is knowing what to call itself. It cannot label itself as for 'the demented' because of the awful stigma attached to that word and our concern to guard the feelings and sensitivities of families and sufferers. On the other hand, titles simply using the adjective 'elderly' suggest just another club for those of retirement age. We have as a consequence stayed with our original title of Elderly Support Group, sometimes accompanying it with the expression 'caring for Alzheimer's sufferers in our community'. Although Alzheimer's disease is the most common cause of dementia it is not the only cause of the illness our clients suffer. However, as a shorthand expression it at least gives us the opportunity to explain what we are about. Talking about an illness that is often untalkable about is one of the crucial issues of the group's work. Here perhaps is an opportunity for the church to make such things more bearable by talking more about them. The difficulties around naming our work also has implications for funding it. Public appeals for donations are difficult to handle because it is hard to convey what we are about simply and shortly.

Turning to the practicalities, there are several basic things essential to the success of the project. The room available for the group must be warm and have easy access to toilets. Ideally the building should have no steps to make entry difficult. Safe car parking off the roadside is also useful as many of our clients take a long time to get in or out of a car. We have found a wheelchair to be a handy back-up tool. Kitchen facilities are required even if a meal cooked professionally elsewhere is used. Suitable seats are necessary; we found the stacking chairs often used in church halls to be unsuitable. A local government grant provided us with padded chairs of the right height. All the equipment and utensils used are as homely as we can make them, every effort is made to counter an institutional feel to our day. We aim to make it much more like a day out with friends. Volunteers are needed at the ratio of about one per client. The support, advice and help of the statutory services is crucial and we have found it to be always most readily given.

I am grateful to Mrs Hazel Wilson, the present voluntary group organizer, for the following description of a typical group day:

> At Present we have six to nine clients each week and usually six all-day volunteers. Other volunteers help for part of the day transporting clients, fetching meals and helping with the washing up. This extra help is much appreciated as it leaves the all-day volunteers free to stay with the clients all the time.
>
> Clients start arriving at the Church Centre at about 10.10 am, when we sit and talk and have our first cup of tea. The professionals tell us that many elderly people do not drink enough, so we encourage the taking of drinks whilst they are with us. During this first session we talk about current news items. News about the Royal family and our own families are firm favourites as topics of conversation. Everyone is included. Old photographs and old books, along with grocery items for price comparisons, are also recurring topics. Some of the stimulation material used is commercially produced for this specific task, and the group has had to purchase it. Other things volunteers have devised themselves. A simple thing like talking through the day's newspaper can be very productive. Such memory stimulation is vital to the group's work. It is amazing how much even the most confused individual can remember from the very distant past, although the immediate past is often problematic. This kind of memory impairment is typical of the disease. These activities usually last until about 11.15 am.
>
> The next session consists of more physical activities. We feel these are particularly important as some of our clients spend all day most days simply sitting. For the games the clients sit in a large circle. We try to exercise all the parts of the body by the use of various games. Favourites are chair football, bouncing balls to each other, hitting balloons across the circle, and hoop-la. Some of the games become quite competitive, and it is always a noisy time with much laughter. After about thirty minutes of this kind of activity we have a breather and exercise our brains with proverbs, old sayings, and the singing of popular songs. Once again long-distance memory recall is used to the full to make up for the shortcomings of immediate memory.
>
> During these periods the behind-the-scenes work of washing up cups and laying tables for a meal has been going on. Lunch arrives around midday. Most of the clients like to use the toilet before the meal and so volunteers need to accompany the unsteady. One lady in a wheelchair needs the assistance of two volunteers and it can take as long as ten

minutes to accomplish this simple task. We feel a properly designed disabled toilet would be a great advantage, but unfortunately we do not have this facility in our church.

During the meal time we play records, using the kind of music that is likely to be familiar to the clients from their younger days. One lady who was extremely forgetful found the music particularly encouraging and always wanted to dance, which she could still do, much to her delight and ours. Although the living skills of all our clients are very seriously impaired we are often able to dig out some one thing that they are still capable of, which is a great encouragement to the whole group.

After lunch and another drink we turn our attention to table games like dominoes, bingo, snakes and ladders. Some of our clients find it very difficult to concentrate on these games, but they soon realize that going up a ladder is better than going down a snake! One to one assistance is often needed at this time, along with lots of encouragement at the picking out of colours, counting moves, and spotting numbers. It's surprising that nobody complains on receiving a chocolate bar as a prize, when all through the game we had been assured that the prize was a holiday in the Bahamas! Occasionally we have tried handicrafts in this slot in our timetable but this has often ended with the clients becoming spectators as the volunteers complete a task which needed rather too much dexterity.

It is now 2.30 pm and time for our last cup of tea, by 3.00 am we are all cleared away and ready for home. Our days are very busy but very worthwhile, not only to our clients and their families, but to us as well. There is a great deal of enjoyment had by all. Persistence with even the most confused of our clients usually has its rewards. Finally, I would like to stress the vital importance of regular commitment by the volunteers; without such commitment the group becomes impossible to manage.

Many of the group volunteers are church members with no previous experience of this kind of work. The hesitancy when first beginning is quickly overcome as the value of the work becomes evident, and consequently our turnover of volunteers is very small. Sometimes local schools and colleges send students to us on assessed placement. Although this adds further written work on the organizer's shoulders, the contribution of these young people has been of great benefit. Other volunteers are people with a particular interest in this illness, or people who have retired from professional work in this field. The group leader is herself a volunteer who has trained herself for the job whilst actually doing it. We have had a great deal of assistance in designing the programme and planning particular activities from local hospitals and other caring agencies. A wealth of advice and help has been readily and freely available simply for the asking. Such encouragement from professionals has been a great fillip to the whole project.

This professional help has also been essential in finding clients for the group. Many of our referrals come from the local community psychiatric nurse, although doctors and social workers use us also. Sometimes referrals come via the local clergy, and occasionally families approach us directly. Each potential client is visited in his or her own home by the group organizer. This personal contact is essential, although it may take several calls to secure willingness to attend. In a world that is often totally confusing to the person with dementia the attempt is made to build a bridge into a new experience by getting the person used to the leader's face. Hopefully the person will therefore be ready to accompany this new found friend to the group, but it may take weeks to build this familiarity. On other occasions no such painstaking preparation is necessary, either because the person is ready and eager for a new interest or because confusion is so severe that the implications of a car journey with someone new cannot be understood.

This contact also enables other family members who know who we are and to be assured that we will take good care of their frail loved one. Sufferers may have been taken to other old people's clubs and organizations but not have been able to cope with them because of their particular difficulties. Difficulty in mixing with other people coupled with erratic behaviour often leads to the isolation of the confused. The high level of volunteers in relation to clients and our concentration on the specific difficulties of dementia makes our approach different, so that even the most confused person may find a home with us for a few hours per week. That said, sometimes the severity of the symptoms displayed or other health complications make a person beyond the scope of our group. This is a hard issue, but one that must be tackled honestly if the group is to function well. Regular volunteer meetings outside the group's working day are used to discuss confidentially how we plan to work with particular individuals. Incontinence usually means the person is beyond our capabilities, although we aim to cope in an unembarrassing way with any possible accidents that might occur. Fortunately, professionals involved often realize that a person is beyond the capabilities of such a voluntary group and consequently do not make a referral. Similar support is also given to clients who deteriorate in health, so that some of those we care for are eventually permanently hospitalized. This is never regarded as a failure; rather we look at the group's work as a positive contribution to that person's ability to cope at home until such coping has become impossible. A few of our clients spend short periods in hospital on a regular basis. In these instances we keep in close contact with the family so that our day out is readily available again when the person returns to being cared for at home.

In various ways we try to encourage contact with a wider community of people than many confused individuals usually have access to. Each year, the group day nearest Christmas becomes an all day Christmas party when all kinds of people are invited in to share the celebration with us. Particularly popular with the clients is the visit of the choir from the local first school. The empathy so often noted between very old people and very young people applies just as well to those with dementia, and the children's presence seems to trigger great joy. Local musicians able to play 'the old songs' are also popular. Trips out into the community have also been attempted, but not often due to the added demands of transport and supervision. A visit to the corner supermarket has sometimes been appropriate with mobile and interested clients, although added confusion caused by bright lights and unfamiliar surroundings is always a risk.

The group is relatively cheap to run, and is most certainly a very effective way of providing resources for this needy group of people. But even with a subsidy from the local church, and a small charge for the meal provided for the clients there are still outstanding costs. None of the volunteers receive any payment but we do reimburse transport costs at an agreed rate for those who use their cars in the group's work. We have received cash help from local government, from national charities, and from local clubs and associations. The volunteers, however, still find themselves in the position of having to run fund raising events to resource the work the group does. In this area we find ourselves really stretched, both in terms of time available and new ideas to use. We have attempted to meet the challenge and extend our work by offering to provide speakers for the meetings of associations that might support us financially. In this way we hope not only to raise funds but increase awareness of dementia in our community.

We hope that the group's work is a small but very positive challenge to the hopelessness and dismay that surrounds dementia. We aim to provide worthwhile assistance to those who are very hard pressed in caring for a sufferer, a few hours respite amidst their constant round of care. We offer a community resource that enables much needed statutory provision to be spread a little further. But above all, we aim to help sufferers to use the life skills they still have to the utmost. In this the work is rewarding and often joyful, particularly when the client does not continue to decline but holds her own for months or maybe longer. We cannot pretend to mend destroyed brain cells, but we can claim to aid the amazing God-given adaptability of the human being. In this there is much hard work but also much excitement, and a great sense of achievement. Edith has really enjoyed her time with us.

Part IV
Outreach

Community Involvement

WILLIAM D. HORTON, M.A.
Wesley College, Bristol

COMMUNITY involvement is a Christian imperative. Not only is the redemption of society as much a keynote of the gospel as the salvation of the individual, our faith gives pastors no encouragement to believe that the corporate aspect of their ministry is to be exercised solely within the fellowship of the church. The world beyond that fellowship must equally be their concern, because it is God's concern. God is the Lord of all life; he is its creator; he is present in the total human experience and there is no area of our existence in which his writ doesn't run. To drive a wedge between church and community, sacred and secular, is to create a false dichotomy which denies the incarnation. Only as they minister in the context of life's wholeness do pastors serve the all-embracing purposes of God's Kingdom.

Needless to say, this understanding of the pastor's relationship to the community is not shared by everybody! Some pastors themselves, while paying lip-service to the wholeness of life, do not always give it practical expression: they shelter behind the church structures where their role is clearly defined and their authority unchallenged rather than venture out into the more dangerous waters of the community at large. Isn't their time fully occupied (they argue) with the internal affairs of church life? Isn't it the responsibility of the laypeople, rather than of the pastor, to be involved in community life? Some congregations encourage their pastor in this attitude; he or she is *their* pastor, a private chaplain paid by them to minister to their spiritual needs and time given to a wider ministry is resented. And, of course, many people who have little sympathy for the Christian faith and even less for the institutional church (but who are prepared to be active in community affairs) see the pastor's involvement as an unwelcome interference, the long arm of the church meddling in matters not of its concern.

This tension between theological perceptions of wholeness and forces which further the fragmentation of society is the backcloth to the present chapter. What follows highlights local opportunities for involvement rather than national issues of church/state relationships with which most pastors are not directly concerned. It assumes that the pastor acts in a representative rather than a personal capacity, sharing the ministry of outreach with the whole congregation rather than working alone. It seeks, first, to identify those aspects of the pastor's calling which are theologically important in community involvement. It then (in the larger part of the essay) indicates how the pastor can put these concepts into practice, both by encouraging the community's involvement in the church and the church's involvement in the community.

Evangelistic missions are regarded as beyond the scope of this paper and such involvement of the church in the community is not, therefore, discussed.

The Pastor's Calling

There are three aspects of a pastor's calling which have an important bearing on the nature of Christian ministry within the community. First, the pastor is a 'reconciler'. The gospel for which the pastor stands is a message of reconciliation and, in itself, is the means of achieving reconciliation. Primarily, of course, this reconciliation is between God and sinful men and women, through the cross of Christ. But firmly linked with this divine-human reconciliation is reconciliation between estranged people; those who are reconciled to God thereby become reconciled to each other. Although the church is (or should be) the fellowship of the reconciled, the gospel cannot be contained within an ecclesiastical framework. The message must be proclaimed and given 'flesh' in the world at large, for the purpose of God is that all people and the whole of creation should ultimately be reconciled in Christ. The pastor's responsibility, therefore, is to share in Christ's reconciling ministry within the community as much as within the church. Opportunities for reconciling opposing factions, for acting as

mediator in disputes, for helping many diverse interests in society
to co-operate for the common good, for breaking down barriers of
suspicion between different groups of community workers and
establishing good inter-disciplinary relationships, these and other
opportunities must be seized whenever (and wherever) they occur.

Second, the pastor is a mediator, mediating the life of God to
men and women. This, of course, is not only the pastor's calling, it
is that of the whole church. In biblical terms, the church is the
fellowship of him who is 'the Lord and Giver of life', the Holy
Spirit. This doesn't mean that every local church automatically
demonstrates God's life within it or that the Holy Spirit's activity is
restricted to the life of the church. Nor does it mean that the
pastor's sole responsibility is to work for a spiritually 'live' *church*.
Clearly none of these propositions is true. It does mean, however,
that a church faithful to the Lord experiences in its fellowship the
dynamic presence of the living Christ. But being 'faithful to its
Lord' commits the church to living and, if need be, giving its life
for others, as Christ did. So, paradoxically, the church only lives
spiritually when it is prepared to die.

The pastor's responsibility is to be the spearhead of this life-giving
ministry in the community. Some communities (new towns,
amorphous suburbs, ribbon developments, perhaps) scarcely warrant
the name. They are held together simply by a common
geographical location and by the one local authority to which
everybody pays rates; they have little or no community spirit, few
communal activities and no real sense of corporate identity. Other
communities which do have a common life find that, with the
passing of the years, their life becomes weaker; they seek new
challenges, new inspiration and new insights into the meaning of
community. Other communities flourish and grow as life begets
life; as their activities increase, so does their need for skilled
leadership and people fully committed to their community's
development. All these situations are opportunities for the pastor to
mediate the life of God in the human situation; creating, reviving
or sustaining community life is the work of the Holy Spirit in
whose name the pastor ministers.

Third, the pastor is a servant. Again, the pattern is Christ who 'came not to be ministered unto but to minister'. The gospels make it clear that Christ's only criterion for serving people was human need; nothing else mattered. His love and compassion extended beyond his own immediate circle of family and friends, beyond his fellow Jews, to embrace all who needed his help. The implication for the pastor is obvious: no boundaries can be imposed on Christian service. The pastor's ministry to the needy cannot stop at the church doors as if those beyond them were the responsibility of others. To imagine that the pastor can remain aloof from the community until such time as a financial appeal has to be made to the public for the repair of the church steeple is to deny the social implication of the gospel. For the pastor to refuse to take part in community affairs unless given a position of authority and enabled to command events is to betray the servanthood of Christ. Without losing identity as a minister of the gospel and without attempting to assume anyone else's role (e.g. that of the social worker) the pastors's responsibility is to serve the community.

Practical Matters

We now ask how, in practice, the pastor can exercise these aspects of ministry in the community. In spite of what was said earlier about the pastor's involvement often being regarded as an interference by those working in the community, there are occasions when the community itself takes the initiative in seeking the pastor's co-operation; these are valuable opportunities not to be missed. National occasions such as Remembrance Day and royal celebrations and local events of a civic, historical or traditional character often prompt community leaders to request a special church service to mark the event. By responding sympathetically to the request, by being sensitive to the requirements of the organizers, by offering a warm welcome to the congregation and by conducting an appropriate service, the pastor forges a link between church and community and paves the way for further such co-operation in the future. As a result, many people who do not normally attend worship enter the church building at their request and are reminded of the Christian faith's relevance to every part of life. When they meet the pastor afterwards, in other contexts, it is not as a complete stranger and this, undoubtedly, helps the pastor to become integrated into the community's life.

While some community initiatives are centred on the church, most invite the pastor to leave the home ground for the community's territory. These initiatives cover a wide range of involvement – from being merely a figurehead whose name and title are thought to add dignity to the group's printed notepaper, through being asked to offer the occasional prayer at meetings or saying grace at annual dinners, to active chaplaincies and membership of hard-working local committees. Those which require little from the pastor can open doors for further involvement later. Those which demand more in time and effort enable the pastor to extend the church's ministry (often at a deep level) to people not otherwise touched by it. Invitations to chaplaincy work, if taken seriously by both sides, are among the most demanding and rewarding. Whether it be the scout group, Toc H, the old peoples' home or to the town mayor, time is well-spent if it helps to break down the barrier between church and community and to remove the spirit of mistrust founded in ignorance which sometimes mars their relationship. Relating easily to children and young people may not be every pastor's forte but invitations to speak at school assemblies, harvest festivals and carol services and to share in the school's special occasions provide a valuable opportunity, not only for offering the children a Christian interpretation of life but also for supporting the staff in their work and meeting parents who claim that family commitments allow them no time to participate in church worship or fellowship. For people of goodwill who recognize that the church has a part to play in the community and invite the pastor to be involved in what they do, the Lord be praised!

In many situations, however, the initiative for community involvement has to come from the pastor; opportunities have to be seized and, sometimes, created. Again, some of these opportunities are centred on the church while others are community based. Among the former is the opportunity of using the church buildings for community purposes. The availability, today, of many secular halls and meeting places makes a return to the mediaeval practice of *all* community activities being held in the church unlikely! None the less, the church hall and ancillary rooms have considerable potential for the church's social outreach, a fact which not every pastor or church council appreciates. Often, 'our' premises are firmly locked for the greater part of the week because they are not being used by the *church*, while organizations in the community may be searching desperately for accommodation. By inviting such organizations to use its premises, the church can deploy its resources more effectively and give a valuable service to the community. But it is not only building resources that can be offered in this way. A group struggling through lack of sufficient leaders can be offered the help of church members to maintain (but not to control!) its work. If it's a recently formed group the full financial cost of its use of the church premises can be subsidized by the church until it is able to be self-sufficient. When such opportunities are seen and welcomed, links are forged between church and community to their mutual advantage.

Other opportunities for involvement arise when the pastor includes community affairs in the church's regular concerns for prayer and action. Praying for the local community during the Sunday worship should be no mere formality, nor should it be confined to vague generalities. Informing the congregation about specific issues and particular needs before prayers are offered brings an immediacy and relevance to the petitions and stimulates the church members into action afterwards. A similar positive interest is created when the pastor includes a page of community news in the church magazine or devotes a section of the church noticeboard to the announcement of forthcoming local events. When different church groups ask speakers from the community to talk to their members the link between church and community is further strengthened, as it is on those occasions when the pastor invites a community worker to preach at a service and a collection is taken for a special community project.

Yet another kind of church-based opportunity for involvement often occurs in new towns and large modern housing estates when, as frequently is the case, the pastor is the only 'leader' who lives as well as works locally. Before 9.00 a.m. and after 5.00 p.m. when the social workers are not generally available, the pastor is left to tackle any problems and emergencies which may arise – and is then much involved in community affairs! By acting as the link between people in need and both statutory and voluntary helping agencies the pastor exercises a valuable serving ministry. Holding a regular 'surgery' in the church and welcoming anybody to it assists this ministry. It may indeed be time-consuming but it expresses the church's involvement in the realities of the community situation.

What initiatives can the pastor take by going into the community? Three areas of involvement must receive a brief mention. The first is that of social welfare. Happily, the time is long since past when the only welfare available was the charity dispensed by the vicar's wife and that grudgingly given by the Poor Law institution. Today, many non-church agencies, statutory and voluntary, care for the vulnerable members of the community, and many individual Christians are part of their serving ministry; this, of course, is the church at work. But *corporate* involvement should also have its place in the church's outreach, both in supporting what is already being done and in initiating new projects where there is a need not being met. An 'official' offer of help from the church council forges a stronger link between church and community than support given by church members on a purely personal basis. Such an offer, however, presupposes serious commitment and should only be made if the promised help can be delivered. It also demands sensitivity on the church's part; no community group appreciates what may appear to its leaders to be a take-over bid! It must be clearly understood that the church is offering service and not seeking control; that it is prepared to work alongside others whatever their beliefs and to accept that the job in hand is a good (Christian) end in itself and not just a means of promoting the claims of the church. The pastor must recognize the professional skills of workers in other disciplines and not claim omni-competence; the clerical collar doesn't compensate for a lack of expertise nor does the pastor's office guarantee acceptance by the community. Only as a *person* with particular gifts will the pastor's involvement be welcomed.

The second area is politics. Here is a dilemma! On the one hand, the political arena is the place where things happen and decisions affecting everybody's life are taken; if the church is to be an instrument of change for the Kingdom of God then, somehow, it must engage in political action. On the other hand, politics are divisive and sincere Christians are to be found in all political parties; there is never likely to be a 'Christian' consensus about any political issue. What is the pastor to do? Some ministers exercise a distinguished preaching and pastoral ministry without making any secret of their political allegiance or of their work for their party. Most pastors, however, believe in the best interests of their ministry not to 'go public' about their personal convictions nor to take an active part in political life. Paradoxically, their detachment from politics creates opportunities for involvement; not being tied to one party the pastor is free to support or criticize any party as the situation may demand, without being accused of acting with prejudice. When, in the Sunday worship, the pastor prays for the government, for parliament, for the nation and for the local council and community, the church's concern for every part of life is being expressed without that concern creating divisions in the congregation. Church members who are active in politics (would that there were more of them!) should be encouraged in their involvement and not made to feel that their time would be better spent on 'church' business. On those occasions when a particular issue grips people's attention (as the question of Sunday shopping did, recently) there is the opportunity to make the local member of parliament aware of the strength of Christian feeling and to ask the member to bear this in mind when the matter comes to a vote. In this case it is better for many individual letters to be written rather than just one from the church as a whole. Politicians take more notice of a flood of letters sent by people concerned enough to write than they do of a formal letter from a church council which may have been written at the instigation of only one or two champions of the cause.

The third area is that of race and inter-faith relations. Many churches today have people of other races and religions as their neighbours and Christians often find themselves a minority of the local population. This presents both a challenge to the church and a further opportunity for the pastor's involvement in community affairs. Christians of past generations would, no doubt, have regarded today's situation as a God-given opportunity to win converts for the true faith and to rescue heathens from the darkness and errors of their ways. Present day Christians, however, have learned to recognize the insights of other faiths into the nature of God and to respect the spirituality and holy living of other believers with whom they are friends. So, while in no way betraying their own belief in the lordship of Christ and the uniqueness of God's revelation in him, most pastors, today, do not see proselytizing as their main concern; they are content to let Christianity shine in its own light and to make its witness through the lives of Christian believers. This doesn't of course, preclude a theological dialogue between Christians and people of other faiths, or an exploration of each other's beliefs, traditions and ways of life and worship. Such engagement inevitably leads to a growth in mutual understanding on which good community relations are based.

There are also opportunities for practical as well as theological involvement open to the pastor in a multi-racial society. Church halls can be offered to ethnic groups for social activities; advice centres can be set up and language classes organized for those who are at a disadvantage because of their poor English. Sometimes, at the official level, the hard-pressed statutory bodies are unable to meet every situation of need. The pastor's ministry, then, is to affirm the dignity of every human being, regardless of colour or creed, by mediating between those who need help and the authorities, by seeking to right wrongs and by supporting those action groups which work for a more just and equitable society. On those occasions when, sadly, community relations break down and racial prejudice and hatred lead to violence, the pastor's role is that of peacemaker. It is a costly role but, modelled on Christ himself, it is the only role open to the Christian in an evil situation. But out of suffering and death come resurrection! If the pastor's involvement leads to that (both for the community and for every individual in it) then the purposes of God's Kingdom are faithfully served.

Towards a Theology of Paid Employment

ANTONY HURST, M.A., M.Sc. (Econ.)
Southwark

How much do parochial clergy actually know about what their parishioners actually do? In particular, how much do they know about that large proportion of their parishioners' time that is spent outside the home, and probably outside the parish, in paid employment? Most people spend most of their waking hours for most of their lives working for money, and this amounts to an ingredient that the church cannot afford to ignore. But sadly parochial clergy are often ill-equipped to relate to people's work experiences, and the parochial church is often inhibited in making an impact on people's working lives.

The reasons for this are not hard to surmise. The parochial church has traditionally focused its attention on people in their homes rather than on people in their places of work, parishioners are defined in terms of where people happen to live and not in terms of where they happen to be employed, and services traditionally happen on Sundays when most workplaces are closed. And this tradition has become self-reinforcing in that it has meant that the parochial church has failed to develop a whole area of experience and expertise so that, on the few occasions when it has been presented with opportunities for involvement in the world of work, it has been unable to capitalize on them.

The assumption that the parochial church seems to make, and what most Christians seem to feel, is that, however relevant people's beliefs may be to what goes on in their homes and in their home communities, these beliefs somehow do not apply to what goes on at work. This split not only ignores reality but also means that important opportunities are lost for appreciating the extent of

God's presence in the world, and for witness, for wonder, for worship, for loving and for prayer. What is needed is a theological framework within which these two separate worlds can be integrated with each other and be made sense of. The theology needs to take account of the purpose of work, the nature of paid employment, and the realities of people's experiences in the workplace. It needs to be pluralist and inclusive, since one of the characteristics of paid employment is that it provides an environment where people of all religions and none share the same experience on equal terms.

There is no better place to start than at the beginning. The story of Creation in Genesis chapter 1 might almost be the story of the first working week, and like most working weeks it starts in chaos and ends in a well earned day off. God's creative task is to transform that chaos into order, and during the first five days he orders the world and everything in it. And then on the sixth day he creates man, and he gives man a very special charge which is that he should cultivate the earth and make it fruitful. And then, because he has accomplished what he had set himself to do, God rests from his labours and in so doing there is a clear implication he delegates to man a responsibility for the continuation of the creative task, for transforming chaos into order and for cultivating the earth and making it fruitful.

This starting point explains the objective importance of work, and since a great deal of the world's work is now performed in the context of paid employment, it explains the positive contribution that paid employment makes to mankind's fulfilment of the divine charge. And it also explains the subjective importance of work as a means of self-expression since the charge is of divine origin. One of the most endearing aspects of the creation story is the way that God, at the end of each day's labour, stands back with a sense of almost smug satisfaction and says 'That's good'; almost everybody who has successfully completed a job that needed to be done will have experienced this same sensation. And it also explains how work is a necessity for all people by virtue of their being God's creations, irrespective of whether or not the work they do is done in his name.

But there are a number of things that the Creation story doesn't explain. Although paid employment carries with it a number of benefits, there are disbenefits also and the two cannot be separated either from each other or from unemployment which is paid employment's reverse side. The most obvious benefit of paid employment is the money; this enables a person to support himself and his family and to buy things that have nothing whatsoever to do his job. And his job also gives him status, both the status that is inherent in his position as an employee and also the status that results from his being able to spend the money he earns. And it also provides him with the scope for personal self-fulfilment. The scope for creativity is more obvious in some forms of employment than in others, but it must not be thought that the opportunities for working with people enjoyed by doctors and teachers, or the opportunities for being artistic enjoyed by film directors and violinists are the only forms of creativity; there is plenty of scope for self-expression in negotiating a deal, in taking the minutes of a meeting, or in operating a lathe. Another benefit is that a contract of employment relieves a person of a great deal of the responsibility for making his own decisions; the nature of his employment will in large measure dictate what time he gets up in the morning, what clothes he wears and what opinions he holds on a variety of issues.

In entering into a contract of employment, an employee undertakes to perform a number of tasks, and these tasks are defined by the employing institution. The institution will have been established for a particular purpose, and in order to realize this purpose it will have defined for itself a number of objectives. The tasks which the employee undertakes to perform will be the means by which these objectives are achieved. The purpose of some institutions, particularly those in the public sector, is defined in terms of meeting particular needs, such as the need for ill people to have their illnesses cured or the need for children to be educated, and a finite amount of money will have been allocated to the institutions to enable these purposes to be realized. Since these purposes are open-ended and the resources limited, the objectives will be expressed in terms of achieving value for money, of attaching priorities to the needs and deploying the available resources to best advantage. The purpose of institutions in the commercial sector will be expressed in terms of producing goods or services at prices that customers or clients will be willing to pay and thus remaining commercially viable.

As his part of the contract, an employee agrees not just to perform his defined tasks, but also to perform them competently and to behave in such a way that is conducive to competent performance; if he fails in any of this he will be in breach of his contract. He also agrees to work towards the achievement of the institution's objectives and this requires at least a minimal commitment to the value-system implied by the institution's purpose. He will need to make at least some sort of commitment to achieving value for money, maximizing output and containing costs, and this in turn will affect his attitudes in his performance of his tasks. So contractual requirements make heavy demands upon an employee, and there are inevitably some people who find the burdens too great and who buckle under the strain.

And there are disbenefits inherent in paid employment too, which are so significant that any theological framework cannot but take them into account. In entering into a contract of employment a person surrenders a great deal of his time and energy; he can no longer wander off and do what he chooses in the middle of the working day. And the commitment to institutional values involves a more subtle loss; each institution implies its own particular attitudes and culture, and conformity requires the surrender of a degree of personal autonomy. And there are difficulties inherent in working within an institution's limitations. There are the limitations implied by restricted objectives, the limitations implied by a shortage of resources, and the limitations that are inevitably consequent upon the fact that institutions are staffed by human beings of flawed perception and partial competence. All these are painful, but perhaps the greatest source of pain in paid employment is that a requirement to love is not, and cannot be, written into anybody's job description.

And the reverse side of the coin of paid employment is unemployment; a theology which took paid employment into account would need to take account of unemployment also. A person who is unemployed is deprived of all of paid employment's benefits. The effects of long term unemployment have been spelled out by a large number of commentators, and most parochial clergy will have met them at first hand. Diminished income matters, and the loss of a framework that shapes the day matters, but what matters most is the loss of self-esteem, that combination of status and a sense of worthwhileness that comes from having something to do which is recognized as useful. Some commentators have used this to decry the benefits that are inherent in paid employment but this is a dangerous course; the civilization that we take for granted is the outcome of the cumulative work of generations of employees and the more subjective benefits of the experience of employment are too real to be wished away. But the benefits of the experience of work are limited and there is no harm in drawing attention to these limitations. Viewed objectively, work has increased our knowledge of the created world and of the human beings who inhabit it, but it has not enabled us to eliminate unhappiness. Viewed subjectively, work gives people the opportunity for being successful, but it is a fragile success within a limited context; keeping a company commercially viable or keeping a public sector institution on the road means having to discount whole areas of the human predicament, and the sense of well-being that paid employment engenders is all too vulnerable to chance events like sickness or redundancy, and it has a finite end when retirement age is reached.

Perhaps the greatest difficulty in incorporating all this within a theology of Creation is the apparent conflict in values; at work people are expected to commit themselves to the objectives of their employing institution single-mindedly and often assertively and even aggressively, and this seems seriously at variance with the values implied in the Sermon on the Mount. On two other occasions in the Gospels, Jesus makes statements which, on a superficial assessment at least, seem to imply that being a Christian and being a committed employee don't mix. He says that you cannot serve God and mammon, and that we should render unto Caesar the things that are Caesar's and unto God the things that are God's. Presumably most of the things that we do during the course of our paid employment fall within the domains of mammon and

Caesar, and any comprehensive theology would need to accord these domains a recognized place.

This apparent conflict stems from the fact that paid employment is essentially contractual. Most people who work for money are employed by institutions and in entering into a contract of employment they undertake to perform an agreed series of tasks in return for an agreed number of benefits, most obviously a specified amount of money. People who are not employees include free-lance workers, like some journalists or plumbers, and a number who work for fees or commissions, like solicitors or estate agents but their work is even more obviously contractual; they agree with their clients or customers to do in return for payment something that the clients or customers want done. Even parochial clergy, in return for accepting an incumbency which has a stipend attached, are bound by some sort of expectation as to what they will do in return, but there can be few people whose contractual obligations are so obliquely expressed. They may, nevertheless have something to learn about their own jobs if they increase their understanding of the nature of the obligations that bind others.

The commodities in which these contracts are expressed are finite, and the most obvious of them is, money. Love, on the other hand is an infinite commodity and is not amenable to contract. More money can be given to one person only if some is taken away from somebody else, whereas if a person is capable of loving another person he is more able rather than less able to love other people as a result, And if love is traded in the context of a contractual relationship it becomes something other than love. And God's love is absolutely infinite. When we talk about everybody being paid an equal wage what we mean is that everybody is paid an average amount, which means that some people have to give up something of what they already have. But when we talk of everybody being equal in God's love we don't mean that God loves each person an average amount, but that he loves each person totally.

Because of these differences, love and money operate in accordance with different sets of rules. In the allocation of money what matters is fairness, that each person should receive his fair share since anything else would mean some people getting less than they deserved. And what matters is efficiency, that money should be allocated where it is most needed since anything else would mean that it was being frittered away on inessentials. And what matters is cost-effectiveness, that it should be allocated where it will yield the best return since anything else would mean that it was not being used to best advantage. In the money world, fairness, efficiency and cost-effectiveness are virtues, but in the love world they are evil constraints. If love were to be allocated fairly, some people would have to receive less; what matters is generosity. If love were to be allocated efficiently it would have to be denied to those who most needed it; what matters is compassion. And if it were to be allocated cost-effectively it would have to be denied to those who were unable to show love in return; what matters is a willingness to be vulnerable. In the parable of the labourers in the vineyard, where all the labours are paid the same amount of money for doing different amounts of work, Jesus is either talking about real money, in which case every personnel manager worth his salt would reject the message as a crazy basis for an industrial relations strategy, or he is talking about money as a metaphor for love, in which case he is making this very point. It is probable that this was a point that needed making in a commercially minded world but the difficulty is that he didn't follow the story by offering guidance to people motivated by generosity, compassion and a willingness to be vulnerable on how to combine this with running a commercially viable vineyard.

Because of all this, there is a strong temptation for Christians either to reject the whole value system associated with paid employment, or to keep their Christian beliefs and their experiences in paid employment in separate watertight compartments with no dialogue between the two. And yet institutions go on employing people and people go on being employed. There has to be a framework within which our work experiences can be integrated with the rest of what we do; our home lives and our work lives both happen within the same God-created world, and it isn't as though we become totally different people the moment we cross the workplace threshold at the start of each working day.

The theological framework that began with Creation needs to be extended to take account of the disbenefits and the pain. Genesis chapter 1 is followed by Genesis chapters 2 and 3. The day that Eve ate the apple is perceived in some Christian circles as a moment of disaster for the human race, but it is also possible to see it as a great step forward for mankind. What makes man uniquely capable of assuming the responsibility for the continuation of God's creative task is God's unique gift to humanity, the gift of free will. This is fundamental to man's capacity for work; all other species are instinctually programmed to do whatever is necessary to ensure their own survival, but man alone is capable of choosing not to do so, and this means that whatever he does to keep himself and his species alive becomes work. And the application of this capacity for choice to the work that he does is the beginning of civilization; even in prehistoric times man was capable of thinking up a whole variety of ways of applying his work effort, and he soon became able not only to ensure his own survival but also to have sufficient time, energy and resources to spare to do other things as well. If Eve's apple had stayed on the tree, we would still be gathering berries and hunting game.

God's will for human beings is that they should exercise a will of their own and this indicates that mankind is the object of God's special trust. But man is capable of living up to that trust only some of the time; he is capable of exercising his God-given freedom to choose to do what is not God's will. The earth's resources are finite, so there is competition for them and man is capable of choosing not to put into practice whatever method of allocating them equitably God's will might imply. It is necessary therefore for man to think up ways of protecting himself and society from the abuses that stem from selfishness and greed, and to establish methods of regulating interactions. If money had not been developed as a currency for regulating commerce something very like it would have had to have been invented, and if paid employment had not been developed as a means for regulating effort man would have had to have invented something very similar. Perhaps this explains how it was that mankind came to invent them in the first place.

It is unrealistic to expect perfection in a fallen world, and paid employment is one of the ways that makes it possible for society to function within this imperfection. Living with the benefits of paid employment has to be tempered by an acceptance of its drawbacks, both the drawbacks that become apparent when the system is working badly and the drawbacks that are inherent in the system even when it is working well. Our vision of the Kingdom, and our knowledge of God's love, cannot but make us aware of the joy that happens whenever the earth is enabled to give of its goodness and when people are enriched by the opportunities that paid employment gives them to put themselves effectively into practice as human beings, much of the worship that is inherent in paid employment is unarticulated, but the value of it is enhanced by a conscious awareness of what is happening.

And this awareness is equally powerful and probably more valuable on paid employment's darker side. There is the tedium of clocking into work on Tuesday and doing all over again what we did on Monday. There are the incessant demands on our time which mean that we are not free to respond to something we may feel that God has called us to do because we are under a contractual obligation to be getting on with the job. There are the conflicts of values when we are obliged to promote company interest when the obligations of Christian witness suggest that we do exactly the opposite. And perhaps most important there is the knowledge that in doing our jobs conscientiously and well we are very often implicated in the suffering and damage to other people and to the created world that our employing institutions perpetrate. This includes the knowledge that very often our own employment is contributing to the deprivations inherent in the unemployment of others.

So Christians in paid employment have a double responsibility. There is the contractual responsibility placed upon them by their employer, and there is also the responsibility that results from an awareness of the extent to which what goes on in their imperfect corner of their imperfect world is loved by God whether or not it is an appropriate manifestation of his will. This would be an intolerable burden if there were not a means of sharing it, and if we did not know that God had already experienced it in the person of his Son. Christianity is a religion of the world as it exists and not a religion that turns its back on it. An important ingredient of the world as it exists is paid employment, and the experience of paid employment, like all other human experiences, requires the perspective of the Cross. Intercession and the eucharist are necessary as means of offering up these experiences, and of sharing in the joys and of bearing the burden of an awareness of the pain. The church needs to affirm the value of the positive contribution of the institutions that employ us, and to help those of us who are employed in sharing our burden.

Welcoming the Newcomer

LESLIE J. FRANCIS, M.A., M.TH., M.SC., PH.D.
Trinity College, Carmarthen

WHEN we live in the same house for any length of time, we become so familiar with where things are and how things work that we easily forget how much we take for granted in our environment. Visitors, however, do not automatically know where we keep the coffee or where we hide the spare key. When the electric lights go out, they do not automatically know where to locate the trip switch. When the radio refuses to work, they do not automatically know whether to tap it gently or to shake it violently.

When we get to know another person well, we become so familiar with their habits, their likes and their dislikes, their way of doing things and saying things that we easily forget just how much we take for granted in our relationships. Strangers, however, do not automatically know our ways, anticipate our tastes, appreciate our habits, grasp our meaning or even forgive our unspoken assumptions.

The church where we are accustomed to worship shares all the advantages of familiarity we experience in our home and runs equal risks of unfamiliarity for the visitor. The congregation with whom we worship week by week shares all the advantages of deep and slowly formed personal relationships and runs equal risks of excluding the stranger. In many senses, the clergy who are so active in ordering the church and pastoring the congregation may have even more difficulty than the laity in perceiving the barriers which our very familiarity erects against the newcomer.

Becoming strangers
As a way of increasing sensitivity to this particular problem, I have gradually developed over the past few years a training experience

which I use in theological colleges and ministry training courses. The programme is known as 'Church Watch Weekend'. During this weekend we deliberately and consciously put ourselves into the position of visitors and strangers in order to try to experience at first hand what churches and church services feel like and are seen to be proclaiming to the visitor.

On Saturday we choose an area which we do not know and where we are not known. Our aim is to discover where the churches are in this area, to find out about the pattern of Sunday services and to explore what the buildings are saying about their ministry and about the gospel of Christ.

What really surprised me when I first began this exercise is just how careless many of our churches are in telling newcomers about their ministry. In the first deanery which I studied, a quarter of the churches gave no public information about the times of Sunday services and only half gave the name or address of their minister.[1] In some areas the newcomer may have to be quite persistent to overcome the first obstacle of discovering if and when the church building is used for public worship.

Second, I began to examine what the church building itself was proclaiming about the local Christian community. Traditionally the majority of Free Churches seem to be kept locked apart from occasions when they are used for public worship. Many Anglican churches and a few Catholic churches are now also following this pattern. The argument is that in today's society it is no longer safe to keep churches open for the public to use. The insurance companies deliberately discourage the open door policy. The locked door, however, proclaims that the building has ceased to be a truly public place open to all newcomers. Instead it has become more like a private home, a place available to members of the family who own the key to the door. Only some locked churches let it be known where newcomers may obtain the key. It is not generally thought that newcomers will want to use the church building as a place for quiet meditation and prayer.

Third, once the newcomer has entered a church, what then is being proclaimed about the church's function and message? I suspect that many more Anglican churches provide useful guidebooks to their architecture than guidebooks to the local Christian community or to the Christian way of life. Two particularly powerful illustrations come to mind from recent 'Church Watch Weekends'.

In a certain market town one mediaeval church remained in use, while the other had been declared redundant. Inside the active church the bookstall displayed a lavishly produced history and guidebook to the church, but no other Christian literature. Inside the redundant church there was no architectural guide, but a pile of free leaflets suggesting how time in the church could be used in prayer. In one large village the parish church was kept locked and no notices were displayed outside. The persistent visitor tracked down the vicarage and was reluctantly entrusted with the key. Inside she was welcomed by the most attractive display describing the life and witness of the local church. The display included a detailed map of the community, even pinpointing the homes of members of the congregation where newcomers could find a welcome, but the problem was getting into the church in the first place.

As others see us

Having spent Saturday looking at churches and trying to find out about the Sunday services, on the second day of the 'Church Watch Weekend' we try to attend as many of these services as possible. Course students are encouraged to attend a range of services, close to and dissimilar from their own tradition. In this way those of us who are used to feeling at home in our own church services are forced to experience what it is like to be the newcomer in the strange place. Listening to the students' accounts of their experiences, three key problems facing the newcomer come to light.

First, there is the question of welcome. A smile and a handshake at the door can break the ice and begin to establish a personal relationship. More importantly, the correct books and leaflets can be placed in the visitor's hands and advice given about where aspects of the service can be found in these books. Many churches, however, do not seem to expect newcomers and the visitors are left to find their own books. This is particularly confusing when the newcomer has to choose between competing piles of the *Book of Common Prayer* and *Alternative Service Book 1980*, copies of *Hymns Ancient and Modern* and *Hymns for Today*.

Second, there is the question of finding a seat. A steward can help the visitor to find the most appropriate place to sit, avoiding the churchwarden's pew, the broken kneeler and the pier which obscures the preacher. Many churches, however, seem to expect newcomers to find their own way about. If newcomers arrive early they may inadvertently choose the most inappropriate spot, not knowing the dynamics of the church, and then feel too embarrassed to move. If newcomers arrive late they may inadvertently find themselves sitting in the front, since the regulars have already filled the back rows, and then be unable to take their cues from those more accustomed to the local practices.

Third, there is the question of following the service. Those who know their way through a Free Church service may feel thoroughly lost when first confronted with the structure of the Catholic mass or the many routes through the *Alternative Service Book 1980* or *The Book of Common Prayer*. At the same time, those who feel secure in their own explicit liturgical structure may be equally puzzled by the implicit liturgical structure in the Free Church services. In either case, helpful signposting during the service, giving out page numbers and short explanations, can help newcomers to follow and to participate. This is particularly important when the service books contain a wide range of optional material and the newcomer has to recognize which pages are being passed over.

Culture gap

If members of one denominational tradition find it difficult to feel at home in another church tradition, how much greater is the difficulty experienced by the unchurched newcomers when they first cross the threshold into the worshipping community. In some senses this is a problem which has taken on a new complexity and urgency for the churches as they move increasingly into a post-Christian culture.[2]

The close relationship between the churches and the state maintained educational system in England encouraged the churches for a long time to assume a general and widespread familiarity with their cultural presuppositions. However superficial this familiarity, it assured some essential points of contact between the churches and those who did not attend them.

For example, as a child in the 1950s, I experienced no discontinuity between church and school. All the children in my neighbourhood, whether they came from churchgoing backgrounds or not, began their school day with a Christian act of worship and our regular religious education lessons were Bible based. At school we learnt to say the prayers which were said in the local parish church, sing the hymns and some of the canticles which were sung in the local parish church and hear scripture read from the same translation as used in the local parish church. By the end of the primary school, we knew the Lord's Prayer and the Ten Commandments off by heart. In the top year, the vicar came in once a week to exercise his right in a Church of England voluntary controlled school to teach the catechism to the children of those parents who requested that provision.

During the past decade or two, schools are becoming increasingly uncertain about the appropriateness of sharing the church's task through daily worship and religious education in a secular and multi-faith society. For example, John Hull's influential book, *School Worship: an obituary*, published in 1975, marshals a range of powerful arguments why schools should no longer expect their pupils to engage in Christian acts of worship. The Schools Council working paper 36, published in 1971, marshals the case why religious education in the state maintained school should concentrate on teaching about religions rather than nurturing into a specific religious tradition. The Swann Report, *Education for All*, published in 1985, marshals the case why specific faith based schools should be seen as socially divisive in multi-cultural Britain.

Increasingly, therefore, the churches cannot assume that their liturgy, language, imagery and hymnody will be immediately familiar to the newcomer. In other words, the cultural divide between the language and the presuppositions of the churches and the unchurched is widening. When churches launch into something as familiar as the Lord's Prayer, they cannot assume that the newcomer will know it off by heart. This simple problem is now exacerbated by the range of translations in which the Lord's Prayer is used. When churches draw on the rich imagery and language of scripture, they cannot be sure that it will resonate with the newcomer. Even when basic powerful natural symbols like bread and wine are used in the eucharist, we cannot assume that the newcomer will be able to cut through language like 'this our sacrifice of thanks and praise'. Even when basic powerful natural symbols like water and light are used in the baptism service, we cannot assume that the newcomer will be familiar with the significance of 'waters of the Red Sea' and 'the River of Jordan'.

If this analysis of the growing culture-gap between the churches and the unchurched is taken seriously, it puts a very different perspective on the issue of welcoming newcomers. While the welcome at the door and the careful signposting throughout the services are important, they are not in themselves sufficient to bridge the culture-gap. What is needed is a much more radical strategy. In my own experience, such a strategy might usefully include three components, Family Services, Project Learning and House Groups.

Family Services
Although the Church of England's new service book makes no provision for Sunday public worship in addition to Matins, Evensong and Holy Communion, a number of Anglican parishes seem to be experimenting with Family Services. This practice is also taking place in the Free Churches.

As often happens when the development of a new practice precedes the development of theory, there are a number of problems with the growing trend with Family Services. In some cases the emphasis has been placed too much on attracting young children, to the point that adults and especially teenagers feel out of place. Family Services can degenerate into children's services. In some cases the emphasis on attracting newcomers has produced a very partial and insubstantial gospel. Family Services can degenerate into entertainment. In some cases the discontinuity between Family Services and the other liturgy of the church is so marked that the regular members of the congregation would never dream of going to the Family Service, while the Family Service attenders are never recruited into fuller church membership. Family services can develop into an alternative church.

Given the proper preparation and a carefully thought through rationale, however, Family Services can provide the essential bridge which is able to introduce the unchurched into the mainline worship of the church. The key, I believe, lies in emphasizing the continuity between the Family Service and what happens in the church on other occasions. For example, in my own small parishes, where the main form of worship was the parish communion, I consciously developed a liturgical framework for the non-eucharistic Family Services using components from the Rite A eucharist. This meant that children and adults who were not familiar with the parish eucharist gradually acquired the concepts and language necessary to help them make the transition into the communion service. It also meant that members of the regular congregation did not feel out of place at the Family Service. They, too, recognized the familiar liturgical landmarks.[3]

Project Learning

Often church services are planned, arranged and conducted by just a few people on behalf of the many who they hope will share in the worship itself. We need to recognize that this is not always good educational practice. More people can learn to appreciate the deeper significance of Sunday worship by actually being involved in the preparation. This may be especially true for newcomers who can be helped to recognize that the worshipping community values and needs their own special skills and contributions. Project Learning provides an opportunity for this sort of involvement.

An example of what I have in mind is provided by a parish I visited last Pentecost. The local church decided to try to involve as many adults and children as possible on the Saturday before Whit Sunday in preparation for the following day's parish communion. Well in advance of the day the theme of Pentecost was discussed and the two images of fire and wind were chosen to provide the basis for a Project Learning experience. The project day was structured particularly with children and young people in mind. This emphasis on children gave adults a good excuse to enjoy themselves as well.

On the Saturday morning regular churchgoers and casual churchgoers alike were caught up in exploring those powerful images of wind and fire. Different members of the local community had volunteered to share things that were important to them and to lead outings to explore different aspects of wind and fire. A sailing enthusiast took a group to the nearest sailing club. A steam enthusiast led a party to the nearest steam railway. A model aeroplane enthusiast arranged a display. A local craftsman opened up his forge. A local fireman arranged a visit to the fire station. During the afternoon a range of workshops concentrated on music, dance and drama, to contribute to the Sunday service. A group of people made vestments and an altar frontal on the themes of fire and wind. Children decorated the church with their model windmills, kites and balloons. In this very practical way some of the historic imagery of Pentecost was renewed and revitalized for the regular worshippers and a number of fringe church members at last felt they had something important to offer to the worship of their local church from their own experience, interests and skills. They were encouraged to think afresh about the pervasive power of God's Holy Spirit throughout his creation.

House Groups
Churches which welcome newcomers need also to be able to provide them with opportunities for spiritual growth and religious learning, as well as occasions when they can build up friendships with other members of the worshipping community. If the culture gap is as great as I have argued, it will not be bridged simply by attendance at Sunday services. Nor is the Sunday church service the best medium for learning anyway. Often the greater the emphasis placed on teaching in the Sunday service, the less opportunity there is for real worship and celebration. Somehow other contexts have to be provided.

An example of what I have in mind is provided in the Anglican context by the house eucharist groups. Here regular churchgoers and the unchurched can explore in a more relaxed and flexible way than in church the central act of Christian worship. The carefully arranged house eucharist provides contexts for worship, prayer, meditation, direct teaching, questioning, discussion and expressions of social friendship. One of the major strengths is in fact the very range and variety of what can take place. Unlike the Bible study, discussion group or prayer meeting, the house eucharist is not so cerebral and does not rely so heavily on articulacy. Individuals can remain silent and not feel conspicuous by their silence. Unlike the confirmation class or training group, the house eucharist is able to accommodate individuals who are at a range of different stages in their personal faith development. Individuals can contribute at their own level and derive benefit at different levels as well.

Conclusion

If our churches are going to grow, we need to be able to welcome newcomers. If our churches are committed to a theology of the incarnation, it is surely appropriate that we should begin by identifying and taking seriously where individual newcomers have already arrived on their spiritual pilgrimage and then patiently share with them in their journey.

---

[1] Fuller details about this survey appear in *Rural Anglicanism* (Collins Liturgical [1985]).

[2] See A. D. Gilbert, *The Making of Post-Christian Britain* (Longman [1980]).

[3] Fuller argument about the design of family services appears in *Making Contact* (Collins Liturgical [1986]): the order of family service described is published as *Come and Worship* (Mowbrays [1987]).

Hospitality

WILLIAM D. HORTON, M.A.
Wesley College, Bristol

MOST pastors in the full-time, paid service of their church are provided with accommodation. They may regard a 'tied' house as an asset or a liability, but, in either case, it gives them a home for themselves and their family for the duration of their ministry without the problem of finding their own house or the responsibility of property ownership. Pastors differ in how they use this accommodation. Some use it simply as a private residence, a home separate from their work, a place of retreat for their off-duty hours to which church members are rarely, if ever, invited. Others use it as an extension of the church premises and the nerve centre of their ministry. Their study, in one of the 'reception' rooms, is used for interviews, counselling, administration and many other church activities. 'Open-house' is kept, meals are shared and visitors given a bed for the night; no one is made to feel unwelcome and hospitality is offered to all.

Taken to extremes, both these ways of using the accommodation provided betray a misunderstanding of the nature of ministry, its opportunities and demands. If the door of the pastor's house is always shut to visitors, then an important area of the pastor's life and ministry is cut off from the people the pastor is called to serve. However attractive the idea of distinguishing between home and work the pastor cannot keep them apart in watertight compartments. Ministry is not a nine-to-five occupation which can be forgotten once the pastor leaves the church building to return home after work. It is a sharing of life experiences, a mutuality of relationships between pastor and people. For the pastor to put limits on his or her involvement with the congregation is to define ministry as a job rather than a vocation. The pastor's home is part of ministry.

On the other hand, the cause of ministry is not best served by
the pastor's total availability to the congregation. Like everybody
else, pastors need times and places for leisure and relaxation if they
are to sustain their ministry without suffering premature 'burn-out'.
Their home is the natural place for re-charging the batteries and if,
there, they are never free from church people and church
commitments they themselves become diminished. The needs of
the pastor's family must be respected, too. The pastor's spouse may
not appreciate having to share the pastor with the church all the
time; the children may resent constant intrusion on their privacy
and the restrictions imposed on them by a never ending flow of
visitors into what they rightly regard as *their* home. Neither the
Christian faith nor the ministry is served if the pastor's over-
generous hospitality alienates the family.

Clearly, a balance needs to be struck between two extremes. The
purpose of this article is to suggest how the opportunities of
hospitality may be seized and the dangers avoided so that this can
be done. The paper then discusses both the art and the cost of
hospitality before concluding with a brief reference to Christ's
ministry as a model for ours.

Giving hospitality provides the pastor with many opportunities
of ministry. However frequently the pastor meets people on church
premises, shakes hands with them after Sunday worship or talks to
them at mid-week meetings, it is impossible to know them at
depth in this way; the individual becomes absorbed in the crowd.
By inviting them home a more personal relationship is established;
a cup of tea or coffee immediately sets the conversation going,
often with unforeseen results for pastoral ministry. Too many
people must not be invited at the same time or there will be no real
meeting and only superficial conversation. Nor must the pastor be
selective in issuing invitations. While most church members are
happy for their minister to have special friends, resentment is caused
and divisions occur if some are welcome in the pastor's home and
others are not. It is important, too, that hospitality is not used by
the pastor for purposes other than the deepening of fellowship
unless, of course, those purposes are openly stated in the invitation.
The pastor may want to hold evangelistic or fund raising meetings

at home and is entitled to do so, provided the captive audience is not invited under false pretences.

Offering hospitality not only gives opportunity for pastor and people to get to know each other better, it also enables church members themselves to grow closer together. By providing a common meeting ground for mutual fellowship the pastor helps to break down barriers between young and old and between people of differing backgrounds and interests. Church life is strengthened as people listen to and learn from each other and begin to appreciate the contributions others can make to their common fellowship. If they are invited to the pastor's home newcomers to the church are integrated into the church's life from the beginning and made to feel that they belong. When one or two of the church leaders are invited at the same time the newcomers will be introduced to people they will recognize and chat to when next they meet on church premises.

In addition to the hospitality which is a normal part of ministry, from time to time special opportunities arise. Visiting preachers who need entertaining for the Sunday, church dignitaries who require a meal and a chance to relax on their itinerary, delegates to conferences for whom homes are required for longer periods, overseas Christians on holiday who seek contact with the local church, these and other visitors contribute to life's rich tapestry and enjoyment. The pastor receives as well as gives! A visitors' book is a happy and useful reminder of these occasions. Of course, the pastor should not assume sole responsibility for the entertainment of special guests; church members should be encouraged to share in it. Many who do so find (sometimes unexpectedly) that they are entertaining angels, God's messengers, unawares; their faith is deepened and their commitment to Christ strengthened. Often, too, long-lasting friendships are forged and hospitality reciprocated to everybody's enrichment.

Offering hospitality is one way of exercising a ministry of love and service to people in need. Every church has its members who live alone and who sometimes find it difficult fitting into a pattern of church life geared to the family. Christmas and Bank Holidays, particularly, can be lonely times for such people and the pastor who is prepared to have an extended family on these occasions performs a valuable service. Widows and widowers, accustomed to going out with their partners as couples, often discover that their social life dries up when they are on their own and no longer conform to the accepted norm of husband/wife entertaining. The pastor who is sensitive to their needs can do much to enhance the quality of their life. But, again, sole responsibility in this matter is not the pastor's. The church as a whole must be made aware of the vital importance of fully including the 'singles' in their programme. The 'singles' themselves must be encouraged to form self-help groups for mutual friendship and entertaining. Enabling these things to happen is as much the pastor's task as providing the hospitality.

People who are temporarily away from home and family appreciate 'adoption' into a welcoming home environment. Students, nurses, members of the forces, business people staying in a hotel all value an invitation to a meal and the opportunity of sharing in the pastor's family life. Where young people are concerned, how they are received by the pastor and the local church when they are away from home has long-term consequences for their Christian faith. If they are welcomed, their commitment to Christ and his church is strengthened; if they are cold-shouldered who can wonder that they turn elsewhere for friendship and care?

There are times in the lives of normally self-sufficient people when the pastor can help meet a temporary need by offering hospitality. Bereaved members of the congregation and those with family or business worries see their situation in clearer perspective over a meal in the pastor's home. People just out of hospital are cushioned against life's demands until the day of full recovery, when the pastor's guest room is placed at their disposal. Loving care is a ministry for Christ.

Hospitality towards chance callers at the door presents problems as well as opportunities. Experience teaches that the majority of such visitors regard the pastor as a 'soft touch' from whom money for alcoholic refreshment can be extracted by a hard-luck story. The busy pastor is tempted to give money as the quickest way of dealing with an unwelcome interruption. This, however, stores up trouble for the future! Not only will the caller return on other occasions but his friends, hearing of the pastor's generosity, will be encouraged to try their luck also! Refusing money does not preclude offering a cup of tea and something to eat (or a meal voucher redeemable at a local cafe) and attempting to discover (and meet) the *real* need of the caller. The pastor should think carefully before inviting a stranger indoors; the family should be warned about the risk of doing so when the pastor is out. It is foolish for the pastor's vulnerability, or that of the family, to be exposed more than necessary.

What of the minority of callers in genuine distress? In spite of the fact that most needy people are reluctant to ask for help and have to be sought out, some do make their way to the pastor's home. The church's resources, however, are usually only sufficient to provide palliative and temporary help. That being the case, the pastor's ministry is to activate the appropriate assistance from statutory and voluntary organizations alike. It may also be to campaign on behalf of the underprivileged and seek to remove the *root causes* of poverty and distress in our society.

Church business meetings and committees can be offered the hospitality of the pastor's home, if there is a suitable room and the family is not inconvenienced. Even with today's higher standards of comfort in church premises the pastor's home usually offers a more attractive meeting place and the business can be conducted in a less formal and more relaxed atmosphere. But let the chairman beware! Sitting in the comfort of a home the members are not always anxious to deal with the business expeditiously and it can take longer to transact.

We turn, now, to the art and cost of hospitality. If the pastor is willing to seize the opportunities for ministry arising from hospitality, then the art must be learned and the cost counted. Hospitality *is* an art and its practice requires Christian grace. What do we look for when we *receive* hospitality? We want to feel 'at home', to be relaxed, to be ourselves and to be allowed to contribute something to the fellowship. We don't want to feel that our presence is an imposition on our hosts. So the art of hospitality involves sensitivity to the feelings and needs of the guest. The pastor, in order to exercise an effective ministry of hospitality, must cultivate this sensitivity. A lavish demonstration of welcome is as unnecessary as an over-provision of food; a readiness to share the home as it is and to put it at the guest's disposal is all that is required. If more than one guest is present, the sensitive pastor strikes a balance between those who are naturally shy and those who are of an extrovert disposition, 'drawing out' the former and ensuring that the latter don't monopolize the conversation. It is unnecessary to fill every moment of a guest's stay with conversation or activity. Most guests (particularly preachers who are due to lead services) appreciate a time of rest and quiet and don't want constant 'entertaining'. For the host to leave the guest alone for a while is an act of kindness and not a dereliction of duty. Different guests have different needs and the pastor must be alert to them all.

It is important, too, that the pastor learns the art of *accepting* hospitality. The example of Jesus is sufficient proof that there is a ministry *to* people through receiving *from* them; publicans and sinners were brought into God's kingdom when Christ entered their homes for a meal. In fact, a pastor's ministry may be undermined by an unwillingness to accept hospitality. Elderly people and those living on their own find help in giving their visitor a cup of tea during a pastoral call; their loneliness is forgotten and their worth as people is affirmed. The pastor's time in waiting for the kettle to boil is not entirely wasted! People who have a problem to discuss often prefer to invite the pastor into their home than discuss it elsewhere; they find it easier to unburden themselves in familiar surroundings. In those homes where alcohol is a normal part of social intercourse, the pastor's personal convictions will determine whether the inevitable glass of sherry is accepted. If it is declined, let it not be declined aggressively! Hospitality graciously offered should not be ungraciously refused. Sensitivity to the feelings of others is a ground rule for ministry in every situation and governs the receiving as well as the giving of hospitality.

If hospitality is an art it isn't practised without cost. The pastor on a limited income must consider this before embarking on a ministry of hospitality; even a cup of coffee cannot be provided for nothing! But apart from the financial cost there is the cost in effort. The married male pastor may want to offer hospitality to all-comers but the strain on his partner, particularly if she has a full-time job outside the home and employs no domestic help, must not be under-estimated. The preparation of meals and of rooms for overnight guests with the consequent clearing up when they have gone can tax the patience of someone who may not be as convinced of the value of entertaining as her husband. The Christian cause is not served if for the sake of something good a better thing, the marriage relationship, is placed under threat.

Effort, too, has to be expended in making guests feel welcome. Some guests are difficult to entertain because they do not respond easily to the hospitality offered; conversation is laborious and the strained atmosphere drains the host emotionally. Other guests are fastidious about their food and demanding in their requirements. Others present problems of conscience! What is the pastor to do if an un-married but co-habiting couple come to stay? Should the visitors be given separate rooms or allowed to share? Should traditional standards be invariably maintained? Is Christian morality betrayed by tacitly accepting the situation as it is? Such questions may not have to be faced often, but occasions do arise when an attempt has to be made to answer them as a practical necessity. Taking second place in one's own home, behaving with tact and patience, giving 'space' and time to guests are all part of the cost of hospitality which cannot be lightly dismissed.

In practising hospitality (as in every aspect of ministry) the pastor's model is Jesus. Though, as a wandering preacher, our Lord had no settled home and was unable to give hospitality precisely as defined in this article, he was none the less hospitable. He satisfied the hunger of the crowd who had been with him all day. He ministered to the needs of his disciples as he shared a meal with them on the night of his betrayal. He welcomed all-comers, giving himself to them in loving service and blessing them with spiritual treasures. Children, sufferers in body and mind, social outcasts, people with questions, problems and concerns all found him to be a person of sensitive spirit, warm heart and clear perception. Life took on new meaning for those who responded to his invitation and shared his company.

Christ's sensitivity to others was reflected as much in the way he accepted hospitality as in his manner of giving it. He wanted little and preferred to relax in people's company than to keep them busy over-providing for his needs (Luke 10:41, 42). He declined to force himself on people who were unwilling to receive him and was not prepared to call down God's wrath on the inhospitable (Luke 9:54, 55). He did not assume that he would be invited into their home when he joined the travellers to Emmaus on the day of his resurrection (Luke 24:28). On this occasion, however, he was invited in and doubtless received the normal courtesies extended to a guest. But Jesus showed himself to be more than a guest; when the meal was ready he became the host, breaking, blessing and distributing the bread (Luke 24:30). At this, the disciples, now guests in their own home, realized their blindness in not recognizing Christ earlier.

The pastor's responsibility is to make the risen Christ known through hospitality given and received in Christ's name. Beginners in the Christian life sometimes imagine that discipleship means being host to a demanding Lord; that theirs is the burdensome duty of serving an honoured guest and providing for him from their own inadequate resources. The true gospel understanding is made clear when the pastor faithfully ministers Christ's grace to people through worship, prayer, Eucharist and the normal routine of daily life in which Christian hospitality has an important part to play. Christ is the host and we are his guests! The pastor who acts for Christ in the ministry of hospitality is privileged indeed.

The Church Family Week

JAMES B. BATES, B.A.
Ilfracombe

THE idea is a very simple one, and it is its simplicity, as well as its directness which appeals. So much time and effort is spent by the church on discussing mission and training, and so seldom is this worked out in actual situations with the people for whom it is intended. A 'Church Family Week' involves, in this case, a team of a dozen or so students, living in a church, and sharing, with the church, its life, and witness to the community around. The students claim no special expertise or experience, they have come to learn, but they do have a willingness to work with the church as it seeks to carry out its mission to its neighbourhood. Similarly, the church need not be a copy-book example of the flourishing Christian community. In fact these weeks have been just as successful in struggling inner-city churches as in the thriving congregations of commuter-belt towns. When two groups of people with a common concern meet to work together as host and guest, the encounter is bound to be creative. The former could feel threatened by a group claiming specialist knowledge intruding upon their normal work, but they will welcome a group of inexperienced students whose primary objective is to learn what it means to be involved in the work and mission of the church. The students, on their part, will appreciate the hospitality of the host church and the opportunity it is giving them to try out in practice ideas they have discussed in theory. Educationally the week is valuable; for the church, because it can explore certain ways of mission which it could not carry out on its own; for the students because they are learning from practical experience what it means to be a member of an active church.

The concept of a Church Family Week developed from the campaigning methods of the Order of Christian Witness, a mainly Methodist organization founded by Lord Soper during the last years of the Second World War. The aims of OCW can be neatly summed up under the three 'C's'. The first aim of an OCW campaign was that of 'Communication', of putting the 'case for Christianity' to people outside the church in every way possible, but by argument and conversation as well as by proclamation. The second was 'Community'. The unit of the campaign was the team, living in community as a family in a church, under a rule as a kind of religious order. The great pacifist quite happily used such military terms as 'commandant' and 'quartermaster', but there was a monastic flavour about the life of the family, living and catering for itself in spartan conditions in church halls and schools. The financial question was solved by the good Christian (and socialist) principle that members paid what they could and took what they needed. There were no great money demands made on the host church. The final 'C' was 'Communion'. Long before the Eucharist became the typical form of Christian worship, Soper insisted on the centrality of the Communion as expressing both the corporate life of the community and the aim of its mission.

Early campaigns were large and ambitious, involving many churches and, in some cases, whole towns. They were ecumenical, and people of national standing were invited to take part. If, in the long term, their effect on the locality was limited, they proved excellent training ground for people who were later to become leaders of the church, and this was especially true of Methodism. For twenty years the Order flourished, but more sophisticated concepts of mission and hesitation among many over the value of evangelical confrontation led to a decline of numbers and change of emphasis. 'Campaigns' tended to be limited to a single congregation, and the objective to work within and through the continuing witness of the church. The nucleus was still a visiting 'family', and the church and its neighbourhood the sphere of activity.

While it was possible and very worth-while to invite students to take part in campaigns of the earlier kind, such campaigns were beyond the capabilities of student groups. So, when OCW virtually ceased to offer campaign possibilities and churches approached me as a college chaplain to bring a team of students to work in their churches, it was to the latter form of 'campaign' that I turned. The term 'Church Family Week' developed from our experience as the most effective way of presenting the invitation to students to take part, of showing the local church what our aims were, and of advertising the week in the neighbourhood in which we worked. In each case it minimized that stress on confrontation which can make mission so misunderstood and resented. Instead the emphasis was on education, education in the context of exploring the meaning of mission, in sharing in the life of a church and its witness. It was an exercise in what Wesley might have called 'experimental and practical divinity'.

As we go through the preparation and conduct of the week, it will be apparent how much the whole enterprise is indebted to OCW, both in its aims and methods. The whole process usually begins with an invitation by a minister, or a church, to come and bring a team of students for a week's campaign. Sometimes the invitation has been prompted by a student in the home church, sometimes, when no invitations have been forthcoming, offers have been made to likely churches. A meeting between chaplain and local minister, or church leaders is then essential so that there is a clear understanding of what is on offer and whether this is what the church has in mind. All being well, this can be followed up by a preliminary visit by some of the student team some months before the planned week. This allows for introductions, discussion of possibilities and consideration of practicalities (facilities for sleeping, cooking, washing, among other things). Usually this will be when the team comes to lead a Sunday service. At this stage options should be kept open so that either party can withdraw should it feel that it cannot meet what is being required, or accept what is being offered.

If both parties are happy to proceed with the week, the preparations can go ahead with the student team and with the church. Matters will not have reached this stage without the chaplain having interested a nucleus of students, usually from the chaplaincy group. Further recruitment can be helped by a visit from the minister of the church to be visited, but the best recruiters are those students who have already had some experience of this kind of work. Their enthusiasm will say much more than the chaplain's pleading. A deadline date should be given by which time definite commitments must be made, and offers must not be made unless the commitment is serious. Even so, as anyone who has worked with students knows, there are the hazards of last minute changes of plan. If it seems that a team of less than ten is all that is possible, then it may be wiser to call the week off.

The team, then, can meet for a regular training class over about a period of six weeks. This may seem very short, but it is assumed that members of the team will already be involved in such group activity as preaching or worship teams. The sessions need not be long, and they will aim to introduce topics rather than to exhaust them. The week itself is a training week. People will learn through doing, and there will be group work during that time.

The first session will deal with aims. Here one will find that students approach the week with different ideas. There will be those of an evangelical persuasion who will see this week as mainly a chance for personal evangelism; others, especially if it is to be in an inner-city church, will be more interested in the social and community aspects of mission; others again may be drawn by the attraction of living as a community. None need be discouraged, each has something to offer, but each needs to see it in the context of learning from a real situation and from practical experience. That is why the session on aims should be linked to a session on 'meeting people' in which sensitivities are developed as to how to listen and respect before speaking and acting. The team will have to meet each other and live and work together, they will meet the host congregation and learn from them about the church and community in which they work, they will meet people intentionally on the doorstep or casually in the street and must know how to approach them without offending them.

Other sessions will cover the techniques of visiting (in this case, a matter of informing and inviting people – avoiding persuading or preaching on the doorstep), and sharing in house-group discussion (here a prepared statement on 'what the Christian faith means to me' is useful). It is assumed that some of the team will have had experience of leading worship and speaking in meetings. Students with talents in drama and music should be encouraged to work out items which could be used either in worship or in the week's activities.

During these preparatory sessions the leader will find out what special interests the students have and appoint them to special responsibilities. Officers will be appointed: the cook (clearly most important, both to keep the team happy and to work with church contacts); the quartermaster (who sees to the effective running of the week, making rotas of jobs to be done, helping the cook and working with the caretaker of the church); the treasurer (who will receive team contributions – up to this year the suggested amount has been £10 – and pay out for the catering); and the student in charge of visiting (who will carry out the scheme prepared by the minister and keep a strict record of all that is done, or not done, so that there can be an effective follow-up). It may be useful to have someone in charge of the women's quarters and the men's. Students will bring personal things and a sleeping bag along with any literature or equipment they think will be useful during the week.

On its part the church will work out a programme for the week, planning for the team to take part in, or to lead, the worship and normal activities. This can include the team's meeting and working with outside groups that use the church premises, from playgroups to Judo clubs. There will be special youth work, morning coffee for mums and toddlers, after-school children's hour, a teen-age youth night, barbecue or ramble, one special evening when the whole church can come together to share in a social and devotional evening with the team, and possibly a public meeting (with a well-known speaker or a production of a gospel musical shared by church and team). The week should be planned from Sunday to Sunday, giving an opportunity to introduce and wind up the week when the church normally gathers in strength.

The minister and church will plan the visiting to be done. This could take the form of house-to-house visiting in a specified area, the streets around the church, or a new housing estate; or it could provide a chance to follow up contacts that have been made through baptisms, weddings, families of children who come to Sunday School or youth organizations. It will be made clear that this visiting is to inform and to invite, so the church will provide two leaflets, one about the normal life of the church and another about the special activities of the week. It will be of great advantage if there are church members who are free to share in the visiting with the team.

On the practical side the church should provide for the domestic needs of a dozen or so young people living on the church premises, seeing that sleeping (camp beds), eating and washing facilities are adequate. The team will cater for itself, but will be grateful for invitations to Sunday lunches which will provide a chance for students and church members to meet. Contacts should be appointed for the officers of the team so that the cook, the quartermaster and treasurer will have someone with local information. There should be someone responsible for liaising with team members about each of the activities of the week so that, although church members may not be free to take part in the daytime events, they will know what is going on and be aware of what may come out of them. The church should be ready to bear the cost of any printing or publicity (not forgetting the local press or radio), and travel.

As with the team, the most important part of the preparation will be to clarify the understanding of the church about the aims of the week and to see that as many members as possible are informed and involved. More than one visit by the team leader and some of the students may be necessary. It is all too easy for the majority of a congregation to dissociate itself from the week, giving the team a feeling that it is working in isolation. For both team and church prayerful commitment and openness to God's leading are essential.

The week itself can be best described under its aims:

1. It is a celebration of the family of the church. For this week especially the church, with and through the team, will keep 'open house'. The fact that a team is living as a family in the church will give it the feeling of a home where everyone is welcome. Something will be going on and someone will be there almost all through the week. The porch, the forecourt or garden will become a coffee bar, and as much as possible will be done there during the mornings, or at other times, so that passers-by will see that the

church is alive and they are welcome. Artists and musicians can work to make the place attractive, and, if needs be, everyone can share in tidying and trimming and cheering up what is, all to often, a dreary facade. No one will be pressurized, but visitors are almost bound to ask why the students are doing what they are doing and the door will be open to useful conversation. Not many may venture in, but the sight of an attractive and active church will convey its own message. It will be made clear that everyone is welcome to all that is happening, and perhaps especially to the daily Bible Study and Family Prayers at the end of the day.

From the porch it is natural to move into the church, and the church should be kept open, re-arranged if possible, to make it a natural meeting place for people, for conversation, for enquiry or for devotion. Pray for chairs so that the church can be set out to provide for these, and for a carpet before the altar rail so that prayers can be informal and, as in a mosque, the floor a natural place for gathering and prayer.

2. It is an exploration of what it means to be the church in the world. Each day there will be Bible study, usually in the mornings leading up to coffee time. Study takes on new meaning when in the context of a practical exercise in mission. The teaching of Jesus, the letters of Paul, the oracles of the prophets were all the outcome of mission, so it is not surprising that they come alive as one attempts to share in it. The house groups and the Church Family Night will also provide opportunities to explore the mission of the church, in the context of this specific church and with the experience (limited though it is) and ideas (raw though they may be) of the team. The Church Family Night offers a chance for the different groups, either age or interest groups, to come together and learn from each other. Churches, like society at large, can easily become segregated, and therefore suspicious of each other. Some successful themes for these were: 'From Cradle to Grave', 'This is our Life', and 'Guess the Parable' (acting out a modernized charade by a random group). As the team visits each of the normal meetings of the church, it will seek not so much to present a message, but to ask questions. They will, of course, be open to questioning themselves, and in seeking to answer, the message will emerge.

3. It is an experiment in witness. The church and team, in opening themselves up to the world, will be tested as to how they can live up to the offer they have made. This must call for full commitment and deep preparation for an adventure in meeting people, in listening to them and in seeking to respond to them creatively. Visiting can be daunting (and one must always remember one's own reactions to doorstep pedlars of various creeds), but a simple statement and a gracious invitation, leaving the householder the complete and unembarrassed freedom to terminate the conversation then and there, will not go amiss. Very often it will lead to a question and sometimes the disclosure of an interest or need. The visitor must be aware of his own limitations, avoiding the offer of advice beyond his competence, or promises beyond his capabilities to fulfil, but he comes in the name of a church and he can offer the visit of the minister. Here meticulous recording of detail is essential. At the very least, visiting is a demonstration of concern and friendship. In some places this will mean a great deal; there are lonely and frightened people who crave the kind of friendship the church can offer.

There are many forms of outreach a team can explore. Invitations to and through the children who come to the after-school play-hour, conversation with the people who use the church, and chatting to the people who drop in for coffee. There can be street witness, especially if there is a precinct or area where activity can take place without intruding upon the public. Street drama, or Gospel folk can attract and intrigue, provoking questions that can lead to conversations. Only the more accomplished and experienced can speak effectively in the open air.

4. The whole enterprise is an educational experience for the church, but especially for the team. The communal life of a group, catering for itself, sharing in the work of the church, thinking about the message and mission of the church, adventuring in various experiments of outreach will give the team members a new understanding of the faith, the Christian community, and of themselves. The family meeting each morning, when the activities of the previous day are evaluated and the plans for the present day are announced, when the officers make their reports and any

member is free to comment, brings the team into a deep and open relationship. The contacts with many different people, mature church members, young people, casual acquaintances from the street or on the doorstep, will all challenge and enrich. The minister may wish to take team members with him on chaplaincy visits to hospitals, homes, schools, or other institutions. Visiting will reveal the misery of some people's lives through loneliness, fear or poverty. It is not surprising that some of the students who have taken part in these weeks have later opted to live and work in areas similar to those visited, especially where there has been a community house. Team members will also have developed skills and gained experience of activities they would never otherwise have ventured upon. It is easier to try something out for the first time in a place where you are not known, and then to bring back that skill to the home church, and in a team one will be ready to share in things that otherwise would prove too daunting.

The church will gain from having played host to the team and from the planning and involvement the week's activities have demanded. It cannot have avoided thinking about the faith and the role the church should be playing, and it will have been encouraged and enheartened by the enthusiasm and commitment of the team. The young people of the church will have become closely involved with the team, some of them coming and living as lay members before the end of the week. Friendships will be formed which often continue over many years, visitors and visited having come to know one another in depth through the intensity of the week.

The key person, of course, is the team leader. Apart from the introductory session, the leader's work is to keep a low profile and to work through the team and the church. In this there will be very close cooperation with the minister, or the church leaders. The leader should plan things so that every task and every activity is carried out by someone else so that he or she can be free to watch over developments, seize opportunities and note potential crises. If the week can so be planned that everything is in hand and the leader can be relaxed and confident, that spirit will be conveyed to the team, the church and whoever appears on the scene. The leader will, of course, always be ready to step into the breach or rescue a situation, explaining and reconciling where there has been misunderstanding. His is the responsibility – to hold the team together, to give it a vision of its task, to build up and maintain good relationships with the church. He needs to pray and to be prayed for. It helps if he can have a room on his own, the minister's vestry is ideal, so that the team can relax and he can prepare at the end of the day. Personally I have always found it effective to begin the day with the leader waking the team with cups of tea, long before they would wish to rise!

As the week proceeds two events will dominate and determine the programme. One is the last Sunday morning service which should grow out of the week's work and bring in the team and church as they celebrate what they have learned during the week. The children who have come to the play hour can contribute, as can other groups who have met and shared with the team. The leader can give out the hymn books (this proved invaluable in one church, where he nursed the fractious baby of a mother who had dropped casually into the church during the week, and had turned up at the Sunday service).

Secondly, at a tea provided by the team, both church members and team can attempt to assess and evaluate the week, giving reports and asking questions. Both will given an account of themselves to the other. Although it is a brief encounter, the shared experience, the full commitment, and the intense activity will almost inevitably have made the week significant in the continuing life of the church and certainly in the future lives of the team.

Special Occasions, 1

EDWARD H. PATEY
Dean Emeritus of Liverpool

THOSE who go through the doors of their local church to take part in acts of worship can be divided into three groups. There are the 'regulars'. These are the paid-up members who know that they belong, and who see their membership as an important part of their way of life. There is a second group of people who claim to belong but whose attendance is less regular. They say that they have other claims on their lives, especially at weekends. If they are honest they have to admit that on the spasmodic occasions when they make an effort to attend, they do not find what goes on in church particularly attractive or compelling. Yet if they were told that they really cannot be counted as church members but only as casual visitors, they would be mightily offended. They would insist that the local church from which they so frequently absent themselves is indeed *their* church. This claim is considerably reinforced when they wish their daughter to have a church wedding with all the trimmings!

There is a third group. They would admit that their appearances in church were very few and far between. This gives them no feeling of shame. They do not feel that they belong there. Yet for a variety of reasons, which are hard to define, they may be seen in church from time to time. They may be among the many unfamiliar faces at a midnight mass or carol service because this is a traditional part of their family Christmas celebrations along with a turkey dinner and a visit to the local pantomime. They probably form the greater part of the attendance at a school Founder's Day service, coming in their best clothes at the invitation of the headmaster and governors. Perhaps one of their children is singing in the school choir or playing in the orchestra. They may reappear on Remembrance Sunday, particularly if there are ex-servicemen or women in the family or they are associated with the Royal British Legion. They may form part of the congregation when various organizations, professional bodies, community groups or charities have asked 'to have a service' marking some special occasion such as a centenary, or simply to celebrate their work. They are often there in force as family, friends or colleagues at a wedding, funeral or memorial service. On many such occasions there are likely to be more people in church than at a normal routine Sunday service.

It is tempting to dismiss these fleeting *ad hoc* worshippers as survivors of a past 'folk religion'. But to do this is to fail to understand the role of the church in our modern secular community. For if the purpose of the church is to proclaim God's concern for all people in every aspect of their lives, the fact that, even in a land where religious observance appears to be on the decline, so many occasional visitors should willingly come through the church door for special events should be welcomed as a great opportunity not lightly to be jettisoned. Yet sadly this opportunity is often thrown away, either because the clergy and church officials lack the imagination or skill to take the best possible advantage of the occasion, or because the sectarian outlook, increasingly evident in today's church, causes them to show little interest in 'those who do not belong to us'. They focus much the greater part of their care and attention on the 'little flock' which is their diminishing church membership, and are not willing to spare much time or energy on those who obviously are not ready to commit themselves wholeheartedly to the Christian cause. By such means the life of the church congregation isolates itself increasingly from the secular community. Such is the sect mentality, and it is destructive of genuine Christian mission.

There was a time when worship was the characteristic activity of the whole community, and the sacred and the secular were intimately woven within it. The liturgy was closely associated with the rhythm of the seasons – ploughing the fields, sowing the corn, reaping the harvest. Year by year these basic events in the working lives of the parishioners were celebrated by Plough Sunday, Rogation Days and Lammas tide. These earthy observations probably made a bigger impact on popular imagination and devotion than did the major biblical festival of the church. Familiar faces from the workaday world were portrayed (or caricatured) on the corbels jutting out from the walls of the church buildings. Beneath the miserere seats in the choir stalls local craftsmen did wonderful carvings which often displayed lively and even erotic scenes from secular life. Commerce was linked with the parish church with the annual fairs and feasts associated with its dedication or patronal saint's day. Dramatic and social events, often of a lively and even bawdy character, took place either in the churchyard, or (as with Church Ales) within the church building itself. In some places vestiges of these links still remain. Ancient parochial charities (often still recorded on boards at the west end of old churches) were the forerunners of the modern welfare state and the great national voluntary charities. The homes of the people were grouped around the church with almshouses for the sick and elderly, and the rhythm of life and death in the whole community was reflected in the baptisms and burials which took place there. Even the churchyard provided a kind of continuation of the life of the community the other side of death awaiting the Day of Judgment, reflecting the hierarchy of earthly existence by the splendour or modesty of the tombs and memorials. It could be argued that the red brick municipal crematorium hidden behind local authority cypress trees provides a poor substitute. Our mediaeval ancestors lived out their lives closer to the rough and tumble of reality than we do, and the local church was involved in all that was going on in the community around it.

Today the normal diet of worship provided by the church is more remote and makes little impact on the greater part of the community it is supposed to serve. In Britain a great number of people live out their lives hardly aware of the existence of the church except when there is a royal wedding, a state funeral, or when a bishop hits the headlines because of his supposedly heterodox views or an ecclesiastical report is published critical of government policy. No effective equivalent has generally been found in our industrial and urban society to take the place of rural observances such as Plough Sunday, Rogation or Lammas. The

Harvest Festival which, in its Victorian hey-day, attracted large crowds, has in recent years been on the decline. It never was very obviously relevant in an inner city parish and today only a few of those who live in villages are themselves workers on the land. Schools, particularly if they are of ancient foundation, still hold services to commemorate founders and benefactors. Such occasions generally look back wistfully to the old ideals of 'godliness and good learning', but such observances appear to mean very little to the boys and girls compelled to be present, or to their parents who come out of loyalty to the school rather than with any very strong convictions about the place of religion in the education of their offspring. These are primarily social occasions, or exercises in nostalgia, designed to stress the need to maintain the *status quo* in the face of more progressive educational policies. Each year members of the Royal British Legion dutifully attend services in their local churches or at war memorials but the numbers steadily decline as the years go by.

It is not surprising that in response to the impact of secularism upon traditional popular religious observances the church should be tempted to retreat into a pious sectarianism placing its major attention on the 'converted' and the 'committed' and with less interest on those who are classified as 'outsiders'. If 'special occasions' threaten to conflict with the regular provision of congregational worship or the observance of the traditional ecclesiastical calendar, then it is the 'special occasion' which must give way and be shunted into the side-lines of the timetable so that 'our own people' will not be disturbed. But to do this is not only to throw away the opportunity for showing Christian hospitality. It may also be to lose a valued occasion for preaching the gospel to those who do not usually hear it. The opportunities for holding special services should be nurtured when and where they occur. They also need to be given new life.

There is a profounder reason why this matter merits careful consideration. Is there not evidence to suggest that many people who consider themselves to be 'outside the church' live their lives more in accordance with the Kingdom of God than some of those who occupy the pews in church with pious regularity? This point has been forcibly made by the great Jesuit theologian, Karl Rahner, in one of the remarkable series of addresses he gave to the synod of the Roman Catholic bishops in Germany. He was at great pains to point out 'those signs of the effective grace of God visible outside the boundaries of the visible Church and its sacraments'. He spoke of the 'marginal settlers' who cannot identify themselves with the church through their faith, but regard her with positive good will. It was his belief that some of these outsiders had a better understanding of the church 'than those inside who are there by virtue of their tradition, family habits, childhood influences and a kind of folklore'. He spoke theologically of the church having open doors whose extent is by no means clearly defined. If Rahner is right (as surely he must be), it means that many of these 'marginal settlers' are precisely the kind of people who choose to come to church from time to time for occasions of celebration, commemoration, and dedication, yet cannot bring themselves to identify with the ecclesiastical institution as they see it in action in their own neighbourhood. Not only must we see these 'marginal settlers' as worthy of the same care and attention as is given to the committed. We must go further and say that the church itself needs contact with these fringe groups for the good of its own health and for a better understanding of this ministry and mission. For such people have much to bring to the rather myopic vision of the average church congregation. Special occasions can widen their horizons and give a new impetus to the corporate life of the 'little flock' which too easily prefers the safety of their familiar pews, wishing not to be disturbed by 'outsiders'.

What are these 'special occasions', what is the purpose of encouraging their celebration, and what preparation must be brought to their fulfilment? Some of the opportunities are already provided in the calendar of annual events. The major festivals of the church and the 'occasional offices' of baptism, marriage and burial are observed regularly in every local church and are too familiar to need elaboration here. Suffice it to say that the most obvious and most frequently repeated of these observances need the utmost care in preparation and presentation if they are to be rescued from the staleness of familiarity and given fresh vitality and meaning. The Week of Prayer for Christian Unity, One World Week, and Remembrance Day all give opportunities for proclaiming the Christian good news of reconciliation both in a divided church and in a divided world. Florence Nightingale's birthday in May and St Luke's day in October can be used to invite members of the medical profession, the nursing service, medical auxiliaries and health administrators to come together in worship and dedication in their task of bringing healing and wholeness to the sick in mind and body. Each year the United Nations Organization designates a special theme, and this can provide pretext and inspiration for another worthwhile special occasion, possibly on the Sunday nearest to United Nations Day. 1986 was named the Year of Industry. An observance of this essential aspect of daily life could involve members of local management and trades union organizations, chambers of commerce and trades councils. In such a way people from many walks of life might be surprised to discover that the church is entrusted with a gospel which has a deep concern for men and women in their places of work. A service of this kind would require careful planning and clear purpose if those really involved in the world of industry were to be persuaded that such a venture was worth their interest and active support. Without such thoughtful preparation special services will only succeed in attracting the usual faithful 'stage army' of supporters, and will be ignored by the 'marginal settlers' for whom the occasion is primarily intended.

But there are many organizations which take the initiative themselves and ask to come to church for a special service. Such initiative should be warmly encouraged. Among them are likely to be the Townswomen's Guild, the Royal British Legion, the Rotary Club, the Red Cross, Soroptimists, youth organizations, schools and colleges. In some towns the annual carnival or arts' festival includes a united service in its official programme, providing the local churches with the great opportunity of doing some imaginative planning together. Whenever possible these services should be planned and conducted ecumenically. Matters of public concern can also provide themes for special acts of worship. Such themes might include concern for the elderly and handicapped people, law and order, racial equality and much else. Some of these opportunities will be discussed in more detail in the next chapter.

How are such occasions to be arranged? Careful preparation is always essential, and this must include serious consultation with the people who are most likely to be concerned. This can be illustrated by a service in Liverpool Cathedral arranged to celebrate the tenth anniversary of the founding of the city's Polytechnic. This is a large secular institution with students from all over the world, of many faiths and none. They wanted to have some kind of celebration to mark this milestone in their history. They already made a practice of coming to the cathedral each year for the presentation of degrees and awards, so this seemed an obvious venue for their anniversary celebrations. The event was prepared with great care over many months. The heads of the faculties of Art and Design, Business and Management Studies, Construction, Education and Community Studies, Engineering, Humanities, Social Studies and Science met with me and my colleagues on a number of occasions. We had to discover what it was we wanted to celebrate. In what kind of way could this wide diversity of secular interest be acknowledged in a church and in an act of worship? We discovered that the common factor was our concern to be creative in this material world and to give thanks for the many opportunities open to us. As the introduction to the service eventually put it, 'This is an act of thanksgiving in which are woven sounds from many voices inside and outside the Church, a dialogue in which both Polytechnic and Cathedral will be challenged'. There were readings not only from the Bible (Christian and Jewish), but also from the literature of Islam, Hinduism, Sikhism and Humanism. So a creative meeting point was discovered and given expression between a Christian community and a great secular institution. Everyone drew spiritual power from the encounter in a shared celebration.

This kind of consultation, essential before any special act of worship, provides an opportunity not only for positive and practical contact with those on the fringe of the church, or completely outside it, but also for initiating Christian dialogue. Basic questions have to be asked and discussed. Why do we want to have such a service? What is it that we want to express in terms of thanksgiving, penitence, intercession and dedication? How does God fit into the picture? Initially it is essential that basic theological questions must be honestly raised and faced. Only when the serious talking has been done is it possible to begin to plan the details of the service, choosing hymns, readings and prayers and deciding who will take part. So the preparation for a special act of worship can become a shared experience.

A civic service at the beginning of a new municipal year can provide a splendid opportunity for this kind of shared consultation with the officials of the local authority. Liverpool is a city of great tradition and splendid achievements. But it also faces many pressing social and political problems. There is no difficulty here in finding an agenda for worship when representatives of the community come together with their elected leaders to pray for the welfare of their city. Thanksgiving must come first.

> God be praised for our city
> for its great contribution to industry and commerce
>
> for those who in the past have planned its civic life, raised up its great buildings and endowed its institutions.
>
> for its University, Colleges and Schools and for all those who have promoted its educational and cultural life.
>
> for its vitality, born of the meeting of many races, traditions and temperaments. For its music and drama; for its art and literature; for its entertainers and comedians; and for its many-sided enjoyment of sport.

Thanksgiving must lead to admission of failure. In so many ways the high ideals of the city have been marred.

> O Lord forgive
> whenever our political life has been spoilt by partisanship and prejudice, by self-seeking and the enjoyment of power and privilege for its own sake.
>
> whenever our commercial life has been more concerned with profits for the few, rather than the welfare of the many.

whenever our industrial life has been the place where confrontation and rivalry have taken the place of brotherhood.

whenever men and women have been denied the right to decent housing, reasonable employment and an adequate standard of living.

whenever entertainment has become debased and sordid, and sport has lost its spirit of fair play
O Lord forgive.

From thanksgiving and penitence the service moves to the central affirmation of the Christian faith in readings, hymns and sermon. The climax is reached in the final act of intercession for the well-being of the city. Here the whole life of the community can be reflected in prayer – the city government, the judiciary, members of parliament, the police, the social and health services, community organizations, local press and radio, entertainment and sport, the pressing needs of those who live and work in the city, and the role of the church. Such a special occasion need not be confined to the celebration of a great city. District, borough and parish councils can be equally involved, demonstrating that the church exists both to serve the local community, and to provide it with inspiration and a sense of purpose. But the desired result will only be achieved by painstaking preparation in consultation with the appropriate authorities, and carefully executed by all who are involved.

Remembrance Sunday is another occasion which provides the local church both with opportunities and problems. The opportunities are obvious. There are many people not often seen in the pews on a Sunday who come to church wearing their poppies, and perhaps their medals, for this act of remembrance. Those who saw active service during the second world war or who lost friends and relatives in that great conflict are a diminishing number. But the service continues to hold poignant memories for them, some mourning the loss of comrades, others recalling the comradeship of those days either on the battlefield or at home during the air raids. The church rightly responds year by year to this mood. But often in the congregation there are also scouts, guides and members of brigades, for this is their 'church parade Sunday'. They have no personal memories on which to focus their attention. The service seems to them to be concerned only with 'old unhappy far-off things and battles long ago'. Some of the more cynical or thoughtful of the younger people present may think that the church is here succumbing to the nostalgia of the occasion, and even encouraging the glorification of war. They may wonder what all this has to do with the One who said 'Blessed are the peacemakers'. So the opportunity must be taken at Remembrance Day services not only to speak about sacrifice but also about forgiveness and reconciliation. Along with grateful remembrance of those who have given their lives for their country in war there must also be recognition of the evil in men's hearts which is the cause of conflict. There is need for penitence for the sins of national pride, economic greed and the lust for power which divided the members of the human race into warring camps. It must be proclaimed that only in Jesus Christ can men and women be drawn to one another as they are drawn to him by the cross.

Yet this 'christianizing' of Remembrance Day is sometimes strongly criticized by the more traditionally minded members of the congregation who assemble in church for this annual observance. The Archbishop of Canterbury was taken to task by some Members of Parliament and by the more jingoistic sections of the press because the order of service for the St Paul's Cathedral thanksgiving service following the Falklands conflict included an act of penitence as well as thanksgiving, and offered prayers for the dead of Argentina as well as for the British. The BBC probably disturbed some viewers by having its Songs of Praise television programme on Remembrance Sunday 1986 relayed both from Dresden and Coventry. In Liverpool the congregation of the German church were always invited to join the cathedral congregation for the annual Remembrance Sunday service, and notable preachers on that occasion have included the great German church leader Dr Martin Niemöller.

Remembrance Sunday remains a 'special occasion' to be welcomed by the church. But in planning the service the cutting-edge of the Christian gospel must be clearly evident. It must not be obscured by nostalgia or tradition. The theme should be boldly announced in the introductory welcome in some such words as:

We come each year on this day to remember those who gave their lives for their country in time of war. The silence will give us the opportunity to pay tribute to their sacrifice. But the Christian faith also speaks of the duty of forgiveness and reconciliation. This is the theme of the second part of our service today.

Special Occasions, 2

EDWARD H. PATEY
Dean Emeritus of Liverpool

In the previous chapter I made a plea to ministers and their congregations of 'regulars' to take seriously any opportunity to have a service in their church for the kind of 'special occasion' at which a number of those who are not regular church attenders are likely to be present. I gave examples, among others, of a civic service at the start of a new municipal year, an act of worship for those working in the health service which could be held near St Luke's Day in October, services to mark One World Week, United Nations Day, a school occasion, or the annual Remembrance Day observance in November. If these events can be imaginatively and thoughtfully used, they provide a valuable opportunity for bringing the good news of Jesus Christ to those who rarely hear it.

Some of these occasions present themselves in the regular course of the annual calendar. Others have to be sought. If so, by what criteria? Look around you at the life of your local community and neighbourhood. What are the things which give people concern and bring them together for discussion and action? What are the bodies which provide people with the opportunity to meet one another to share their particular interests and to put their ideas into practice? Among the organizations which spring quickly to mind are the Townswomen's Guild, Women's Institutes, Rotary Clubs, Soroptimists, civic associations, professional bodies, art, music, drama and dance societies, and many others. Not all these organizations will want to 'have a service', though some will certainly welcome the suggestion. Others will be ready to cooperate in other ways, delighted to discover that the local church shares their concern for the welfare of their fellow human beings, and for the good ordering of society and the world around us. The great Dutch theologian. Edward Schillebeeckx, is fond of reiterating his slogan: 'God's concern is man's concern: man's concern is God's concern'. There is no way of making this simple but profound truth more evident than through an act of corporate worship in which man's response (or lack of it) to God's concern is celebrated in acts of thanksgiving, penitence, intercession, petition and dedication.

I illustrate this thesis with a brief description of two special services in which I was involved when ministering at Liverpool Cathedral. Each required months of consultation and preparation. Each caused considerable public interest because it was considered to be unusual, and each was able to focus strongly on some basic aspect of Christian faith and life. The first was given the title 'Christian Responsibility and Road Safety'. The thinking behind the service was clear. Everyone is either a motorist, a cyclist or a pedestrian. Many people are all three. The statistics of death and serious injury through road accidents remain a national scandal. Far more people are killed on the road each year than die in much more publicized air crashes. All this not only causes tragic bereavement, permanent injury and much personal suffering. It also represents a huge outlay of time, expenditure and personal skill in the casualty departments of our hospitals. Many accidents are the result of pride ('see how fast I can go'), impatience, bad temper, and a wilful disregard of the laws regulating speed and other safety measures. Even more irresponsible is the correlation between road accidents and the consumption of alcohol. Pedestrians, including the elderly and children, contribute to this sad story by their lack of thought. Among the guilty who add to this sorry tale are those who call themselves Christians. It does not appear to occur to some of them that there are few areas of life where the biblical command to 'love your neighbour as yourself' is more relevant than when sitting in the driving seat of a car. Even upright citizens feel no particular stigma if they are summonsed for speeding on the motorway. It is just bad luck if they are caught. Yet these things are sinful because they put other people in danger as well as oneself. It is a Christian responsibility not only to avoid accidents as far as it is humanly possible to do so; it is the moral responsibility of the church to be seen supporting all those who are involved in

promoting road safety. Before the service was held a large number
of people and organizations were contacted and invited to be
involved. They included members of the Transportation and Basic
Services committee of the local council, the Road Safety officer,
the police and ambulance services, the fire and salvage officers, the
Automobile Association and the Royal Automobile Club, hospitals
and schools. There was no difficulty in determining the theme of
the service and the address to be given. It was well summed up in
the hymn by Giles Ambrose which includes the lines

> We offer in simplicity
> Our loving gift and labour;
> And what we do we do to thee,
> Incarnate in our neighbour.

Children carried road safety banners which they had designed and
made in their schools. For the Bible reading verses from
Ecclesiasticus 32 had an extraordinary appropriateness:

> Do not travel by a road full of obstacles
> and stumble along through its boulders.
> Do not be careless on a clear road
> but watch where you are going.
> Whatever you are doing, rely on yourself,
> for this too is a way of keeping the commandments.
> To rely on the law is to heed its commandments,
> and to trust in the Lord is to want for nothing.

The service around the theme 'The Care of the Offender – The
Christian Responsibility expressed as an Act of Worship' happened
as the result of a conversation with the Roman Catholic chaplain at
the local prison and with a senior probation officer. The
introduction, which was printed in full in the Order of Service,
described the purpose of this 'special occasion'.

> Offenders in our community are frequently the objects of obloquy and
> abuse since many people believe that they are simply a nuisance and
> deserve to be punished. Some of them do deserve to be punished as
> they commit crime for what they can get out of it; but not all of them
> are like this. Many people who become offenders have had the cards of
> life stacked against them in such a manner that most of us would have

fallen foul of the law had we been so unfortunate as to be born into their circumstances. For all these folk, and there are many, the people of the Church must surely care. If they do not, who else can be expected to do so?

Statutory services such as the Prison Service and the Probation Service exist to help people back into the community, but unless the ordinary members of the community are willing to help them too, the job can only be half done. All of us need jobs, homes, friendship. Only the people who form the community itself can provide these basic necessities.

That is what this Act of Worship is all about. You will hear ordinary people saying how, in their different ways, they can help probationers and ex-prisoners to get back on their feet so that they can once again contribute like everyone else to the corporate life of the community. And you will be invited to respond in heartfelt prayer and practical action.

The service included a series of statements about the needs of the offender and the response of the community. These were given by a prison officer, a probation officer, a volunteer after-care auxiliary, the warden of an ex-prisoners' hostel, an ex-Borstal boy. The congregation also heard recorded statements taken in the prison by two prisoners, one beginning a long sentence, and one due shortly for release after a long stay behind bars. The Christian response to all this was summed up in a reading from Romans 12:

Love in all sincerity, loathing evil and clinging to the good. . . . Have equal regard for one another. Do not be haughty, but go about with humble folk. Do not keep thinking how wise you are. Never pay back evil for evil. Let your aims be such as all men count honourable. If possible, so far as it lies with you, live at peace with all men. My dear friends, do not seek revenge, but leave a place for divine retribution; for there is a text that reads, 'Justice is mine, says the Lord, I will repay.' But there is another text: 'If your enemy is hungry, feed him; if he is thirsty, give him a drink: by doing this you will heap live coals on his head.' Do not let evil conquer you, but use good to defeat evil.

These two services were on a large scale in a big city. But services designed on a much smaller scale for special occasions in the local church can be equally impressive as vehicles for evangelism through worship. But to be effective they need to be equally carefully prepared and presented. It is when there are many in the congregation who are not accustomed to taking part regularly in public worship that the church must be seen to know precisely what it is doing, and doing it with efficiency and conviction. There is no room for the slipshod and the careless. All those taking part should be carefully rehearsed. If visitors to the church are carrying flags or symbols in procession, or bringing up an offertory either of alms or tokens, they should know well in advance what is expected of them. This is particularly essential if lay people are to read lessons and lead prayers. It is fitting that they should do so, especially if in their persons they represent in some way the theme or purpose of the occasion. But the impact of the whole service may be ruined if the reading of the lesson is inaudible or unintelligible. Readers need to be rehearsed thoroughly in advance, and should know what the passage they are reading means. It is often helpful to them to have the passage typed out in full, preferably in a translation which is both simple to understand and to read.

Preaching on these occasions requires a special kind of preparation. There are a number of essential questions the preacher must ask himself or herself. What sort of people are expected to be in the congregation? What is the concern which brings them to church on this occasion? What are the meeting points between their concern and the gospel of Jesus Christ? These questions may seem elementary, but they are often neglected. Sermons are not infrequently given on these special occasions when the subject matter has nothing to do with the theme of the service, and the preacher has quite obviously failed to do his homework. This kind of 'occasional preaching' requires much more careful and painstaking preparation than the ordinary Sunday sermon. Here either the time of the year (Christmas, Lent, Easter, Pentecost, Advent etc.) or the lectionary of set readings provide the preacher with his theme. He does not have to wonder what he should preach about. His task is to expound that part of the story of our creation and redemption as recorded in the passages of Holy Scripture appointed for the day. But when he is asked to organize a special service it is the world which sets the agenda. War and peace, world hunger, death on the roads, health and disease, the life of a city or village, crime and punishment – these may be the themes which attract 'outsiders' to come through the church doors to share in worship. Whatever the occasion the preacher must make sure that he knows what he is talking about, and this will only come after careful study of the relevant information. If his sermon reveals ignorance or naivety (and this not infrequently happens) it will probably go unheard, however important the core of his message may seem to him to be.

On these occasions it is probable that the congregation will consist of men and women of different denominations. The preacher must avoid beating the drum of his own particular churchmanship or ecclesiastical tradition. Some of his hearers may have no church allegiance of any sort. They will be quite unfamiliar with Bible texts or 'churchy' language. So there must be spare use of the kind of religious vocabulary and pulpit talk familiar enough to regular churchgoers. It is a mistake to believe that a sermon is devoid of theological content unless it is generously peppered with Bible texts and ecclesiastical phrases. On the kind of special occasions described in this article the business of the preacher is to proclaim the gospel within the context of the shared interest which brings his hearers together, and in the language of everyday use. Nor should preaching be seen in isolation from the devotional setting in which it is placed. The significance of the special occasion and the address which expounds it should have a clear focus in the acts of thanksgiving, penitence, intercession and dedication which precede or follow the sermon. Special occasions generally demand specially prepared acts of worship. Anglicans usually make the mistake of trying to adapt the ordinary pattern of Sunday worship (such as Evensong) by adding a hymn, prayer or reading in the hope of making the old order relevant to the occasion. This often gives the impression that a piece of new cloth is being badly stitched to an old garment. Evenson is not an all-purpose order of service, though it is often treated as such. To do this nearly always produces a liturgical mess. To an even greater extent, the familiar Free Church 'hymn sandwich' is treated as an all-purpose worship order. Obviously it is more adaptable than the set 'Prayer Book' liturgy.

But it can become equally stereotyped. The production of worship for special occasions calls for fresh and imaginative thinking. For example, it may sometimes be more appropriate to have the address at the very beginning of the service, with the worship which follows being clearly designed as a response to the message which has been proclaimed.

In the previous chapter I gave an account of a service which was prepared to celebrate the tenth anniversary of the Liverpool Polytechnic. I described how many academic departments had collaborated in the preparation of this act of worship which was centred on the theme of Creativity. But there were certain aspects of the curriculum which could not be easily incorporated into the order of service but which had an obvious place in the overall theme. These departments were invited to exhibit evidence of their work in the cathedral. So the transepts and side-chapels provided an unusual setting for a display of computer technology, laser beams, engineering work, fabric printing, dress-making and a whole selection of electronic gadgetry. Many other examples could be given. To coincide with the service to express concern for the care of the offender, already described, the Prison Department together with the Probation Service collaborated to mount an exhibition relevant to the occasion. For the Road Safety service there were visual displays by the police and road safety organizations, and a huge mural was mounted, the work of children from a number of schools who both designed and painted it. At another service of dedication for those concerned with the welfare of animals and the conservation of nature, there was a large exhibition organized by a whole variety of environmental and animal welfare organizations, most of whom had never worked together before. School services can provide an opportunity for the display of children's work in their local church. Christian Aid, Traidcraft and similar 'third world' organizations can provide posters and other display material for a Christian Aid, One World Week or Harvest service. Most child care organizations like Dr Barnardo's, the National Children's Home and the Children's Society are glad to collaborate with churches in the organization of acts of worship designed to stimulate Christian concern for children at risk in our society and the work of those involved in child care. The impact of many special services can be greatly enhanced by the addition of a visual dimension. Already many churches have brought a new meaning to Harvest Thanksgiving by involving local commerce and industry in their celebration. In such ways the church can again be seen to be a place relevant to the needs and aspirations of the community in which it is set.

'Special occasions' in church need not be acts of worship – at least not in the generally accepted sense. Recent years have seen a considerable increase in the use of church buildings for art, music, drama, dance, exhibitions, flower arrangements, and social gatherings. These are happenings which in one dimension might be classed as 'secular' but which take on a new meaning when held in a setting which is known primarily as a place of prayer and worship. Two examples can illustrate this point, but readers should have no great difficulty in translating these rather special events into the context of their own local church. The same basic principles obtain whether such events are made for a great city cathedral or a small country chapel.

When the Liverpool folk group 'The Spinners' agreed to give a concert in the cathedral to support the work of the local Community Relations Council, it was decided to include between their musical items readings from the sacred writings and philosophies of a number of world religions. A large multi-racial audience listened with rapt attention to both words and music and later spoke of it as a deeply spiritual experience. What had been intended as a 'non-religious' money-raising concert had become a significant act of worship for many.

When in 1975 the German electronic rock group 'Tangerine Dream' did an English tour they not only booked to appear in the city halls of Birmingham, Sheffield and Glasgow, they also approached three English cathedrals, York Minster, Coventry and Liverpool. They wanted to give concerts in these buildings because they knew from experience of playing at Rheims and Munster that great cathedrals can give a perfect acoustic setting for the sound produced by their quadrophonic synthesizers. In a press interview the leader of the group explained 'Cathedrals have incredible acoustic possibilities, particularly as most of them were built when amplifiers did not exist. In no way are we trying to create religious events, but in these buildings the atmosphere is more conducive to concentration. The intrinsic beauty of cathedrals goes without saying, and it is sad that these buildings are underused.' Before agreeing to the Liverpool concert I listened with great care to their recordings. I reached the conclusion that their music came from an entirely different world from that of the commercial 'pops', and that it could fittingly be played in a cathedral setting. The cathedral was a sell-out, most of the audience being of student age. I prepared a short leaflet which was given to everyone as they came in, welcoming them and sharing my own beliefs why I thought this event fitted within the purpose for which the cathedral was built.

> Obviously Tangerine Dream's special sound will be heard at great advantage in a building of this size and with our kind of acoustic. That is why they have asked to come here. And we readily agreed to their visit because we believe that their musical style has something to say about the spiritual purpose for which this cathedral was built. They are a genuinely creative group, using the latest electronic techniques and creating a style which is all their own. In this cathedral we stand for God the Creator who has made mankind to share with him in the creation of all that is beautiful and true. The music of this group is also reconciling; people with musical tastes which range from 'classical' to rock find themselves sharing in their enjoyment of this music. We stand here for a faith in Christ which exists to break down barriers which divide people into opposing camps. We hope you will enjoy tonight's concert for its own sake – and for the sake of the spiritual truths of creativity and reconciliation for which Liverpool cathedral has been built.

Our churches in Europe are the heirs of a remarkable heritage in liturgical, musical, artistic and community care tradition. The best of these things must be preserved even when changing tastes make them temporarily unfashionable. This article is not a plea to jettison all that is good in its past. But the church must not rest content to justify its continuing existence on the strength of past glories alone. There is an essential task for each succeeding generation to make the local church a centre of creative expression and a focal point for the hopes and fears of the community in which it is set. Here liturgy and worship can be placed at the disposal of the people and not left in the hands of traditionalists, conservatives and antiquarians. Here drama, music, dance, painting, poetry and liturgy can speak powerfully to the condition of modern man even in our materialistic and secular society. Here it can be seen that the church where these things are offered is also a workshop for an adventurous compassion, springing out of the experience of worship to meet the concrete needs of those at greatest risk in society. Here will be found a compelling witness to the living ever-present God whom to worship in word and action is the chief end of man.

Evangelism in the City

LESSLIE NEWBIGIN
Birmingham

THE Editor has invited me to contribute a chapter with the above title to this volume. He has coupled the request with a reference to my book *Foolishness to the Greeks* in which I had tried to suggest what would be involved in a genuinely missionary encounter of the gospel with our contemporary western culture. In reviewing this book in his 'Talking Points' he pointedly asked: 'What do you do about this in practice?' In pursuit of an answer to that very legitimate question, and remembering that my present ministry is in what we are learning to call an 'Urban Priority Area', he has asked me to reflect on the way in which the gospel is to be communicated in such situations. I feel bound to respond, not because I pretend to know the answers, but because I cannot escape the question.

The small congregation with which I now minister worships in a Victorian building situated immediately opposite the Winson Green Prison. In an early document the area served was defined by the following boundaries: 'HM Prison, the Lunatic Asylum, the railway and James Watt's famous factory'. It is now an area of very high unemployment, an exceptionally high proportion of single-parent families, and a rich ethnic mix in which native Anglo-Saxons form a minority. In relation to the nation as a whole it would be described as an area of relative deprivation. In terms of absolute poverty, or – for example – in comparison with the Indian villages where most of my ministry has been exercised, its people have considerable material resources. Every home has a television and this provides, for most of the time, the visible centre of life in the home. The commodity in shortest supply is hope.

The older inhabitants speak much of earlier times when there was a closely packed community in which neighbours knew and helped each other. Much of this was destroyed in the name of 'improvement'. The terrace houses were pulled down and their inhabitants forced to move to the suburbs. One 18-storey tower-block was built; those who inhabit it have one main ambition, namely to escape. Older people comfort themselves with nostalgic memories of the past, and are fearful of the present. For young people, especially for those of the Afro-Caribbean community, there is little reason for hope about the future. There is a famine of hope.

We have good news to tell. Before we begin to think about how it is communicated, it is well that one begins with a negative point. It is *not* communicated if the question uppermost in our minds is about the survival of the church in the inner city. Because our society is a pagan society, and because Christians have – in general – failed to realize how radical is the contradiction between the Christian vision of what is the case and the assumptions that we breathe in from every part of our shared existence, we allow ourselves to be deceived into thinking of the church as one of the many 'good causes' which need our support and which will collapse if they are not adequately supported. If our 'evangelism' is at bottom an effort to shore up the tottering fabric of the church (and it sometimes looks like that) then it will not be heard as good news. The church is in God's keeping. We do not have the right to be anxious about it. We have our Lord's word that the gates of hell shall not prevail against it. The nub of the matter is that we have been chosen to be the bearers of good news for the whole world, and the question is simply whether we are faithful in communicating it.

But how to communicate? In my experience the hardest part is trying to communicate to the native Anglo-Saxon. The others are – in general – people who know that God is the great reality, even if we may judge that their knowledge of him is imperfect. To the Muslim the gospel is shocking but at least it is significant. To Hindus and Sikhs it is something really worth listening to – even if one finally decides that it is just another version of the 'religion' which is common to us all. Many of the Afro-Caribbean people in our inner cities are devout Christians whose faith, hope and love put most of us to shame. But for the majority of the natives, the

Christian story is an old fairy-tale which they have put behind them. It is not even worth listening to. One shuts the door and turns back to the TV screen where endless images of the 'good life' are on tap at all hours.

How can this strange story of God made man, of a crucified saviour, of resurrection and new creation become credible for those whose entire mental training has conditioned them to believe that the real world is the world which can be satisfactorily explained and managed without the hypothesis of God? I know of only one clue to the answering of that question, only one real hermeneutic of the gospel: a congregation which believes it.

Does that sound too simplistic? I don't believe it is. Evangelism is not some kind of technique by means of which people are persuaded to change their minds and think like us. Evangelism is the telling of good news, but what changes people's minds and converts their wills is always a mysterious work of the sovereign Holy Spirit and we are not permitted to know more than a little of his secret working. But – and this is the point – the Holy Spirit is present in the believing congregation gathered for praise and the offering up of spiritual sacrifice, scattered throughout the community to bear the love of God into every secular happening and meeting. It is they who scatter the seeds of hope around, and even if the greater part falls on barren ground, there will be a few that begin to germinate, to create at least a questioning and a seeking, and perhaps to lead someone to enquire about the source from which these germs of hope came. Although it may seem simplistic, I most deeply believe that it is fundamental to recognize that what brings men and women and children to know Jesus as Lord and Saviour is always the mysterious work of the Holy Spirit, always beyond our understanding or control, always the result of a presence, a reality which both draws and challenges – the reality who is in fact the living God himself. And his presence is promised and granted in the midst of the believing, worshipping, celebrating, caring congregation. There is no hermeneutic for the gospel but that.

The first priority, therefore, is the cherishing and nourishing of such a congregation in a life of worship, of teaching and mutual pastoral care so that the new life in Christ becomes more and more

for them the great and controlling reality. That life will necessarily
be different from the life of the neighbourhood, but the important
thing is that it be different in the right way and not in the wrong
way. It is different in the wrong way if it reflects cultural norms
and assumptions that belong to another time or place; its language
and style must be that of the neighbourhood. But yet if it is *not*
different from the life around it, it is salt which has lost the saltness.
We ought to recognize, perhaps more sharply than we often do,
that there *must* be a profound difference between a community
which adores God as the great reality, and one where it is assumed
that he can be ignored.

But here a problem arises which is perhaps specially pressing in
deprived areas. It happens over and over again, and it has happened
throughout history, that the effect of conversion and Christian
nurture is that a man or woman acquires new energies, a new hope
and a new sense of dignity. And it can follow that his next step is
to leave the area where he sees only depression and despair and seek
a better place. He leaves the inner city and moves to the leafy
suburb. The congregation which bears the good news is weakened
by its very success.

This means, surely, that in all our preaching and teaching about
the hope which the gospel makes possible, we have to keep steadily
in view the fact that what the gospel offers is not just hope for the
individual but hope for the world. Concretely I think this means
that the congregation must be so deeply and intimately involved in
the secular concerns of the neighbourhood that it becomes clear to
everyone that no one and nothing is outside the range of God's
love in Jesus. Christ's message, the original gospel, was about the
coming of the kingdom of God, that is to say God's kingly rule
over the whole of his creation and the whole of human kind. That
is the only authentic gospel. And that means that every part of
human life is within the range of the gospel message; in respect of
everything the gospel brings the necessity for choice between the
rule of God and the negation of his rule. If the good news is to be
authentically communicated, it must be clear that the church is
concerned about the rule of God and not about itself. It must be
clear, that is, that the local congregation cares for the well-being of

the whole community and not just for itself. This will – in the contemporary situation of such areas as Winson Green – lead to much involvement in local issues of all kinds of which it is not necessary in an article of this kind to give examples.

But, and this reminder is very necessary, this involvement must not become something that muffles the distinctive note of the gospel. The church ought not to fit so comfortably into the situation that it is simply welcomed as one of the well-meaning agencies of philanthropy. I think this warning is necessary because of the frequency with which I hear 'kingdom' set against 'church' in discussions about our role in society. I have insisted that the church's message is about the kingdom. The church is called to be a sign, foretaste and instrument of God's kingly rule. But it is the *church* to which this calling is given. We have too often heard 'kingdom issues' set against 'church issues' in a way which conceals the fact that 'kingdom issues' are being conceived not in terms of the crucified and risen Jesus, but in terms of contemporary ideology. In the heyday of progressive liberal capitalism, 'advancing the kingdom' meant enabling more and more people to share in its blessings. Today the ideas are more generally coloured by Marxist ideals about the oppressed as the bearers of liberation. One has much sympathy with this in view of the contemporary attempt to persuade us that the way to maximize public good is to give free rein to private greed. We live in a society which is being ideologically polarized by this attempt as never before. It is not easy to keep one's head. But it is essential to keep all our thinking centred in the fact that the kingdom of God is present in Jesus – incarnate, crucified, risen and coming in judgment. The life of the church in the midst of the world is to be a sign and foretaste of the kingdom only in so far as its whole life is centred in that reality. Every other concept of the kingdom belongs to the category of false messiahs about which the Gospels have much to say.

To put it even more sharply: the hope of which the church is called to be the bearer in the midst of a famine of hope, is a radically other-worldly hope. Knowing that Jesus *is* king and that he *will* come to reign, it fashions its life and invites the whole community to fashion its life in the light of this reality, because every other way of living is based on illusion. It thus creates signs, parables, foretastes, appetizers of the kingdom in the midst of the hopelessness of the world. It makes it possible to act both hopefully and realistically in a world without hope, a world which trades in illusions. If this radically other-worldly dimension of the church's witness is missing, then all its efforts in the life of the community are merely a series of minor eddies in a current which sweeps relentlessly in the opposite direction.

But if one insists as I am doing upon the radically other-worldly nature of the Christian hope, it is necessary at once to protect this against a misunderstanding which has brought this aspect of the Christian message into disrepute. A recognition of this other-worldly element has often been linked with a privatization of religion characteristic of our post-Enlightenment culture. When this happens, the church is seen not as a bearer of hope for the whole community, but as a group of people concerned about their own ultimate safety. It is thus seen as something essentially anti-social. And, especially in a religiously plural society, this attracts justifiable censure. 'Evangelism' is then easily identified as 'proselytism' – the natural attempt of every human community to add to its own strength at the expense of others. From the point of view of people concerned with the total welfare of a human community, 'evangelism' is seen as something at best irrelevant and at worst destructive of human unity.

Is there a valid distinction between 'evangelism' and 'proselytism'? It must be admitted that in many discussions of this subject I have sensed that the distinction was very simple: evangelism is what we do and proselytism is what the others do. But I think it is possible to get beyond this obvious illusion. Everything depends upon the point which I made at the beginning, namely that the conversion of a human mind and will to acknowledge Jesus as Lord and Saviour is strictly a work of the sovereign Holy Spirit of God, a mystery always beyond our full comprehension, for which our words and deeds may be – by the grace of God – the occasions but never the sufficient causes. Anything in the nature of manipulation, any exploiting of weakness, any use of coercion, anything other than 'the manifestation of the truth in the sight of God' (2 Cor 4:2) has no place in true evangelism. Of course anyone who knows Jesus as Lord and Saviour will rejoice when the company of those who love him grows. But he will also know that Jesus is much greater than any of our understanding of him and that it therefore behoves us to make no final judgments until the Judge himself comes. It is he alone who decides whom he will summon to be with us in the company of witnesses.

If we are clear about the distinction between evangelism and proselytism we shall be in a position to say something constructive about the matter of evangelism among people of other faiths. I have mentioned the fact that in the area of my present pastoral charge there is a large proportion of families of Muslim, Hindu or Sikh faith. I have said that I find it much easier to talk with them on matters of religious faith than with most of the natives. But I am also frequently told, sometimes by Christian clergymen, that evangelism among my neighbours of other faiths is an improper activity and that I ought to confine myself to 'dialogue'. I find this exceedingly odd. We live in one neighbourhood. For weal or woe we share the same life. We wrestle with the same problems. It is, surely, a very peculiar form of racism which would affirm that the good news entrusted to us is strictly for white Anglo-Saxons! After the last annual Assembly of the United Reformed Church which had given much attention to evangelism, one of the participants wrote to the Church's monthly paper to ask why it was that this word was reserved for our relations with unchurched Anglo-Saxons while in respect of our relations with people of other faiths we spoke only of 'dialogue'. The question was not answered.

How has it come that 'evangelism' and 'dialogue' are presented as opposed alternatives? Surely because both have been misunderstood. 'Evangelism' has been misunderstood as proselytism. There is reason for this and all of us who seek to be true bearers of the gospel need to take note. If 'evangelism' is the attempt of a religious group to enlarge itself by cajoling or manipulating those unable to resist, then it is rightly suspect. But a believing, celebrating, loving Christian fellowship, fully involved in the life of the wider community and sharing its burdens and sorrows, cannot withhold from others the secret of its hope and certainly cannot commit the monstrous absurdity of supposing that the hope by which it lives applies only to those of a particular ethnic origin.

And the word 'dialogue' too needs to be examined. No sharing of the good news takes place except in the context of a shared human life, and that means in part the context of shared conversation. In such conversation we talk about real things and we try both to communicate what we know and to learn what we do not know. The sharing of the good news about the kingdom is part of that conversation and cannot happen without it. But why do we have to substitute the high-sounding word 'dialogue' at this point? Is it because we fail in the simple business of ordinary human conversation? I confess that in the Winson Green neighbourhood we have not established any 'dialogue' between representatives of the different faiths, but we do have quite a lot of conversation. And it is the kind of conversation which is not an alternative to but the occasion for sharing our hope. And it leads some people to ask the sort of questions that lead further.

Some, but not many. I certainly cannot tell any story of 'success' in terms of numbers. I guess that this is the experience of many working in such areas. The church remains small and vulnerable. I do not find in this ground for much discouragement. The kingdom is not ours. The times and seasons are not in our management. It is enough to know that Jesus reigns and shall reign, and to be privileged to share this assurance with our neighbours and to be able to do and say the small deeds and words that make it possible for others to believe.

Sharing Ministry on a Large Council Estate

TREVOR N. STUBBS, Dip.Min., A.K.C.
Middleton, Leeds

The suggestion of a sharing in Christian ministry between the laity and the clergy often meets more resistance from the laity than it does from clergymen. This is no less true in Urban Priority Areas. My own experience is based on a council estate in the north but I believe the following holds true for most of the large council estates that surround our cities.

The resistance to shared ministry springs mainly from two sources. First from those who in days gone by have been taught to hold their pastors in awe and look up to them as a kind of 'priestly aristocracy'. For these people even the thought that a local boy could one day be ordained is difficult to come to terms with. However this objection is dying out fast. The second source of resistance is a pervading lack of confidence – in society, in oneself and in God.

Lack of Faith in Society. There is a feeling, not without some justification, that those who have power both despise the poorer sections of society and seek to keep them down. This 'us-them' feeling is a hurt that underlies the basic assumptions of the majority of the poorest on our estates. It undermines anything that anyone from outside (or even inside sometimes) attempts to do to ameliorate the situation. Society as a whole is not seen to care, and authorities of any kind, temporal or spiritual, are regarded with suspicion.

Lack of Faith in Oneself. A large proportion of estate residents often have a deep lack of faith in themselves to cope with life at all – let alone cope with other people's needs as would be met in a 'ministry' situation. Frequent personal crises are expected. People believe they will fail in their efforts – they mostly do! For the vast majority the secret is to become involved in as little as possible or just dabble on the edges so that you can make a hasty withdrawal when things start to cave in. Some withdraw from society altogether where it is safest. Others believe the best thing you can do is to enjoy life while you can – now. Escapism is common mostly through as intense a social life as the cash (and credit) allows. This can manifest itself in excessive drinking, smoking, gambling, pornographic videos, and taking opportunities to indulge in cheap and irresponsible sex. So a section of UPA society, because of their own lack of faith in themselves slip into a degradation that mars the wider society's faith in them. The circle is complete.

Lack of Faith in God. But this lack of faith extends in a third direction – a lack of faith in God. It's not that people do not believe God exists (95 per cent of UPA people do). The belief is that God is on the side of them: the 'haves' and the authorities. God is seen to condemn; he does not like people to have physical pleasures. Anyway he either does not want to, or cannot, do anything to change things for the better. Whether he cannot or just doesn't want to is not known because it just comes down to the same thing in the end – God doesn't really come into the question most of the time. There is perhaps more praying done than meets the eye, especially among women, but more faith is put into folk religion than anything else. Clairvoyants, spiritualists, magical healers (all demanding fees!) are also popular because they prescribe instant remedies that do not require personal confidence.

The most absent ingredient and the most longed for is *hope*. But for the local 'realists' it is an elusive butterfly sought after by the young and proclaimed by the eccentric (including the church).

The estate on which I live with about seven thousand people is not large as council estates go but it is adjacent to others like it. In our city (Leeds) there are hundreds of thousands of people living on similar estates. Yet it is not the size that matters as much as the insularity.

There is very little social interaction with people of different socio-economic classes. Very few professional, managerial or university graduates live on the estates. Contact with such people is only as clients. The only exceptions to this are church ministers. Again few local estate people ever visit the areas of private housing in the city and visa versa. Some do have relatives who have 'made good' with whom they keep in close contact, but these are a minority.

There is, therefore, a great need for the professionals who are available. Solicitors, advice workers, social workers, doctors and health visitors are in constant demand. They are often used as social props to help people cope with their 'problems' (including lack of hope!). The young have most opportunities and dedicated teachers put great efforts into young people who show interest and determination and a few do well and go on to take 'A' levels and leave the estate for good. The majority do not show such potential and some would prefer to continue to live in the estate anyway. However, there remain a large number who do leave – especially the most educated and most able who would make the most dependable leaders. Few people elect to come onto the estate from outside. Most incomers are placed here by the council – often people who are desperate for housing.

The local clergy have therefore fitted into the scene as professionals, provided to help cope with the difficult patches of life. (They would soon become a source of cash if they didn't quickly learn to say no!) The clergy are looked upon as the persons who will help keep people going. Most, of course, (including men) are glad they are there but do not want to have to call upon them. However there are a large number of people who 'latch on' to the church (and the clergy in particular) as a place to release responsibilities. Many church people like and expect the clergy to take responsibility for everything. Sadly there is often more faith placed in the clergy to keep things going than in God. 'A good vicar is one you can depend on' means a man who will shoulder the burdens. A vicar who 'doesn't care' is one who refuses to prop up at every turn. Traditionally it is for the vicar that things are done rather than for God or others. 'We've polished the chairs for you today, vicar!' – even though the vicar is not expected to sit on the chairs in the nave himself. The church belongs to the vicar and in return he is to look after his flock and feed them. Of course not

all church members think like this but most do. (The established
church does not help people to think otherwise either, when
incumbents are inducted into the 'real and actual possession' of the
building, its contents and curtilage!)

How, then, does one begin with shared ministry in this context?
Perhaps the best place to begin is to suggest how not to do it
because, like many another experiment, we began in our church by
getting it wrong! We started where the professionals would, by
outlining the structures of shared ministry. We felt that we had to
establish the theory, work together on an agreed aim and devise a
plan that would get us there. So we got as many church members
together as possible into home groups (not an easy task to begin
with) and set about analysing the purpose of ministry, the current
roles of the clergy and the laity and the possibilities of change. I
firmly believe this is an excellent way to go about things. It involves
lay people from the outset and allows them to determine the
process, the 'set up' and the priorities. The clergy become partners
in ministry right from the planning stage. In theory this should be
even more important in an UPA parish where the clergy are almost
certainly from a totally different background themselves.

However, far from welcoming the opportunity to share, many
people were very much alarmed. Shared planning is seen to involve
too much shared responsibility. The whole process itself is an
imposed model from a different culture. Centuries of division
between the managers and the workforce has left working people
with a culture that does not require decision making or planning.
'That is done by others and that's how it should be.' To be given
the task of working out what is right for oneself or one's
community is not to gain freedom but to be given just another
burden to bear!

In our case a team of local church members was elected –
probably because the vicar thought it was a good idea(!) – with the
responsibility of introducing a shared ministry scheme which would
involve everyone. At the same time they embarked on a two year
training course. The training was both academic in appearance and
very difficult to adapt to the local situation. UPA people do not
work well in a structured plan using technical categories and doing

theoretical training. And so for us the team, the plan and the structure have gradually dissolved away despite a great deal of effort to 'make' it work over two years. In retrospect it should have been clear from the start that it was not going to work because the structures could never be owned by people whose culture does not 'think' in structures.

This is not the same as saying that UPA church members are not ready for shared ministry – they are as ready and as willing as any congregation could ever hope to be – we simply must not begin at the wrong end, along lines that cannot be followed, understood or (most importantly) identified with. The theology of the structures was carefully thought out and the training planned by specialists but it sadly confused rather than enlightened. So the experiment faltered.

The pursuit of shared ministry, however, has not been abandoned. We began to look at where people really 'were at', what church members were already doing, and how and what resources we had. We discovered that church members, as much as any other single group of people, 'neighbour' in the community. They look after in an *ad hoc* way people who live around them – fetching pensions, minding children, getting the doctor, helping with the shopping, etc. No one asks people to do this, it is purely voluntary and doesn't commit them to something controlled by others; not anyone in authority (including the vicar), not God, and not because the Bible or the law says so. It is not seen as particularly God's work or work with any moral obligation. They do it because it is needed now, and the need is perceived, and because it is within their cultural tradition. Very few people link the fact that they can and want to do this with the fact that God is in their lives somewhere, stimulating and enabling. They are not necessarily aware that God is working in and through them – yet to the Christian he clearly is.

This, then, ought to be our starting point – helping people to see that they are already sharing in Christian ministry with the clergy. Once the penny drops that by 'neighbouring' with concern I am truly loving my neighbour (and Christ through that neighbour) then sharing responsibility no longer becomes an extra burden but a new discovery. For many church members shared ministry will remain at that level – simply caring for their immediate neighbours, workmates and family in keeping with cultural patterns. The important thing is that this ministry is seen as, and recognized by themselves and others to be, part of the Church's whole ministry and that God is present ready to pour his strength and love into the situation.

Another important point to make about the 'burden' of ministry or rather the 'burden as perceived' is the problem of long term commitment. UPA people are particularly reluctant to take on long term or open ended commitments because culturally they are 'people of the moment' (the future is generally not planned for), and also because they have trouble with knowing how to relinquish jobs if they need to. (It often occurs with some drama because they are afraid they will be prevailed on further and do not want to lose face. More than a few vicars have arrived home for tea to discover a note of resignation through the letter-box and a plastic carrier bag of ledgers, accounts or minute books on the door step!) It is far wiser to work with culture whenever possible and plan 'one off' events or short term clearly defined projects.

An example of this happened in the hard winter of January 1987 when a quarter of our estate froze and a large number of people were flooded. Twenty or so church members got up a soup kitchen and visiting teams, furniture and bedding was collected and dried, and a hot line developed with the local housing office and social services for two way referrals. A few weeks later a similar team was distributing EEC butter etc. to thirteen hundred people per week. In a series of short term commitments people work much harder with total commitment. For many people this is how they will serve.

But not all ministry can be done in general terms or as one off exercises. Some of it needs training and experience too. This, I believe, is still possible but should be done with twos and threes and begin with the practical. People with some clue about how and why a ministry should be tackled are the raw material. Take for example the ministry to those who bring their children for baptism. It is important to watch and listen to see if there are people who are already interested in this area. They may not have thought they could do anything or indeed that it has anything to do with lay people, but they do have ideas. Once the clergy have talked about what is needed, it may become clear that they have a ministry to perform that no clergy could. A lay ministry among one's neighbours will have an impact in areas that are rarely open to clergy who come from the professional and educated parts of society. These church members can be encouraged to visit families coming to enquire about baptism to just 'get to know' them. Gradually the responsibilities can be increased until maybe the primary contact is with the lay person. It is certainly true that parishioners relate much more readily with their neighbours. They can take on the responsibility of talking about the meaning of baptism in terms the local person can easily understand – lay people do not have the disadvantage of having to translate into language they themselves do not think in. (It doesn't take a college graduate long to learn that there is more than one sort of English – and his sort will not do!) The clergy, of course, are not left out of the ministry and can make their own visits before and after the baptism – but the responsibility of the ministry is truly shared. Ministries to the bereaved and the sick can be built up in the same way. However this may take many years and will always be fragile because it depends on suitable individuals who may not always be available.

It can be seen that a structure of ministry develops, but it is not decided upon at the beginning. It is something that grows out of the practice of ministry. The structures are unique to each situation depending on the individuals who minister and who are ministered to. The lay person may or may not be involved in any ministry for long. The way out and the possibility of a change must be kept open. Situations often change fast on a council estate – a new job, a new baby, a different shift, redundancy, a sudden change in government training schemes or social security legislation which alter the weekly income, family demands of all sorts, illness, or just a feeling of a need for a change. So the ministry stops and the clergy must pick up the reins until someone else comes along and things begin again with a new structure that suits the new worker. If two or three work on a project there is some chance of continuity but often when one member goes the team must stop too. (Twos and threes are no guarantee of continuity.) Frequently no new person comes into view for some time. The former strength and healthy activity is now replaced by a weak point and lack of activity and that which the clergy proudly pointed to a few weeks before now no longer exists! Sometimes it is right for the clergy and other stipendiary ministers to persist with a project when it falters (in which case it becomes, albeit temporarily, a clergy run activity); at other times it is right for the project to cease. Both alternatives call into question the priorities of the clergy and their role, and both may feel like failure – and failure only serves to further undermine the confidence of the laity thinking about working in other areas of ministry.

So we have no clear structures to show for our pains, no labels, no diagrams, no progress charts, and no long term schemes. It could look like failure to those outside the situation as well as inside. That is part of the problem of the large council estate because so much looks like failure to those who think in terms of management and organization. The opinion that, 'These people need to get themselves organized and get stuck in instead of loafing about waiting for someone else to do it or just doing things in bursts in a haphazard sort of way', is often expressed. There may be some truth in this, but the motivation is so often lacking in people because they feel so marginalized, or even excluded by the organized who inadvertently reduce them with their policies, plans, structures and schemes. Sadly the church as a whole is often expected to be yet another set of insensitive and authoritarian organizers. The role of the church outside the UPAs is to encourage, not to judge, and to recognize that not everything can be seen in terms of the need for structures which is taken for granted but which, in reality, is part of an educated, middle-class culture. (This is not to say that education and structure are undesirable, but to recognize that they will never be part of the culture of the large council estate because an individual who becomes aware of their value generally moves away or, if he remains, is in a small minority.)

Shared ministry on a large council estate must therefore not only take account of the local culture but arise from it, (1) taking advantage of the opportunities that present themselves, (2) being extremely adaptable and (3) not being judged as a success or failure in the generally accepted way. The same criteria should be applied to clergy who work in such areas, with the addition of a fourth, (4) remaining faithful to God, the people and the task no matter how difficult things may become. The role of the wider church is to understand and support – and be prepared to become personally involved.

Thoughts on Twinning from the Inner City

TWINNING is usually understood to be the bonded friendship between two churches, usually one rich and one poor, one suburban and one rural or inner city. In this article I am speaking of a group of four or five suburban communities with whom the inner city church has developed friendship.

For more years than I care to remember I was a 'Methodist manse mum'. Now with my family grown up and husband passed heavenward, I live in a tower block in a most depressed inner city area.

I know it is depressed because at the last census we had the most people out of work and the least number of cars, and nothing has changed since then, and because, although a few flowers may appear in council house gardens, the flowering of the people's lives, the growth of community, local leadership, sports, and the attainment of 'O' levels are noticeably missing. The estate is roughly two miles long and half a mile wide. It is surrounded by industry, much of it dying, although there are some new factories. The population is about 25% elderly original inhabitants before reconstruction, about 30% of Caribbean extraction, 10% Irish, 6 or 7% Asian, and the rest English. A high percentage have come to live here because of family misfortune, and only wish to move away.

I cannot remember when the terms 'Inner City' and 'Pluralistic Society' became current in our vocabulary, but certainly from the early '60s we began to focus on blighted places of decay, followed by the new council housing that was often to become the new slums, so that before I came to my high rise flat I had learned a lot about coping with the structures of society and the difficulties of the lives of the poor. I had heard too the question asked in every conceivable way: what about our needy communities? How can these churches live? Without capital where is dignity? One of the new answers in Methodism has been the 'Mission alongside the Poor' fund, which has given a new sense of responsibility to the whole church and a new freedom of expression in hard areas.

Seven years ago I was told to join the nearest Methodist Church. That was easy to find, but any local congregation was almost non-existent. Growth had begun, however, and a small, strong, attractive local community has emerged. We are made up of people of Afro-Caribbean origins, some from the Islands, some first generation British. All could be called deprived in the sense that tough circumstances have robbed them of the opportunity to reach their highest potential. Most are family people suffering the lack of so many of the provisions which they feel money and more adequate circumstances would provide.

A plethora of cultures, a lack of educational expertise, the absence of normal rush-hour hubbub, many one parent and unsupported families, all reinforce a sense of isolation which it is difficult to overcome. Asian and Caribbean incomers have found jobs and started on careers, and have departed for fairer pastures after a stay in poor housing. Very often those who remain in the inner city feel that skin colour is of the utmost importance.

Some churches outside of the cities, and even in the suburbs, have as yet no black members. When I visited a nearby smaller town, a church member said to me, 'I have never spoken to a black person. I have seen them when I visited the city and often wished I could.'

How then can sharing begin? Is it a useful way of spending time? We are still, I believe, in the infancy of experiment, dogged on the one side by the terrible difficulty of keeping commitments because of adverse family circumstances and on the other by an inability to recognize paternalism and avoid it.

Methodism has its own inbuilt system of twinning, in the circuit, and from way back poorer churches have received security and strength from their association with better endowed communities in a successful, though rather delicate adjustment of the financial budget so that none should bear too great a burden. Real friendships develop also. Yet it has to be said that church offices are most often held by the more influential and literate members of society, the poor do not as a rule speak out and feel that their offering would be insignificant, circuit sharing is often paternalistic, and new cultural patterns, emerging in answer to the needs of lifeless areas, may be frowned upon by circuit officials, so that adventurous groups may feel disciplined.

Our church is composed mainly of women in their most active years. Early in our associations we formed a Wholefood Cooperative, initially to deal with handling community money and to move toward simple and substantial living. We did not see it then as a bridge over which we would travel to other churches and groups, but it led to a netball team, a supplementary education project, a cultural meals group, a witnessing and speaking group, an assortment of children's work, and so on. Each has played a part in cementing friendships with suburban areas.

I believe that only very elderly people and perhaps mothers of very large families enjoy being 'taken to places'. The basis of dignified twinning is to capitalize on skills which can be exchanged.

Three small pictures of our associations and their attendant dangers give me food for thought.

(1) The first happy relationship sprang from the enthusiasm of a children's worker and her understanding of need spread through a large church community. A total effort of money and care was to be made for a year. Previously proceeds had been offered for overseas development. All seemed well, and indeed so it has proved, but it was put to me that this project would be more 'exciting' than those in the past since it was, so to speak, 'visible'. Here begins the difficulty. The daily lives of people in depressed areas are often hard and unyielding. Bringing up children with inadequate finances, coping with lack of amenities, and hopelessness could not in any sense promote the stimulus to make the other community find the effort worthwhile.

(2) A most interesting liaison was formed with a dormitory village through our minister's activities on the youth committee.

Children's visits and family evenings followed. Many of our happier adventures have been with this lively group. Then a high-powered worker in middle years felt called to give up all and share the greater load. Here again, however, the reality of the situation is not what it seems. The tremendous sacrifice needed for such a change of outlook mitigates against such a project without due regard to the cultural changes that would be needed.

(3) The third example grew from two or three Christians who felt that more should be achieved in care and interest from a large suburban church with a great number of professional people in its membership. The work was efficiently put in hand and lists of needs and supplies were drawn up. Some wonderful advances were made, but frustration set in when such real needs as a few hours of coaching for 'O' levels by teachers fitted in badly with the list on offer.

All these projects have enriched donor and receiver and all are still alive in one way or another, but I draw the inference that we tread delicate ground. All these experiences highlight the difficulties that well-endowed groups have in comprehending the greyness of the lives of the poor. We cannot be exciting or even in some senses grateful. We may even be embarrassed and shy if we cannot keep the small amount of dignity we have managed to achieve.

Some of our most successful efforts at sharing have developed from invitations to speak that came out of the blue. One such church in a small town outside the conurbation received us with courtesy and paid for our transport, listened as our speakers added to the mosaic of the evening, and gave us a cup of tea. A year later they asked us again. Our effort, more costly in time now since we have no great skills, passed off successfully. And then, behold, they had prepared for us a magnificent meal and treated us as family from afar. They accorded to us the wonderful trapping of pomp laid out for the great preachers of the day. Each one went home glowing from such honour.

So there is a scale of experience from groups cold and formal who want to fill their speaking plan, to those who visit us with a real desire to cross the divide, and on to those one or two special experiences when we have come home warmed that they should see in us 'those who follow the Way'. I am sure these kinds of experiences are current everywhere.

So what has been the use of the activity in which we have involved ourselves?

First, I believe the forming of loving relationships. Two women, one with degrees from Cambridge and destined for the ministry, the other with a large family and large problems, living miles apart, have found a spark of love that will last their lifetime through. Or another person who crosses the city to give time to our small education project is sustained by prayer and a little help by a house meeting. Then there are the two ladies who went as guests to the wedding of a member of the village church and felt they were part of the family. Financially, culturally and in general management it was totally different from their home patch, yet it sealed them into a belonging that remains.

Secondly, there is an increase in our estimation of ourselves and therefore in our dignity. In the beginning, time and again, family problems and shyness prevailed and the minibus was only half filled. Now with some of the skills of socialization in their hands, one or two have put away their small scripts and speak a little from the heart. In many ways we have crossed the cultural barriers.

Above all many have lost the concept that we are an oppressed, hard hit group, although I think we are, and begin to see themselves as a moving people and part of the wider Christian community. None of the these programmes were intended for anything other than to build our church, but I see them now as a prerequisite for the adventures we have shared and a capitalization of the talents of inner city churches which can bring only good.

Some conclusions

Visiting a large women's group in a suburban church I was reminded of the variety in life and churchgoing. In a short time I met one just widowed and enmeshed in suffering, one pregnant, one whose husband was recently unemployed, several middle aged and lonely, two enthusiasts for church community, one an enthusiast for twinning. An average mix. For this reason I believe sharing is better from a small, enthusiastic group than by formal arrangement by minister and stewards. Nothing is worse than expressed expectation unfulfilled. A small group of enthusiasts can maintain a sense of adventure. Those trapped within the problems of the inner city find escape difficult. I can cope with the idea of a new catacombs, through which flow love, courage, and hope from the surrounding communities as people awake to the need.

Some difficulties were expressed by the leader of a housemeeting involved. She doubted whether there would be enough support to make it worthwhile, because her church was fully involved with its own community programme. Problems may be concentrated in the inner city, but they occur everywhere. Further she explained that as part of the inner city church's move towards them they produced a meal and brought the children's choir. It worked well, but almost up to the last moment they did not seem sure that it would take place at all, and their church members were not used to such uncertainty.

What then can be received by the outer churches?

First the mixing of cultures and a better understanding of the 'real' pluralistic world in which we live.

Secondly, sharing of faith, often hard won and simply expressed, together with a knowledge of the children who are our future.

Thirdly, the growth of loving relationships.

And finally, a relief from the fear which followed the heavy media coverage of inner city problems. To many the inner city became a threat. Young men with dreadlocks, dark streets, and the proliferation of drugs reinforce the isolation. Yet from these areas can come balanced Christians who are indeed ambassadors of the kingdom.

This article is written from a Methodist perspective, but similar experiences can doubtless be found in other churches. The writer wishes to remain anonymous to safeguard the integrity of her local inner city church.

Social and Political Issues

ALAN LE GRYS, B.D., A.K.C.
Stoneleigh, Surrey

1. *Facing Conflict*

Anyone who has had the experience of raising social and political issues in church circles will know how easily this can lead to controversy. Both politics and religion deal with sensitive areas of personal belief, and the strong feelings aroused can lead to divisiveness, and a breakdown in personal relationships. It is little wonder if the pastor's natural instinct is to avoid this as much as possible, if only in the interests of self preservation!

Nor does the potential for conflict stop at the church door. Christians involved in political action will often run into disapproval from the wider community. They will be told that the church (which usually means the ordained ministry) has no right to be involved in affairs 'of this world' – and 'should keep out of politics'. Again, the temptation is to avoid controversy by limiting ministry to safer areas of ecclesiastical or charitable interest.

However, it is unlikely that any church will be able to avoid politics entirely. Remembrance Sunday presents the preacher with ethical questions about war and peace; Harvest Festival raises the spectre of world poverty and hunger; Education Sunday points to the politics of educational reform; prayers for the State, or for the world, beg questions about the nature of government – are our prayers the same for the UK and the USA as they are for the Soviet Union or South Africa? Even the Christmas story hints at the problems of the homeless and powerless. Unless the church is to retreat into superficial answers, some sort of response is inevitable; even silence can count as political consent.

But, if the questions are unavoidable, then the corresponding fear of conflict has to be faced. Yet, once accepted, this need not be as difficult as may first appear. Conflict is a common theme

201

throughout the Bible, and it is one of the few things Jesus told his disciples to expect (Mk 13:9-13). His own ministry leads to conflict; he comes to bring 'not peace, but a sword' (Mt 10.34). He sets new priorities, which run contrary to commonly accepted social values. Eventually this leads to the cross; yet this, paradoxically, leads in turn to new life through the resurrection. Thus, in Christ, conflict is creative; and disciples are called to share in this by taking up the cross and following, if necessary, even into death.

In this case, theology would appear to be supported by psychology – maturity is achieved by facing conflict, not avoiding it. If so, pastoral care can actually *require* conflict, as a necessary stage in personal growth. As Kenneth Leech says, 'There is a false assumption that pastoral care . . . is concerned with the reduction of conflict and tension. This view is based on two false assumptions: that it is possible, and that it is desirable. In fact, the nature of personal relationship is one which does not allow us to escape from inner struggle, but rather intensifies it.'[1]

2. The Theology of Engagement

At a clergy conference a few years ago, participants were asked to comment on the programme. One anonymous wit wrote 'The Word became words . . . and died'. Theology can become so wordy that it is in danger of losing the vitality of faith – as someone once said (to misuse another more famous remark) 'it is not that Christianity has been tried and found wanting, but that it has been found boring and not tried'. By contrast, 'the Word of God is sharper than a two-edged sword' (Heb 4:12), and there is an abrasiveness in the gospel which needs to be recognized.

This theological perspective is the unique contribution Christians have to offer. The church is not – or, perhaps, should not – be interested in the pursuit of power, but in the values of God's justice. Christian involvement should be an expression of theology, not political idealism. Doctrine, Biblical Studies, and even Church History, all contribute something to this distinctive Christian ethic; but, very briefly, the theological basis for engagement comes from:

(*a*) The doctrine of creation: Creation 'ex nihilo' is an affirmation of God's involvement in everything. Nothing – not even politics –

exists, except by providence. Christian concern begins as an act of witness to the God of human history. He is not brought in as an optional extra; he is there already.

(b) The concept of sin: The theology of creation, however, is incomplete without an account of sin – that, in some way, mankind distorts God's creative purpose.

Western preoccupation is with the individual, but the Old Testament is equally concerned about the corporate nature of sin, within the context of the covenant. The idea of personal responsibility does not clearly emerge until 6th century BC (Jer 31:29 ; Ezek 18:2); thus, in the prophets, judgment frequently centres on much which we would regard as political – for example, Amos 5:10-24; Isa 1:10-18; Jer 7:1-7, etc.

(c) Redemption: Only once in the Bible is it suggested that God came close to despair over mankind (Gen 6:5-7). Instead, he is loyal to the covenant, and his response to sin is the promise of redemption.

This is shown in specific acts. In the Old Testament, primarily through the Exodus/Sinai cycle. Because he is 'the God who led you out of slavery in Egypt' (e.g.: Ex 20:2), the covenant calls for the reordering of social, as well as personal values. Within the New Testament, action is centred in Christ. His view of redemption is presented in Luke 4:16-21, which has been called 'Christ's manifesto'. Quoting Isaiah 61:1-2, he says:

> The Spirit of the Lord is upon me
> because he has chosen me
> to bring good news to the poor.
> He has sent me to proclaim liberty to captives,
> and recovery of sight for the blind,
> to set free the oppressed,
> and to announce the year of the Lord's favour.

Given that the last reference is to the Law of Jubilee (Lev 25), this one passage links redemption to poverty, justice, health, and economics. In each case, these would be considered political issues in our terms. In the Gospel, they are linked to the work of the Spirit. In Christ, politics can become theology.

(*d*) Sanctification: Professor Cranfield has argued that 'sanctification means the growing freedom to obey God ... (it) is the fulfilment of the promise in Jer 31:33 that God would put his law in his people's hearts, that is, create in them a glad and free commitment to it'.[2]

Sanctification, then, is a process of growth, through the Holy Spirit, into a deeper relationship with God's law, including the demand for social justice. Christ's death is the definitive act of redemption; but it is incomplete until creation is 'changed from glory into glory' (2 Cor 3:18). The work of the Spirit is to bring this process to completion. This is eschatological; but, the church in union with the Holy Spirit is called to share in this by preparing for the Kingdom, and by bearing witness to it. In this, the church continues to proclaim the 'good news' as shown in Christ – including the relationship of the gospel to issues of poverty, justice, health, economics.

Social responsibility is, of course, only one aspect of the Christian life; but, on theological grounds alone, it needs to be recognized as an important part of the Christian response to God, as basic as prayer, worship, and other aspects of Christian ethics. Against this, however, it is often argued that:

(*a*) Christ was never directly involved in politics. When challenged by Pilate (Jn 18:33-38), Jesus said, 'My Kingdom is not of this world'. He teaches his disciples to 'Render unto Caesar the things which belong to Caesar, and to God the things which belong to God' (Mt 22:21). Therefore, 'churchmen dabbling in politics should take note that their only task is to prepare for the world hereafter'.[3]

(*b*) The New Testament Epistles teach submission to government authority (Rom 13:1-5; I Tim 2:1-4). The state exercises power as an agent of God, and the church has no right to challenge this authority.

It must be recognized that there is some substance in these arguments. For example, despite the fact that he was crucified on a political charge, there is no evidence that Jesus was ever concerned about political power. Indeed, it is one of the temptations rejected in Mt 4:8-9. But the church's role is to identify with *the powerless*, and to question those who exercise political control. It was, I think, Dom Heldar Camara who said, 'the task of the church is to be in continual opposition'. That the church finds this difficult, is shown by the continuing attempt to justify the presence of bishops in the House of Lords. It is said they are there to exercise Christian leadership within the political process, and to influence those in power. If so, there is little evidence of its effectiveness. Perhaps it is more likely that they are there because of the church's anxiety to be close to centres of power, rather than alongside the people of the Magnificat.

Submission to the state also needs qualification. Firstly, the same arguments apply to, say, Soviet Russia and Nicaragua as much as, say, South Africa or the UK. And, secondly, biblical passages in favour of submission are balanced by passages such as Rev 13. When civil power becomes demonic, as in Nazi Germany, it is to be opposed and resisted, not obeyed. Christ's kingdom may not be of this world – yet. But 'the kingdoms of this world' are to become 'the kingdom of our Lord' (Rev 11:15). Thus, Christian loyalty is ultimately to God, not to the State. In the end, even the affairs of Caesar belong to God.

The 'two worlds theory', therefore, is difficult to support theologically. Perhaps it needs to be recognized that those who use such arguments often have authoritarian views, and a vested interest in limiting opposition. The attempt to restrict Christianity to personal piety and private morality needs resisting. It is politically motivated, and theologically unsound.

3. Planning a Response

In theory, Christian response is the straightforward application of theological principle. In practice, however, it is at this point that the problems begin. There are so many 'good causes', so much background information and technical detail, so many political calculations, that it is easy to be overwhelmed. It can be only a matter of time before enthusiasm and commitment run out into the sands of frustration.

In the parable of the Unjust Steward (Lk 16:1-8), Jesus commends an otherwise dubious character for shrewd planning. An overall vision is of crucial importance for sustaining hope through inertia and difficulty, but Christians are challenged by the parable to combine high idealism with practical common sense. No one is going to be able to avoid all the problems. But, in my experience, there are some things which can be done to limit the danger of being overwhelmed. These include:

(a) Being patient: Kosuke Koyama speaks about 'the 3 mile an hour God'.[4] The pace of change can be painfully slow, and the urgency of moral injustice can be demanding. Real change, however, is effected by creating a climate of opinion, and this takes time – God's time.

(b) Selecting priorities: It has been said that the characteristic heresy of the English speaking church is individualism. Nothing is more likely to undermine commitment than the sense that each individual is personally responsible for every social injustice. In fact, it is not necessary to save the world single handed. The concept of the body of Christ means that social responsibility is shared throughout the church, like everything else. This ought to be true within a congregation, and within the wider church network (Deanery, Council of Churches, Diocese, etc). It ought to be true ecumenically. Too much energy is wasted in isolated concern or unnecessary duplication. Groups should reach agreement about areas of specialist interest – one group, perhaps concentrating on world development, another on disarmament, Amnesty or Shelter, and so on. That interest is then offered as a ministry on behalf of the whole church. By sharing strengths and weaknesses in this way, it is possible to make sure that most issues are covered within the overall ministry of the church.

(c) Developing a political awareness: Clear objectives need to be combined with an equally clear understanding of the political process.

Lord Hailsham has described British democracy as an 'elected dictatorship'. Once a government has achieved an overall majority, it is relatively secure, and may push through legislation virtually unchecked. The Party Whip system is designed to protect this, and it means, in practice, that most backbench MPs have very little power, except in the broadest terms (which increases in direct ratio to the nearness of the next election!). Even Government Ministers are limited by constraints of 'collective responsibility', the practicalities of policy implementation (otherwise known as the Civil Service), influential power groups (such as financial institutions), and by long term electoral prospects. Then, those involved in policy-making talk about the 'political management' of public opinion, and those called to be 'as wary as serpents, yet as innocent as doves' (Mt 10:16) would do well to realize that they are 'being managed' in this way.

Finally, there are the problems of 'hidden agendas'. Effective campaigning involves careful targeting. Concern about South Africa, for example, tends to focus on the moral issues of apartheid, which the government has no difficulty in accepting. Apart from slight modifications in the presentation of policy, however, in practice this makes little difference. The real agenda, one suspects, has more to do with financial involvement, and political perceptions about regional stability throughout Southern Africa. As long as only moral issues are targeted, little progress is likely to be made.

(d) Information gathering: Many campaigning organizations engaged in research are glad to supply background information. Some of this will be technical, but most of the overall concerns will be clear enough. Effective campaigning needs to be well informed; politicians are skilled in resisting simple moral outrage – they have to be.

One example of this is world development. Few people, Christian or otherwise, could fail to be moved by the appalling pictures of famine in Africa. Public response was magnificent, and yet all of the major Aid agencies would recognize the inadequacy of that response. Poverty in Africa is structural, and determined by economic decisions taken in places like Wall Street or the City of London, and no amount of charity is going to provide more than immediate first aid. 'While we, the people, gave more than ever before in response to the famine in Ethiopia and Sudan, our government gave less help ... than it had five years earlier. British Government Aid fell by more than a quarter in real terms between 1979 and 1985. Our individual efforts, fund raising by all the agencies, by BAND AID, LIVE AID, SPORTS AID put together made up a quarter of the shortfall'.[5] What is needed is structural change, not charity.

It should also be said that the complexity of issues is one device used to prevent effective campaigning. Whilst there is no excuse for outright ignorance, there is no inherent need to have a PhD in Economics before making moral judgments.

(e) Seeking wider support: Background material can be technical, full of jargon, mostly indigestible and highly boring. Most areas, however, have local action groups, or the potential to form such groups; many churches have individual 'experts' within their own congregations, and these human resources should be used. The church needs to 'plug into' existing networks, and to help build up contacts with like-minded people. No one needs to feel isolated – a problem which affected even the mighty prophet Elijah! (1 Kgs 19:14).

(f) Setting goals: The final stage of preparation is the identification of more immediate *achievable* goals. This may be no more than planning a church service or organizing a local exhibition; or it may be more ambitious, such as taking part in a wider national campaign to achieve a small change in, say, government spending priorities. This is important for two reasons: partly because it helps to monitor progress over a period of time; and partly because of the encouragement it offers groups who are able to see some immediate results from their work. Such targets need to be entirely realistic, and within the limits of available resources.

4. *The Pastoral Opportunities*

So, there are practical difficulties in the way of effective campaigning; but, providing the theological commitment is strong enough, it is possible to work through the dual problems of conflict and political complexity, through careful preparation and the use of support networks.

It has been said that the task of a campaigning organization is 'to make people angry' – that is, to stir up the kind of passion which makes political change compelling. It may be that the church is uniquely placed to do this: partly because the motivation is not party political, but theological; partly because of the regular pattern of teaching and preaching offers an opportunity to make social concern a normal part of Christian awareness; and partly because the church has access to decision makers and voters alike, through day to day pastoral contact.

Many churches will have some activists, who, like John the Baptist, play an important role in stirring the conscience and shaking complacency. Nevertheless, there is no need to duplicate the work of other campaigning groups; the church has a distinctive contribution to offer simply through the normal insights and skills of ministry. Social responsibility must not be relegated to the fringes of church activity, for those 'interested in that sort of thing'. It should be integrated into the overall pattern of pastoral ministry, exercised through:

Prayer: Those who presume to speak about God need to spend time in listening to him. Action should be rooted in prayer and contemplative Bible study. This should lead to intercessory prayer – for decision-makers, for the victims of injustice, and for those involved in opposition or lobbying. There is also a need for affirmative prayer – in giving thanks that 'God is working his purpose out', however unlikely that might seem at times.

Witness: Evangelism means 'good news' – not that recruits are needed to fill empty pews, but that God meets us at the point of our vulnerability. Salvation can be practical as well as spiritual. Specifically, it means good news to the poor, the unemployed, the homeless, the hungry, the victims of violence, and so on.

One other aspect of witness is also important: by establishing links with groups such as political parties, campaigning organizations, community action groups, and so on, many people who would normally remain outside any contact with the church are brought within range of pastoral care. The message to all those concerned is the simple: God cares.

Challenge: If it is accepted that conflict can be important for personal growth, then there is a pastoral responsibility to challenge assumptions and lifestyle. This ministry is exercised through preaching, house group discussions, 'teach-ins' and even one-to-one counselling. Christians should learn to enjoy being different in outlook and expectations: to be 'not conformed to the standards of this world, but transformed by God' (Rom 12:2).

Supportive pastoral care: This is often seen in terms of those who have authority or power; but there is at least one other important aspect – that of supporting people who face difficult moral decisions. There is one member of my own congregation who took the decision back in the 1930s to be a pacifist, and he stood by this throughout the last World War. He felt isolated and unsupported by the church for years, and has only recently felt able to speak about this within our own congregation. He also needs pastoral care and support.

Visiting: Most clergy – and pastoral assistants – have had the experience of visiting parishioners, and being presented with a cup of tea, and some off the cuff remarks about the weather and the state of the nation. Sometimes, these casual remarks betray deeply held attitudes which may need to be questioned in the light of the gospel. This is perhaps one of the most routine of pastoral encounters – and yet (speaking for myself!) it can also be one of the most difficult. The temptation is to let the remark pass, and have another biscuit. It may be, however, a heaven sent opportunity to open up a deeper discussion.

Many activists will find this 'low key' approach frustrating, whilst others will be hesitant about any engagement at all. The answer to both may be found in the Arabic proverb: 'It is better to light one candle than to curse the darkness'. Rather like Ezekiel (Ezek 3:16-21; 33:1-9), the church is called to be a faithful witness, whether or not anyone is prepared to listen; the rest is up to God.

Given the odds against success, the temptation is to give up after a lot of effort has yielded nothing in terms of tangible results. This is an effective method of preventing change. The church, however, should be better equipped to cope with disappointment, for God's 'power is strongest when you are weak' (2 Cor 12:9) it is *hupomonē* ('steadfastness/patient endurance') which leads to the victor's crown (Rev 3:10).

None of this is very profound, but what God may be asking is not penetrating insight or the mastery of technical detail, but simple passion and commitment. For too long, the church has allowed other people to set the agenda – the media, the 'moral majority', the government, popular public opinion; and there are worrying signs that some right-wing interests are trying to put further pressure on the church to conform to a pre-determined political agenda. The church must not allow itself to be intimidated. In the end, all that is really needed is more courage in our faith, confidence in our theology, and a passion for God's people.

---

[1] Kenneth Leech: *Spirituality and Pastoral Care* (Sheldon Press [1986]). See also; Alastair Campbell: *The Gospel of Anger* (SPCK [1986]).

[2] C. E. B. Cranfield: 'Preaching on Romans' (*ET* 99 [1987-88]), 39.

[3] Goebbels, Hitler's Minister of Propaganda.

[4] Kosuke Koyama: *Three Mile an Hour God* (SCM [1987]).

[5] *'Walk for the World' Briefing Paper* – for further background information contact: World Development Movement, Bedford Chambers, Covent Garden, London, WC2E 8HA.

Part V
Friendship

Christian Relationships with People of Other Faiths

MARTIN H. F. FORWARD, M.A., M.Litt.
Leicester

I WENT for a first visit to an elderly woman who lived with her ailing husband. I was nonplussed by her comment when she opened the door: 'Oh, I thought you were one of them. *You* can come in.' I discovered that *them* were Hindus who occupied all but four of the hundred or so houses on her road. She drew me into the kitchen where she was preparing dinner: 'They've taken over this place. They don't speak English. All my friends have left the area. I'm alone here, a stranger in my place of birth. I can't get out, except occasionally to the shops, because of my husband's illness. I don't even go to church now.' Her final angry comment: 'Their food smells dreadful. It makes me sick.' This observation carried no weight with me, who felt very queazy sitting near a stove on which, in traditional English fashion, cabbage had been boiling for rather longer than was good for it or for my sense of smell.

It's easy to mock. It's easy to be appalled by the racism of this white, Christian Englishwoman. But perhaps the most helpful response is just to listen to the pain of a bereavement process. Within the last thirty years, the landscape of her youth and early middle-age has changed around her. Large numbers of Indian Hindus displaced her friends, transformed the shops and cinemas she was accustomed to. Her securities were gone, and she had reached a stage in her life when she needed friends, who were elsewhere, and who were replaced by people of very different appearance and habits. Sometimes racism must be instantly condemned, but in this kind of situation, when no particular person has to bear the brunt of blinkered and tribal prejudices, perhaps it is best to listen, to say nothing, to get to know the person and have them like and trust

215

you, waiting a better day for something to be said or done to heal their loss in a more constructive way than cross-cultural abuse and ostrich-like isolation.

Many members of inner-city congregations have, like this woman's friends, left the area. Again, instant judgments are unwise. Some may have left because of, in the words of one man to me, 'the jungle-bunnies next door', a dreadful phrase which I felt I must challenge him about. But others wished to improve their standard of living, and when their income permitted a move, they chose the leafy suburbs, a semi- with a garden rather than a terraced house with an outside toilet. Some come back, out of nostalgia, to worship in the area they left, and couldn't care less about the new makeup of the environs of the church, except perhaps to regret it. But others come back, believing that God has things for the church to do and say in a multifaith community, and believe and hope that they can play their part in his purpose. Some pastors arrive in a church set in a multifaith area, prepared to chivvy and harangue their congregation, assuming that they are introverts and crypto-racists in need of enlightenment. They may discover people who at work and home have every day to cross boundaries of colour, culture, religion and prejudice, and do so, quietly, lovingly, with some setbacks but, after some time, with a wealth of experience from which the pastor can learn.

Those who have crossed the boundaries and have realized that such boundaries are more apparent than real can, by telling their stories, help others trapped by their sense of bereavement into racism and isolation.

Another elderly white woman in my congregation also lived on a road largely inhabited by Hindus. She, too, nursed a sick husband. For a while, she avoided contact with her Hindu neighbours because she did not know what to say to them, and was a little afraid of their very obvious differences from her and her way of life. Suddenly her husband took a turn for the worse, and had to go into hospital for the last weeks of his life. She had no transport, and had to make the journey three times a day by bus. Her Hindu neighbours noticed this. Their little boy came round and told the woman that his dad would take her that night. Came the time, and the boy scrambled into the car with his dad and the woman to act as interpreter for them. Every day he took her. The boy made verbal communication possible, but the woman was surprised how far a smile and a laugh could go in bringing people together. Early one morning, she was phoned to be told that her husband had died. She sat by the fire, icy cold, unable to feel or do anything. The boy, on holiday from school, noticed that she didn't leave the house at the usual time to go shopping. He went next door, let himself in, went up to her and, saying nothing, put his arms around her. Then she began to weep. After a while, he went and fetched his mum, who went into the kitchen and made the woman a cup of tea and an omelette. The woman had no children. Her neighbours helped her sort out the funeral arrangements, and attended the service. She and they became fast friends. She was invited to family weddings and to their religious celebrations. But most of all, she rejoiced that the little boy called her, granny.

It is a pastor's job in a multifaith area, to encourage his people to share their stories with one another. And when he visits his people, he may discover that many of them work alongside or among people of other faiths as teachers, police officers, factory workers, shop assistants or on the staff of the local hospital. Just think what experiences can be shared as stories from such people. Lent meetings or study-groups could hear and ponder tales of living and working interfaith.

What are the ways for a pastor to make relationships with people of other faiths? It is very much worth a visit to the local police station, where the bobby on the beat might know Urdu or some other helpful language, and be willing to arrange introductions and give his impressions of the neighbourhood he serves. Local interfaith groups or Councils of Faiths can be disappointingly insipid and maiden-auntish in their endeavours not to raise issues that can offend (though the best of them, for example, Concord in Leeds and the Wolverhampton Inter-Faith Group, are beyond praise for the integrity of their achievements), but all of them are occasions to meet people of different religions. Take a diary with you, and plan a visit to a local mosque or temple as soon as you can. You will probably find that face to face encounter over a number of visits leads to a mutual honesty which, not unnaturally, individuals are not apt to display at public meetings.

Such honesty can be devastating. A Christian pastor often goes to a multifaith area with a burning conviction to witness to his Lord. Few Christians would deny the importance of such witness. But conversations with a friend from another faith, who was maybe born in another country, will reveal his repugnance of the secularism of modern Britain and his fears that his children will be contaminated by it. (Hence one of the reasons for the demands by some Muslims for separate schools for their children.) One friend put it to me: 'You sent missionaries to our country, and still do, to convert us. Yet few Christians go to church here, and many more do not know their faith. With what integrity do you preach to us?' That there is a measure of truth in such a comment can hardly be denied.

A Christian pastor may also wish to share in community service with his friend of another faith. Here again, that friend may be devastatingly frank: 'We come to this country and you Christians want to be kind to us. We were condescended to in the days of empire. In the modern world, you may keep your good works.' Or, as another Muslim friend said: 'Why is it that your boards of social responsibility think they are best fitted to relate to us? Is this not racism, the assumption that we exist to be helped. We are not like alcohol or drugs. It is not even our difference of colour that most separates us. It is our view of God upon which we differ.' A Hindu or Sikh would take issue with this Muslim over how much our view of God divides us, but not I think over the central issue that belief in God and its consequences in our lives are central to good and honest relationships between people of different faiths. Good community relations depend upon that.

Indeed, the language of Muslims, Hindus and Sikhs is shot through with references to the Almighty; God is acknowledged as a support in daily living, and it is not considered embarrassing or inappropriate to mention him constantly. I can testify to the fact that for a reserved Englishman, conversation with friends of another faith can be immensely liberating, enabling me to speak openly and sincerely about the deepest things of life with those who believe, but differently from me. Would that I could do so with some of my Christian friends. The English language has become irredeemably secularized: God be with you is bastardized as goodbye. At least with my friends of another faith I have been able to mention God, as they do, when we meet and when we part. They are shocked, and I have become so, that many nominal Christians only use God's name in meaningless swearing. Of course, when God is mentioned all the time, he can be invoked as an excuse: I think of the Muslim drug addict who announced that he would give up heroin, if God wills, thereby putting sole responsibility upon God for his cure. Nevertheless, the point remains that if nominal or practising Christians think that relationships can be built between them and people of other faiths on a basis which ignores the religious dimension of everyday living, we shall usually be proved wrong, often even when meeting the younger generation of Muslims, Hindus and Sikhs.

This means that Christians must put their own house in order in terms of belief and practice. There is a lot to be said for spending a year or two running weeknight courses on the essentials of Christian faith for the benefit of churchgoers, who often have the most cursory knowledge of such things. Only thereafter should the minister embark with them on a pilgrimage to mosque, temple and gurdwara, or encourage them to examine Sufism or explore yoga. There are exceptions to every rule. Some Christians, learning from another's faith, are driven to seek a deeper understanding of their own. The point is that to meet another kind of believer involves examining one's own beliefs, unless such meeting is a sport or a diversion. (For a certain sort of person it is. 'Interfaith' is the latest craze, sandwiched between eurythmics and vegan cookery. This article is not written for such people, but one must recognize that they exist, and not be too impressed by their flattery and their desire for your attention.)

A minister whose church is set in a multifaith area will often find the deepest and most agonizing theological questions raised in the rites of passage. Here again, stories might illuminate the issues.

A woman from a suburban church phones me. She once fostered a girl who wants her baby christened. There are problems, but the girl ought to explain them. Would I see her? Off I go. The girl is the child of a white woman, who was a drunk and neglected her, and a Muslim father, who left her mum long ago. The girl was sent to a variety of homes and foster parents. At fifteen she felt able to branch out on her own. She turned to glue-sniffing, lived with her Jewish boyfriend, and had his baby. She determined to be a better mother than hers had been. She gave up glue-sniffing, and settled into motherhood. The baby was a cot death victim. She went to pieces for a while, thinking that God hated her, and was distraught because, shortly before the baby's death, the vicar had refused to baptize him. She became pregnant again, her new baby was born, she contacted a former foster-mother to see if any pastor would christen her child. Enter me. In her, subliminal Christianity and Islam urged her to do something to thank God for his birth, or perhaps simply to avert the divine wrath, the evil eye. Her nominally Jewish boyfriend felt something should be done. Neither of them had a clue about the teachings of any religion, but it was clear that to refuse her would be one more rejection in her life. I did the baptism, knowing that her foster-mother would be a godparent to the child, and making sure that members of the church would keep in touch with her. Did I do right? What else could I have done? These are real and not rhetorical questions to be faced.

A Caribbean Methodist woman had lived with her black rastafarian boyfriend for five years, and had three children by him. She was a regular attender at my church. Her parents had disowned her for marrying a rasta, but grand-children had helped to change the rift into an uneasy tolerance of the situation. Now they wanted to get married, and her parents were very pleased. The man was apparently agreeable to getting married in church. I went to interview them. He could not have been more truculent or macho. Exasperated, I told him that as he wasn't doing me a favour but rather the opposite, he could go take a nosedive. The gist of his reply was that we whities were arrogant, down-putting, untrustworthy, so no wonder we were to be approached like a rattlesnake, with caution. We wouldn't even accept his rum. So I did, and stayed, and we organized the wedding which was a happy and reconciling affair. Should the wedding have happened or not? Again, a real question is here.

A lapsed Catholic woman and her Muslim boyfriend from Iran came to ask me to marry them. Her priest couldn't and wouldn't. Would I? They were obviously in love. But can love, on her side, cope with a return to Iran, involvement in his extended family with its different roles for men and women? If she thought she could cope, would she want such a life for any daughter they might have? What did her parents think? The couple wanted to be married in a church. The man insisted that she and their children could remain Christian. But was that option really open to them if they returned to his family? She had no experience at all of Muslim extended families, but was sure that love, which she seemed to me to confuse with romance (Mills and Boon have a lot to answer for), conquers all. I felt unable to agree to their request. Was I right, I ask myself? And what when a young Christian woman in the congregation asks if she should keep seeing her Muslim boyfriend, of whom she is becoming very fond? Which will be harder, she asks, to face the future without him, or to face together what a future with him implies in terms of religious differences and taking on board a set of in-laws whose expectations seem fearful?

A Hindu friend phones me to ask me to come and pray by the bedside of his dying mother. I go. How do I pray aloud with integrity? On the walls of her bedroom are pictures of Jesus, but also of Rama and Sita, Ganesh and Hanuman. Jesus is revered, but differently understood from Christian devotion. An apparent link between us is in fact a deep divide, if we discuss things openly and honestly. In fact, it's easy to know what to do. These are my friends, God loves them as he loves me, and I can hold the old lady's hand and pray for peace and forgiveness and mercy as she slips away from life.

Issues that are raised by such stories should be shared with members of the church. They can support you with their prayers. They can show the love of the church by follow up visits to people of other faiths who have sought help. Being involved in the pastor's activities can help them to come to terms with the complex theological issues involved in interfaith relationships.

Sometimes the worshipping congregation is involved, willy-nilly, in such issues, and it would have been useful if at least some of them were helping the minister in his relationships with people of other faiths. Two examples may make the point.

A Sikh, faithful in attendance at his gurdwara, comes with his Christian friend to morning worship, which happens to be a service of Holy Communion. He comes up to receive the bread and wine. He has heard the minister say that this is a sacrament for those who love the Lord Jesus, and certainly the Sikh tradition venerates Jesus, though not as Christians do. Heads turn, with some disapproving looks and much curiosity to see what the Methodist minister will do.

So what should he do? According to John Wesley, the Lord's Supper is a converting ordinance. This could be taken to mean that it is not just for the Christian faithful, but a sign which can bring all its participants into a deeper awareness of the grace of God. Granted that Wesley would never have dreamed that a Sikh might draw near for his comfort to this Christian rite, can his theological insight be extended to cover this situation, not as a salve to the minister's conscience but as a proper recognition of the power of this holy mystery to lay bare the nature of God to those who choose to share it?

Moreover, relationships matter. Should the minister courteously refuse to give a Sikh bread and wine, and would this be seen as a snub? One remembers that in the gurdwara, holy food is distributed to all who come, and the Sikh's expectation would therefore be that he was welcome to participate fully in the church's meal. What must the pastor do in this situation to respect the intention of the eucharist and to love his neighbour?

The second story is about the church's carol service, run by the Women's Fellowship on a weeknight evening. Members of the local Hindu temple are invited to come. It is a fully Christian service, with carols, prayers, bible readings, and a short sermon. After the service, tea and vegetarian mince pies (made with vegetable and not beef suet) are served, and greetings of the season exchanged.

After one such service, an elderly Hindu lady went to the Communion table on which were placed models of the nativity scene. She touched the model of the Christ child, and put that hand to her forehead, bowing in deepest respect. She stayed a few moments in prayer, and then moved away. What is one to make of that act of faith and devotion, which so moved many Christians who saw it? What does God make of it? She would not see Jesus as Christians do. To her, he is one *avatar* (incarnation) among many. She had conformed him to the pattern of her religion, and not seen in him all that Christians believe him to be. Yet in an unobtrusive way, she showed more respect and love that night than some Christians ever do.

No Christian worth his salt would want to ban people of other faiths from church premises or services, despite complex issues involved. Interfaith services are another matter, and are best avoided, if at all possible. Faithful people are not in the business of providing Commonwealth Day with a rather spurious sign of divine approval, nor should they be in the business of making incoming Lord Mayors feel that the whole community honours them. Social gatherings are the place for this sort of affirmation, so long as someone in authority has taken the trouble to digest food laws of the several religions. There is no reason why Lord Mayors should not have a service from their own tradition to which people of other faiths come, reverently observing, and participating as they feel able in good conscience to do.

Occasionally, a pastor is involved in the pain of another community's problems. One story. A Muslim girl comes to a pastor and asks him to tell her about Jesus. 'I believe in God', she says, 'but not my parents' God. They want me to leave school, veil up, and marry a boy of their choice. I want to be a doctor.' What must the pastor do? One sort of witness could be seen as taking advantage of her vulnerability. Instead, he knows of a group of Muslim women who follow a western pattern of life, who support each other and remain, a little uneasily, within the fold of Islam. He puts the girl in touch with them. They can talk to her parents and try to help the family through this crisis. The minister believes that he has sown a seed which will not be without fruit, that he has shown Christian love in his act. Has he obeyed or betrayed the gospel?

These stories illustrate the range of opportunities for the Christian pastor in a multifaith area. There are no easy answers to the situations he gets involved in. This pastor has two concluding observations.

First, theology is central to his enterprise. His relationships, his capacity to help and be helped, depend upon a coherent vision of what God has done in Christ. With such a vision, difficult situations can be analysed, acted within, prayed about and justified. Without it he is a mere do-gooder; in my experience, most do-gooders in multifaith areas seek to do what is easiest, not what is right. What the author's coherent vision is may be implied from this article, but remains to be explicated elsewhere.

The second conviction is that he must take his congregation with him, learn from them, seek their prayerful support and prayerfully support them. That means visiting them and getting to know them. This seems to ask a lot, alongside forging relationships with people of other faiths. But, as many of the stories reveal, most pastors in multifaith areas will not, after certain preliminary courtesies, have to seek relationships with Muslims, Hindus and Sikhs. People of other faiths, firm in it or utterly confused about it, will come to him. Of course, the pastor can decline involvement, and explain that there is such a lot of work to be done within the church: 'isn't there somebody else who can talk with you?' We are, of course, back to theology. God loved the *world* so much that to it he sent his Son. To confine the gospel within the church is certainly to betray it.

Relations with Jews

MARCUS BRAYBROOKE
Box, Wiltshire

CHRISTIAN-JEWISH relations should be of importance to all clergy, whether or not there is a Jewish community nearby. How Christians understand their own faith is bound up with Judaism. The shadow of the Holocaust has raised profound issues about our understanding of human nature and of the ways of God. Israel and the West Bank call for our sympathetic prayers. Together, Jews and Christians are starting to speak about vital social and moral issues.

Deicide

For many centuries, Christians have expressed their faith in opposition to Judaism. Traditionally, it has been taught that the Jews rejected and killed their Messiah and that in punishment God banished them from the Land of Promise. The charge of 'deicide' – that the Jews killed God or the 'Son of God' – has been denounced by the Vatican and all mainline churches. It is untrue historically, morally and theologically. Our Lord was crucified, which was a Roman penalty. The High Priest may have colluded with his death, but not all Jews opposed Jesus. Luke tells us that many lamented and mourned when he was led out to death (Lk 23:27, 49), and, of course, the first disciples were Jews. Morally, it is wrong to blame subsequent generations for what their ancestors are alleged to have done (Mt 27:25). For example, all Germans, especially those born since the Second World War, cannot be blamed for what the Nazis did. Theologically, it is widely recognized that God's covenant with Israel abides and has eternal validity. This is not just because through many centuries of persecution, Jews have remained faithful to the covenant, but primarily because God is a faithful God who keeps his promises.

Probably few clergy would now admit to teaching that the Jews

killed Jesus – but certainly on the Continent before the Second
World War, Jews would lock themselves in their houses on Good
Friday 'for fear of the Christians'. Even so, this false teaching still
lurks in our readings and hymns. I remember a Rabbi complaining
about 'The Lord of the Dance'.

> I danced on the Sabbath.
>   and I cured the lame:
> The holy people
>   said it was a shame.
> They whipped and they stripped
>   and they hung me high,
> And they left me there
>   on a cross to die.

I suppose many in our congregations take 'the holy people' as a
'dig' at the clergy – or as a reference to the high priests – but Jews
will at once think it refers to the 'people of Israel'. The second
verse of 'Lo, he comes with clouds descending' has the words,

> Those who set at nought and sold him,
>   Pierced and nailed him to the Tree,
>   Deeply wailing
> Shall the true Messiah see.

Its use during a televised Advent Carol service led to complaints
from some viewers. Again, once when I was listening to choral
evensong on the radio, the lesson from St John included these
words,'. . . and the Jews sought to kill him' (Jn 7:1). Informed
listeners would know that John used 'the Jews' as a term for 'the
opponents of Jesus', but not all listeners are informed and there was
no comment or introduction.

It is very important in our choice of readings and hymns,
especially during Holy Week, that we do not inadvertently
perpetuate the false charge of deicide. Martin Gilbert begins his
long history of the Holocaust with the words, 'For many centuries,
primitive Christian Europe had regarded the Jew as the "Christ
killer", an enemy and a threat, to be converted and so be 'saved',
or to be killed, to be expelled, or to be put to death with sword
and fire'.[1] The evils of Christian anti-Jewish teaching must be

recognized and eradicated before a new relationship can be developed.

Anti-Judaism

Anti-Judaism is hidden in the way our Lord's teaching is often contrasted with Judaism of his time. There is still widespread misunderstanding of the Law (*Torah*), as a burden, with talk of 'works' righteous-ness'. Judaism needs to be understood in terms of covenant. God, of his mercy, chose Israel to be his people and rescued them from slavery in Egypt. It was an act of pure grace. In response, he gave his people a guide to life, the *Torah*. This was freely accepted as a response to his mercy. Psalm 119 shows the joy of a faithful son of the covenant in obeying God's will. The Christian too wishes to respond to God's love in Christ by obeying his commandment to love one another.

It seems that our Lord in his teaching was close to the Pharisees.[2] They were concerned that all God's people should be holy – not just the Temple priests. They therefore tried to interpret the Law's application to the changing circumstances of daily life. Some of the conflicts between Jesus and the Pharisees reported in the Gospels may reflect later arguments between church and synagogue.

Present day Rabbinic Judaism derives from Pharisaism – so again a proper understanding of Judaism of the first two centuries CE, is important for relations today. It is also important to remember that Rabbinic Judaism was a creative religious development and that living Judaism is not 'Old Testament religion'. (You still find those who think the Jews continue to offer animal sacrifices!) Rabbinic Judaism and Christianity were two distinct creative religious developments growing out of Old Testament belief and practice. Sadly, the parting of the ways became embittered and only now are scholars beginning to untangle the sociological and political factors which need no longer poison relations between the two religions.

The Holocaust

That poison showed its deadly venom in the Holocaust. Christians cannot fully enter into the horror and depth of suffering of the

Shoah, although there are films and novels which help one to do so. Yet they should try to understand the anguish and trauma. The 'Final Solution' was a systematic attempt to eliminate Jews and Jewry, which gives it a unique horror in the chronicle of human cruelty. The easy application of the word to other tragedies leaves Jews uneasy, especially as there are those who insinuate that the Holocaust has been greatly exaggerated to win sympathy for Zionism. Forty years is a short time and as survivors grow old they remember the past more vividly. They fear the world would rather forget. The least we can do for the dead is to remember them. In the USA, a number of churches have an annual Holocaust Remembrance service.[3]

Christians have to confess honestly their share in causing Jewish suffering. Centuries of anti-Jewish teaching provided the seed-bed in which the noxious weed of anti-Semitism could grow. Too few Christians opposed Hitler early enough. Christians need also to be careful in interpreting the tragedy in Christian terms of death and resurrection. This is partly why the setting up of a convent at Auschwitz and the beatification of Edith Stein distressed many Jews. Yet, some Christian and Jewish thinkers are together beginning to talk about the lessons to be learned, especially in our understanding of human nature and how we speak of God's love in a world where such evils occur.

Conversion
Recent memories, but also the long history of Christian persecution of and pressure upon Jews, demands that Christians show great sensitivity in any approach to Jews. Many suspect that all Christians really want to convert them and fear that dialogue is a change of tactic rather than a change of heart. To some Jews, Christians seem bent on the spiritual destruction of Judaism, which would be even worse than the crimes of Hitler and his associates. Certainly much effort and money (often from the USA) is still devoted towards missions to Jews, even if mainline churches have become more circumspect. All forms of pressure, deceit or 'targeting' are to be deplored. Jewish students may feel lonely and isolated. An invitation to a '*kosher* lunch' looks attractive, but if it turns out to have been

organized by the Christian Union, they may feel 'tricked'. A 'Prayer for Israel' meeting may create misunderstanding, if the Christian nature of the organization is not made clear on the notices. To stand outside a synagogue giving out tracts, or to put up a big placard on a church which happens to face a synagogue with the words, 'Jesus said, "No one cometh unto the Father but through me" ' confirms Jewish suspicions about Christian intentions. The Council of Christians and Jews, which is committed to dialogue and understanding, has had to make clear that it is not a missionary organization.

Those who believe they are called to engage in mission towards Jews need to be very sensitive in their methods and aware of how their behaviour may be interpreted. A growing number of Christians, however, who affirm that God's covenant with Israel is still valid, believe mission is inappropriate. This relates to the widespread debate about the relation of Christianity to other religions.[4]

Yet, the church is committed to witness. One rabbi said to me, 'I know your religious duty is to convert me and my religious duty is not to be converted.' After that, we had a happy drive for a couple of hours talking deeply about religious matters. In dialogue groups where there is deep trust it is natural to speak of one's faith in Christ (witness), and to listen to a Jew speak of his faith. A Christian is not asked to hide his or her belief, but in dialogue there must be trust and openness and no hidden agenda. Organized mission to the Jews throws in question that trust and threatens dialogue and the search for understanding.

Some individuals do change their religion (and this happens both ways). This possibility should be respected and those who convert should be ministered to. Sadly Jewish Christians sometimes feel unwelcome in dialogue groups.

Israel

To many Jews after the Holocaust, Israel is their only hope of security. Those who come close to Jews, should accept that commitment to Israel is part of Jewish self-understanding today, although many Jews will be highly critical of the actions of particular Israeli governments. The civilized world was unable to protect Jews from the onslaughts of Hitler. They doubt whether it would protect them if the Arab nations gained military superiority. Hence Israeli vigilance and daring, which has won admiration when used against foreign attacks, but condemnation when used against Palestinians in Lebanon, Gaza and the West Bank. The plight of the Palestinian refugees is indeed miserable. The failure of Arab nations, other than Egypt, to negotiate with Israel and to reach a peace agreement prolongs their sufferings and causes a cancer in Israel's democracy.

Christian attitudes to Israel are very varied. Some, with a literalist interpretation of biblical prophecies, identify very strongly with Israel, whilst others who wish to speak for the afflicted identify strongly with the Palestinians. Most local born Christians are Arabs and expect Christians in other parts of the world to support them. Visitors need to listen and to avoid snap answers. The plight of the Palestinians arouses the visitor's sympathies, but it is a mistake to apportion blame without enough knowledge of the complex and tragic history. The great need is to help all who live in the area to escape the shackles of bitter memories and to begin to listen to others. Pilgrims too need to listen and should avoid reinforcing the bitterness of those who speak to them. There are Jews, Muslims and Christians also working for peace and reconciliation, for example at Neve Shalom, who need support and prayer. It is good if pilgrim groups can find time to meet with as wide a variety of the people who live in the Land as possible.

Moral Issues
The contribution of the Jewish community to debate about moral issues was recognized recently with the creation of the Chief Rabbi as a life peer. Last autumn, he was awarded a Lambeth degree by the Archbishop of Canterbury. He has been keen that Christians and Jews should not only understand each other, but speak together out of their shared ethical tradition. In December 1986, the Joint Presidents of the Council of Christians and Jews, who are the Archbishop of Canterbury, the Moderator of the General Assembly of the Church of Scotland, the Cardinal Archbishop of

Westminster, the Moderator of the Free Church Federal Council and the Chief Rabbi, met for the first time to discuss moral issues, such as *Faith in the City*, Aids or the plight of believers in the Soviet Union. This has now become an annual occasion. The Anglican-Jewish consultation last spring also concentrated on *Faith in the City* and the moral issues involved in the spread of Aids. The agreed statement stressed the need for the two communities to speak and act together on social and moral issues.

On many issues, there are sharp disagreements within the Jewish community, as in the churches, especially between Orthodox Jews and Reform and Liberal Jews. On other issues, such as *Shechita*, Christians may feel a clash of principles. They may wonder whether the Jewish method of slaughter of animals does cause unnecessary pain, but they may also be concerned to uphold liberty of religious belief and practice. Even so, Jews and Christians may come closer together by focusing on common problems that face them as members of society, than by discussing the past difficulties between members of the two religions. On these common problems, Jews and Christians are starting to talk especially with Muslims, but also, through the Interfaith Network, with members of all other religious communities in Britain.

Local Contacts

Recent developments are relevant to church members wherever they live, but if there is a Jewish community nearby, they are of particular importance. In many areas there are local Councils of Christians and Jews, through which Christians can meet Jews as people on a friendly basis, learn about their religion and explain their own and begin to talk about the many vital issues in Christian-Jewish dialogue. Elsewhere, Christians could take the initiative in forming a local Council of Christians and Jews.

Local synagogues are usually very hospitable in welcoming groups from churches and schools to show them round the building. Whilst visitors are welcome to attend services, unless they understand Hebrew, they may find them difficult to follow, even though the prayer book provides an English translation. A demonstration *seder*, the ritual Jews observe in their homes at

Passover, is always fascinating. It gives Christians a vivid feel for Judaism, but it also helps them understand more about the origins of the Communion service. Attempts to 'Christianize' a *seder* are, I think, likely to be confusing, as it may mask the distinctiveness of the two faiths.

Because the Jewish community in Great Britain is small (about 350,000) and declining numerically, it is very sensitive about those who 'marry out'. Some clergy are willing to bless a 'mixed marriage', but rabbis will be reluctant to do so (although occasionally this happens in the USA).

Orthodox rabbis are also unlikely to attend an inter-religious service, say, during the Week of Prayer for World Peace. It is sensible to consult privately about what is possible before sending a public invitation. Reform and Liberal Jews, however, are active in interfaith organizations.

Even if there is not a local Jewish community, there are opportunities to engage in dialogue through courses and conferences, arranged by the Council of Christians and Jews, by the Centre for the Study of Judaism and Christian-Jewish relations at Selly Oak or at Ammerdown or elsewhere. Recently, nearly 130 theological College students, from a wide variety of denominations (the largest Christian ecumenical event for theological college students!) spent a weekend in Jewish homes in North London, attending a course at Leo Baeck Rabbinical College.

Dialogue happens at many levels. There are international and scholarly gatherings, conversations between Christian and Jewish leaders, local conferences and meetings. They are breaking down barriers of prejudice and suspicion and allowing people to meet. From the discussion, Christians and Jews are finding old ideas about each other challenged and their own faith quickened and renewed. They are beginning to speak together to society on ethical matters. The fascination and stimulation of such dialogue, however, can only be appreciated by taking part in it. It is demanding but richly rewarding in new friendships and a deeper appreciation of the faithfulness of God.

A Message of Hope
If, indeed, after two thousand years of hostility, Jews and Christians

are being reconciled, they are creating something precious to share with society and the world, in which there are many deep and bitter divisions. 'Dialogue', the Pope told representatives of the International Council of Christians and Jews, 'is a modest, but in the end, effective way to peace'. If Christians and Jews can teach to others what they are learning together, they have a message of hope which is relevant to all.

---

[1] Martin Gilbert: *The Holocaust* (Weidenfeld & Nicholson), 1.
[2] See E. P. Sanders: *Jesus and Judaism* (SCM Press).
[3] M. Littell, ed: *Liturgies on the Holocaust* (The Edwin Mellen Press).
[4] John T. Pawlikowski: *What are they saying about Christian-Jewish relations?* (Paulist Press); Alan Race: *Christians and Religious Pluralism* (SCM Press).

Further information about bibliographies, courses, etc. is available from the Council of Christians and Jews, 1, Dennington Park Road, London NW6 1AX.

Through Another's Eyes: A Christian vision of God in a world of religions

MARTIN H. F. FORWARD, M.A., M.LITT.
Leicester

IT has been my privilege and pleasure to have edited a recent book containing many Christians' experiences of living in a multi-faith society. So many contributors to it have found relationships with people of another religion to be a transforming experience.[1]

My life, too, has been immeasurably blessed and shaped by friendships across the boundaries of religion. When I pause to reflect upon how and why I have become a student of world religions, secretary of the Methodist Church's National Committee for Relations with People of Other Faiths, and the friend of men and women from many faiths and none, I thank God above all for my father, and his friendship with an Indian soldier. They worked together in Aden in the 1940s. Twenty years later, my father was again working in Aden, and he renewed his old friendship. As a result, my family went to dinner at the house of – let us call him – Ali.

I shall never forget that evening, although I was only ten years old, and it was over a quarter of a century ago. That night, my mother's plain and wholesome English cooking gave way to exotic rice, spiced meat and lentils. After it, I burped noisily, and my mother rebuked me. But Ali told her not to: 'You see, to our way of thinking he has shown pleasure in the food he has eaten.' The female members of his family served us but ate separately and later, and they wore beautiful clothes, which I later knew to be *shalwar qamees*. Most moving and wondrous of all, at one point in the evening, quite unselfconsciously, Ali excused himself, went to another part of the room, and said his prayers.

What was I to make of that evening? I could, I suppose, have

235

ignored it and forgotten it. I could have thought how quaint it was, in the condescending manner of so many Britons abroad. I could have been shocked by heathenish practices.

I was too young, I suppose, for these responses, or for any immediate response. Instead, what happened was that I remembered the night's events, and in later years, grew increasingly to wonder what made a person like Ali tick. Curiosity, and not a desire to pass judgment, mastered me.

Years passed. I went to live and work in India, where I made Hindu and Muslim friends, some of whom became to me as dear as if they were my family. Because I loved them, and they me, we tried to see the deep things of life from the other's point of view, through another's eyes.

These personal reminiscences are recorded because of the editor's request that I should describe my 'coherent vision' of God, as I rather generously described it in chapter 22. My Christian vision of God in a world of religions arises out of personal involvement with people of other faith. Sharing another's friendship and love, being involved in their living and sometimes their dying, is very different from taking a detached view of inter-faith relations (by and large, of course, people have relations, faiths don't). The plain fact is that many books about other faiths, including some influential ones, read like worthy masters or doctoral theses. They do not betray the anguish and joy of involvement. This is odd, because the Christian good news is about God involving himself in our living and dying. If Jesus was amazed by, perhaps even willing to learn from, the faith of a Syro-Phoenician woman and a soldier of an occupying power (Mk 7:21-28; Mt 15:21-28; Mt 8:5-13; Lk 7:1-10), we too should be open to what God is saying to us through the faith of others.

But before recounting what he is telling us, let us clear the decks of what he is *not* telling us.

God is not telling us that all religions are the same. Clearly, they are not. Buddhism and Christianity are very different responses to the mystery of life.[2] To be fair, most people who insist to me that all religions are the same, really seem to be meaning that all are acceptable routes to the divine presence. But this is to claim too much. As Professor Bowker puts it: '. . . perhaps all religions are different roads leading to the same truth. That may be so, but we cannot be sure of it. All roads do not necessarily lead to London simply because they are roads. Some lead to more exciting destinations like Wolverhampton, Newcastle and Timbuctoo. What this means is that religions are not necessarily or automatically true, simply because they are religions. If it *is* possible to be religiously right, it must also be possible to be religiously wrong. This means that there *are* issues of truth and choice in the religious exploration.'[3] As a matter of fact, the widely used comparison of religions to ways that all lead to the same destination is very arrogant. Who has seen journey's end in advance, so as to be able to map it out for us less fortunate pilgrims? To be sure, it is possible to claim, with some degree of credibility, that a person's commitment, by faith, to such virtues as love, justice and peace, give him or her 'intimations of immortality', the *same* immortality, but this claim is not best proved by spiritual map-reading. (Another story often told is that of the King of Benares, who caused blind men to touch different parts of the same elephant. They totally failed to describe what it was. One thought he was touching a rope, another a tree trunk, and so on. Who is playing the role of the king, all-seeing and all-knowing? And what a nasty man he is, to play such a cruel joke. This story is as good an example I know of that sneering condescension which some mistake for tolerance.)

Of course, the description of religions as ways to God or transcendent otherness is meant to affirm the presence of God outside one's own faith system. I share that affirmation. However, I want also to allow for the fact of the 'religiously wrong'. I do not mean *just* that religious people interpret their heritage in ways that are often, to say the least, unhelpful. This is undoubtedly true, as is witnessed by, for example, Christians in Ireland and the Lebanon; and by Sikhs in the Punjab; and so on. Rather, I want to make the more fundamental point that all people will find that their religion occasionally contradicts important tenets of another faith. For, example, note Rabbi Michael Hilton's and Fr Gordian Marshall's observations on forgiveness as an issue between Christians and Jews: 'The Gospel narratives are profound in the link they draw between healing and freedom from a sense of sin. The rabbinic analysis of the kind of attitudes which block the path back to God is also profound. Yet there is a world of difference between them. Judaism, in its emphasis that forgiveness comes from God, does not permit people to forgive on behalf of others who have been wronged: Christianity explicitly and clearly has given men that function. These are different perspectives which we must understand, because they cannot be harmonized.'[4] These are frank and truthful words, unclouded by sentimentality. It seems very important to me that the two authors can be honest with each other and to their audience. Friendship can cope with, may indeed be enriched by, differences, even agonizing and fundamental ones. There is no need to resort to pretended similarities or points of convergence.

God does not seem to be telling us something very different, namely that all other religious systems than Christianity are false, misguided at best, the work of the devil at worst. Simple honesty compels the Christian to admit that the church has sometimes done diabolical things; nor, examining its record in the modern world, does it nowadays look like a totally redeemed and redeeming institution. But, putting that on one side, what are the reasons why Christians say that other religions have got it wrong? Appeal is often made to the scriptures. However, the selective use of texts to buttress Christianity's claim to a monopoly on truth, does not convince many people of goodwill. Any Christian who has told a Muslim that Jesus is the only way, will have heard the retort that God will not accept of a person anything other than Islam. Each party to this debate has to come to terms with why the other cannot see what is plain to him: that his scripture is true, and the other's false. As a matter of fact, many scriptures, including the New Testament and the Qur'an, contain a variety of attitudes about true and false faith, (e.g. Jn 14:6 and 1:9; Qur'an 3:85 and 2:62).

Another kind of reference to the falsehood of other faiths, points to their supposed grievous shortcomings as vehicles of God's revelation. In particular, it is often said that all religions other than Christianity are human strivings after God, and that their members therefore have no adequate understanding of grace. A partial exception to this rule is sometimes made for Judaism and Islam, the semitic religions over against the Indian ones. (This common distinction, sometimes regarded as between prophetic and mystical religions, is utterly unhelpful, and more or less meaningless. To be sure, Jews, Christians, and Muslims 'possess' Adam, Abraham, Moses, even Jesus, but what they make of them is very different. If one has a christology which is universal in scope, as I suggest that one should, then there is no reason, why Hindus, Sikhs, and the rest should not believe and live in ways that we can recognize as, in some measure, related to Christian believing and living.) Let this claim be answered by the Christian Klaus Klostermaier's conversation with the Hindu Gopalji:

> 'Gopalji', I asked. 'Is it not presumptuous to choose one's own Ishtadevata, the God one adores?'
>
> 'It is not we who choose our God, it is God who chooses us,' he replied. 'It is in his power to attract or repel us, to let us do good or evil. We cannot do anything on our own . . .'[5]

It is easy to see why Christians think this way. They wish to affirm the truth *they* know. But this need not, indeed must not, restrict the sway of God's truth. The world can do without that sort of tribalism which easily leads to the view of, 'My religion, right or wrong'. Whence truth, in Ireland and the Lebanon? Moreover, the view that other religions are total darkness arises out of ignorance of them. Thomas Thangaraj, a distinguished South Indian theologian, once commented on the lack of knowledge of his Christian college students about Hinduism and Hindus:

> Yes, the villages they come from are Christian villages, or if they come from the town, they will come from the Christian streets. I myself grew up in a street called Christian Street! Most of the students have never really met a Hindu, as for example in my own case. A Hindu never came to our house. It was only when I myself was at Serampore [as a theological college student] that I met Hindus and had my own horizons widened.[6]

Indeed, it has to be said that many missionaries have spent years abroad, learning languages, and studying other religions at great depth, but have learned nothing important about the *faith* of other people. They have not met people at the level of understanding that controls and sustains their living and their dying. They have come to judgments learned in an alien culture, before they have exercised curiosity, or indeed compassion. They have not looked through another's eyes. And because God has seen human beings through the eyes of Jesus, they have misunderstood something at the heart of their own faith. It is important that Christians living in today's multi-Faith Britain do not relive the mistakes of past Christians, however well-known, however well-intentioned, however godly and goodly some of their achievements.

(Pause for a moment to reflect that there are *other* things God is *not* telling us about religions, but space prevents elaboration. However, beware the view, widespread among young Westerners ten or twenty years ago, that Christianity is wrong, and anything east of Suez right. Such people should read Gita Mahta's *Karma Cola* (Fontana [1981]), sub-titled 'Marketing the Mystic East'. The book is very funny indeed, and rather worrying.)

The decks also need to be cleared of the many works which have arisen out of the recent overly-influential exclusivist, inclusivist, pluralist debate.[7] On this view, Christians can either be exclusivists, holding other religions to be false; inclusivists, holding other religions to contain enough truth, by the light of Christ (or Christians), to be acceptable to God; or pluralists, readily acknowledging other religions as legitimate and autonomous vehicles of salvation. It is important to note the centrality of salvation to this debate. I used to argue that I found the debate unhelpful because, if, for the sake of argument, I accepted its categories (which I don't) my meeting with people of other faith led me, over some issues, to be an exclusivist, over others, an inclusivist, and in yet other issues, a pluralist. I now see that the chief point of issue, not always as clearly targeted as its champions should aim at, is whether all religions save. This question highlights why I find the debate academic and narcissistic. Most of the proponents of this debate would call themselves pluralists. Yet really they are inclusivists, seeing another's religion through their own eyes, judging it according to Christian categories. To be sure, salvation is a concept known to, for example, Hindus and Muslims, but they handle it very differently from each other and from Christians. Moreover, in parts of the Christian tradition, salvation has been narrowed in its scope. It has also been over-worked: there are other Christian categories. God is saviour, but he is also king, and lord and father, and shepherd, and much more besides. Christians need to look afresh at what salvation means to and for them, before using it, in one Christian sense, as the controlling image by which to understand the religion of others.

(Another pause here, to ask whether it makes much sense to talk of religions at all, or at least, to compare them. The great Canadian scholar Wilfred Cantwell Smith persuaded most students of world religions to proceed with care in this area. His position, first elaborated in 1962 in *The Meaning and End of Religion* (SPCK [1978 edn]), is that if we are to understand religious traditions, we should cease to reify them. The term 'religion' encourages this reifying, so it should be dropped. Chs 6 and 7 focus on 'cumulative tradition' and 'faith' as his way of understanding the historical religious process. Smith *must* be read; he provides rich intellectual fare for his readers. But his works do rather portray (betray?) him as a Western, Protestant Christian, persuaded, at bottom, that religion/faith is a *personal* matter.[8] As for myself I admire, at a distance, and think that one can and must use the word religion; and that the faith of (let us say) a Muslim depends upon the faith of Islam.)

The retort might be, do we not necessarily look at other religions through our own eyes, judging them by our own deeply held convictions?

Certainly, truly religious people have deep convictions. We may look through another's eyes but, to stretch the metaphor, on our own ground. Yet that view might make us shift our position, at least a little! Moreover, there is another, more important point. I know more *about* Islam than most Muslims, but of course a Muslim will know Islam *experientially* as I never will. Nevertheless, my knowledge about Islam ought to prevent me from 'Christianizing' Islamic concepts and Muslims' beliefs, unless I know what I am doing. My impression is that too many Christian writers about God in a world of many faiths don't know what they are doing. They assume a common framework of desire and expectation and reward. Religious experience and aspiration is more subtle, less to be pigeon-holed, than such an assumption permits. Actually, if one knows what one is doing, 'Christianizing' (perhaps 'Christ-ing') the faith of others is a fruitful and honourable procedure. Kenneth Cragg is the supreme Christian practitioner of this. In his long and distinguished ministry he has wrestled with asking, indeed demanding of Muslims, 'What think ye of the Christ?'[9] He can be accused of reading out of the Qur'an what no Muslim, not even its author, believes to be there. But at least he has shown that discussion between Christians and Muslims need not plough the arid fields of past controversy in the same old ways. Because he knows what Muslims affirm and why, he is able to suggest other responses they could make.

Let us pause for a moment to see where we have come to. I have discussed what, for me, are inadequate visions of God in a world of religions. In the course of describing these, I have at least hinted at things I hold to be true. Let me affirm these. It is in meeting people of other faith that possibilities of understanding arise. My encounter with Ali, brief as it was, led me to seek deeper relationships with people whose religion and culture are very different from my own. Such meetings are, in a multi-faith context, a necessary vocation for those whose religion is incarnational. There is both truth and falsehood in the faith of others, as there is in one's own religious practice. Christians have to wrestle with the fact that whilst gospel values are lived out by others, they are not recognized as related to what God has done in Christ. There are matters of profound disagreement, between Christians and others. We may have to make judgment about another's faith but, setting on one side the question of whether we are able to do so as those who really live out our faith, curiosity and compassion ought to precede judgment; and judgment should be informed by knowledge.

How do I, as a Christian, make sense of these several affirmations? To put it another way, can they offer a coherent vision of God in a world of religions?

Like Kenneth Cragg, I believe Jesus Christ to be at the heart of a truly Christian vision of God. That is tautological, but needs emphasizing. From Bishop Cragg, I have learned to ask myself how other religions can be revelatory of the God whom I have seen in and through the Lord Jesus. I have tried also to know what my friends of other faiths believe, and not to misrepresent that belief, but to suggest other ways in which their faith and mine might speak to them of God, who is *Abba*, Father.

Let us take the case of Islam. On the face of things, speaking of God to a Muslim leads nowhere constructive, if Jesus is mentioned. Muslims find accounts of Jesus in the Qur'an, but there, although he is called the Messiah, that title is emptied of any properly Christian meaning. It is denied that he is the Son of God, and the doctrine of the Trinity is both misunderstood and denied.[10] Yet despite those very great differences. Christians witnessing among Muslims have usually done so by telling the story of Jesus. I wonder whether this is the best way forward. I have tried a different approach. The *logos* passage of John's gospel,[11] Pauline and deutero-Pauline passages about the cosmic Christ, and material from the letter to the Hebrews point to a vision of God who is for all people, everywhere, and at all times, as he was in Jesus. I do not have the space here to describe the implications of these passages for constructing an adequate Christian theology for a multi-faith society. Suffice it to record that, when I speak to a Muslim of God, I feel able, at the start of such conversations, not to mention Jesus at all, so long as what I say about God is consistent with who Jesus revealed him to be. So, Muslims and I can discuss a God who forgives, is merciful, judges, is gracious, without, at first, mentioning Jesus. Of course, at some point, Jesus must be mentioned, because he is the one who focuses and embodies and enriches my knowledge of such attributes of God. Equally, Muslim friends, knowing that I am a Christian, will expect me to talk of Jesus, when I am ready to do so. Because they are friends, they will let me take my time and choose my moment to speak of deepest things (a courtesy I try to return; talking of God requires the sensitiveness of friendship; it is not usually best served by saying too much, too soon, to strangers). When I get to the point of talking about Jesus, I do not feel the need to talk about divinity and trinity. If you have been brought up, as a Muslim, to abhor Christian identifications of Jesus with God, patient Christian explanation is not always going to break down your long believed assumptions. It is often best for the Christian to try another way. The Qur'an has many passages which refer to signs (*ayats*) in the world, which confirm and sustain belief.[12] So I have asked Muslims to try to see Jesus as such a sign for Christians; indeed, as the *crucial* sign; and I have asked whether this description of him makes any sense to them and for them.

Of course, more traditional forms of witness *do* work; but not for everyone. The question is whether Christians have a theology adequate enough and sufficiently imaginative to explore new possibilities of communicating their vision of God.

And that vision of God *must* be communicated. Obviously, witness can be imperialistic, but it needn't be. At best, it is the heartfelt desire to share a transforming experience, to find out if he who has spoken to our deepest hopes and needs, has spoken similarly to another's.

Certainly, my vision of God, or rather, God's disclosures of himself to me, affirms that he is out in the world: in Aden, India, Pakistan, Israel, Leicester. Wherever I have been, I have found him mediating himself to me through friends of many faiths. It is always a joy to me; it never surprises me. After all, God loves the world so much that to it he sent his Son. Christians do not take God to anyone; he is already here, wherever we are, wherever anybody is. Our vocation is to share what we know of him whom we have seen in Christ, which can change lives of others, as he changes ours. As we share what we know, we find him in the goodness and love and faith, the Christ-ly qualities, of those who would not call themselves Christians – and that can change *our* lives.

---

[1] M. H. F. Forward: *God of All Faith* (Methodist Church Home Mission Division [1988]).
[2] So much so that some wonder whether any meaningful comparison can be made. What has Buddhism to do with God or the gods? John Bowker believes that there is a Buddhist sense of God. His *The Religious Imagination and the Sense of God* (Oxford [1978]) seems to me to be a masterly example of understanding the faith and belief of others, yet suggesting something more, fresh insights into the way religious people might interpret their religion in belief and practice.
[3] In his foreword to J. R. S. Whiting's *Religions of Men* (Stanley Thornes [1983]), ix.
[4] M. Hilton with G. Marshall: *The Gospels and Rabbinic Judaism* (SCM [1988]), 152.

[5] K. Klostermaier: *Hindu and Christian in Vrindaban* (SCM [1969]), 84. This is a wonderful book, and ch. 5, 'Yoganandaji, my brother', is a touching tale of meeting, loving, and learning.

[6] K. Cracknell and C. Lamb: *Theology in Full Alert* (BCC [1986]), 72.

[7] The best book on this debate is A. Race: *Christians and Religious Pluralism* (SCM [1983]). It is both a *tour de force* and a *cul de sac*!

[8] A good introduction to him, written by a 'fan', is K. Cracknell: 'What is Faith?' (*Epworth Review* 15 [1988]), 65ff.

[9] The best of his books, indeed a great work, is the early *The Call of the Minaret* (Oxford [1956]). It is telling that it was published in the year of Suez. There are many ways of relating to the world of Islam, some better than others! See also his article 'Islam and Incarnation' in *Truth and Dialogue*, ed. J. Hick (Sheldon Press [1974]).

[10] See G. Parrinder: *Jesus in the Qur'an* (Sheldon Press [1976]), esp. chs 13 and 14.

[11] By far the best discussion of this seminal passage for our purpose is A. C. Bouquet: *The Christian Faith and Non-Christian Religions* (Nisbet [1958]), ch. 6. The author wrote his prefatory note to the book in India. Is this significant? It has been felt that the definitive commentary on John's Gospel would come from South Asia. Sadly, it is not that by L. Newbigin *The Light Has Come* (Eerdmans [1982]), which could have been written by a Barthian who had never set foot in India. This, despite Bishop Newbigin's long and distinguished ministry there, academic knowledge of Hinduism, and conversations with some Hindus about this Gospel. *The* Indian commentary awaits an author. Meanwhile, *India's Search for Reality and the Relevance of the Gospel of John* ed. C. Duraisingh and C. Hargreaves (Indian SPCK [1975]) affords some interesting insights.

[12] E.g. Surah 45:3ff: 'Surely in the heavens and earth there are signs to the believers . . .'